Contents

Contents

Acknowledgements

There were a number of people who were encouraging and helpful during the conception of this book and I thank them for their generosity and willingness to share their time and experience: Janeen Baxter, Michael Emmison, Gavin Kendall, Zlatko Skrbis, Philip Smith and Mark Western gave valuable advice at the planning and preparation stages. A smaller group read and commented upon earlier versions of the work, and their insights, criticisms and suggestions were greatly valued. Thank you to Michael Emmison, Gavin Kendall, Zlatko Skrbis, Philip Smith and Brad West for the time they gave to carefully read these drafts.

Thanks to Griffith University's Centre for Public Culture and Ideas for assistance with the final preparation of the manuscript. Here, I am grateful for Daniel Hourigan's eye for detail. I am also appreciative of the generosity of Yale University's Center for Cultural Sociology, its Directors and Fellows, who hosted me for a spell in 2005 during which I worked on this manuscript. To get there, I thank my senior colleagues at Griffith, Kay Ferres and Wayne Hudson, for their encouragement and assistance.

Preface

Our lives are characterised by innumerable encounters with objects. We pick objects up, use them in myriad ways, act with them to achieve ends as mundane as whisking an egg, sending an e-mail, playing a board game and drinking a cup of coffee, and move on to our next object-mediated encounter. Objects are routinely, mundanely, part of everyday existence. Moreover, beyond this pragmatic view, even the most commonplace object has the capacity to symbolise the deepest human anxieties and aspirations. On the basis of their taken-for-grantedness and ubiquity one should not conclude such everyday objects are unimportant. People tend to think it is they who control and direct objects, electing to use them on their own terms. In a sense this assumption is entirely correct. However, this book tries to show that in important ways objects have a type of power over us. By this it is not meant that objects deceive, disappoint, exploit and command us through rounds of consumerist desire or technological domination. Rather, people require objects to understand and perform aspects of selfhood, and to navigate the terrain of culture more broadly.

This book surveys the field of contemporary material culture through an examination and synthesis of classical and contemporary scholarship on objects, commodities, consumption and symbolisation. Its main goal is to give a concise, but diverse, review of the ways of studying the *material as culture*. The book is not meant to serve as an examination of any one version of contemporary 'material culture studies'. Nevertheless, the interest in people–object relations it develops is distinctly indebted to the recent round of material culture studies that has emanated from London. This oeuvre has been groundbreaking in bringing to bear a large body of relevant anthropological concepts to contemporary consumption. Readers familiar with this body of work will certainly notice its influence here. However, the intention here is to move beyond – and indeed back from – this work to consider a wider range of foundational and contemporary theoretical and empirical literature on objects, including work from the fields of classical social theory, consumer research, psychoanalytic theory, sub-cultural theory and social performance theory. The work originates broadly from what could be called a cultural sociological perspective, though it cannot claim to be a complete application of cultural sociology's strong programme (see Alexander, 2003) in the field of material culture studies. What it does share is cultural sociology's desire to understand social life through the application of structural and hermeneutic approaches to capture discourses, narratives, codes and symbols which situate objects, along with their interpretation, symbolic manipulation and individual performance within a variety of social contexts.

The treatment the book gives to studying objects as elements of culture will be relevant to a diverse audience, but especially those with an interest in consumption, identity and theories of culture generally. Its arguments and coverage develop from a desire to advance consumption studies through investigating objects of consumption. As Mary Douglas and Baron Isherwood pointed out in their important work *The World of Goods* ([1996]1979) – reiterating the principle of *'bonnes á penser'* Claude Lévi-Strauss established in his structural anthropology – people construct a universe of meaning through commodities, they use these objects to make visible and stable cultural categories, to deploy discriminating values and to mark aspects of their self and others. Thus, this book works from a premise that to study the objects themselves, and people's relations with them, is an effective analytic strategy for understanding modern consumption and indeed culture broadly.

The book has four parts.

1. Locating material culture. Chapters 1 and 2 comprise the conceptual and definitional components. They present key terms, principles and concepts for studying objects as culture. Outlines of diverse ways of imagining and studying objects are provided, along with a discussion of key disciplinary fields that study objects. To give readers a feeling for researching object meanings in the field, original research case studies and examples are used to show readers how objects do cultural work, in practice.

2. Theoretical approaches to studying material culture. Chapters 3, 4 and 5 give detailed reviews and interpretations of the three major approaches to thinking about objects: (i) Marxism and critical theory, (ii) structuralism and semiotics, (iii) cultural and symbolic approaches. The discussion in each chapter is generally chronological, picking up on key theorists, major works and the important principles of each of these theoretical frameworks. Each chapter concludes with a critical discussion of major points of the approach, strong and weak points, and an annotated discussion of recommended further readings.

3. Objects in action. Chapters 6, 7 and 8 move from the theoretical bases for studying objects to diverse social and psychological fields of social relations where objects matter. In these chapters people–object relations are investigated in the following fields: (i) status and cultural distinction, (ii) social and personal identity, and (iii) narrative and social performance. These chapters allow readers to consider the complexities of people–object relations in varied contexts, though ones generally framed through fields of consumption, including fashion, the home and material displays of cultural affiliation and identification.

4. Conclusion. Chapter 9 concludes the work, offering a brief summary of key aspects of the book, and develops a theoretical agenda for understanding material culture.

PART I
LOCATING MATERIAL CULTURE

ONE

The Material as Culture.
Definitions, Perspectives, Approaches

SUMMARY OF CHAPTER CONTENTS

This chapter introduces material culture studies and demonstrates the usefulness of the material culture approach. It has two main sections which:

- introduce key principles, terms and associated terminologies in the study of material culture
- demonstrate the application of the material culture approach through case studies.

Living in a material world

Objects are the material things people encounter, interact with and use. Objects are commonly spoken of as material culture. The term 'material culture' emphasises how apparently inanimate things within the environment act on people, and are acted upon by people, for the purposes of carrying out social functions, regulating social relations and giving symbolic meaning to human activity. Objects range in scale and size from discrete items such as a pencil, key, coin or spoon, through to complex, network objects such as an airliner, motor vehicle, shopping mall or computer. Traditionally, however, the term material culture has referred to smaller objects that are portable. Although scholars from a variety of disciplines have studied objects, their uses and meanings since the beginnings of modern social science scholarship, it is only in relatively recent times that the field of 'material culture studies' has been articulated as an area of inquiry.

The field of material culture studies (hereafter abbreviated to MCS) is a recent nomenclature that incorporates a range of scholarly inquiry into the uses and meanings of objects. It affords a multidisciplinary vantage point into human–object relations, where the contributions of anthropology, sociology, psychology, design and cultural studies are valued. Material culture is no longer the sole concern of museum scholars and archaeologists – researchers from a wide range of fields have now colonised the study of objects. As well as fostering productive multidisciplinary approaches to objects, MCS can provide a useful vehicle for synthesis of macro and micro, or structural and interpretive approaches in the social sciences. By studying culture as something created and lived through objects, we can better understand both social structures and larger systemic dimensions such as inequality and social difference, and also human action, emotion and meaning. Objects might be seen then, as a crucial link between the social and economic structure, and the individual actor. If we think of the material culture of consumer societies, they are in fact the point where mass-produced consumer objects are encountered and used by individuals, who must establish and negotiate their own meanings and incorporate such objects into their personal cultural and behavioural repertoires, sometimes challenging and sometimes reproducing social structure.

A primary assertion of MCS is that objects have the ability to signify things – or establish social meanings – on behalf of people, or do 'social work', though this culturally communicative capacity should not be automatically assumed. Objects might signify sub-cultural affinity, occupation, participation in a leisure activity, or social status. Furthermore, objects become incorporated into, and represent, wider social discourses related to extensively held norms and values enshrined in norms and social institutions. In a complimentary fashion, objects also carry personal and emotional meanings, they can facilitate interpersonal interactions and assist a person to act upon him or herself. For example, wearing certain clothing may make a person feel empowered by altering their self-perception. Objects, then, can assist in forming or negating interpersonal and group attachments, mediating the formation of self-identity and esteem, and integrating and differentiating social groups, classes or tribes.

When studying and accounting for material culture, one needs to keep in mind the relative viewpoints of the analyst and actor. For the analyst to perform a virtuoso analytic deconstruction of any given object is by no means easy, but it is uncomplicated by the idiosyncrasies, incoherencies and sheer mundanity of the user's perspective. Take Barthes' (1993[1957]) classic essays on aspects of French culture in his book *Mythologies* as an example. As elegant and instructive as these essays are, one wonders about the equivalence between the manner in which everyday users of such objects perceive them, and Barthes' sophisticated textual 'reading' of them. Furthermore, it is not just a matter of individuals pondering what objects might mean, but individuals reading objects in relation to other individuals within complex intergroup networks patterned by social status and role, and space–time contexts. For the analyst then, the object can be rendered all-powerful, perfectly understandable and historically crucial in the course of any literary reflection. However, once the voice of the user is introduced, clarity and certainty give way to multiple interpretations, practices and manipulations. What was once fixed by analytic measure and conceptual clarity alone melts away.

The current interest in material culture is associated with two key developments in the social sciences: the profusion of research into consumption across a range of disciplines, and the rise of poststructural and interpretive theory. Attention to objects as rudimentary elements of consumer culture has acquired renewed status in socio-cultural accounts of consumption processes in late-modern societies. This interest in consumption objects is also tied up with broader developments in social theory, particularly the so-called 'cultural turn'. Although social scientists have historically had an enduring concern for the material constituents of culture (Goffman, 1951; Mauss, 1967[1954]; Simmel, 1904[1957]; Veblen, 1899[1934]), the recent interest in objects has developed in the context of prominent socio-cultural accounts of modern consumerism, and in turn, the emphasis these have given to the material basis of consumption processes, and the cultural meanings that colonise such objects as they move through social landscapes (Appadurai, 1986; Douglas and Isherwood, [1996]1979; Miller, 1987; Riggins, 1994). The second development is connected to the general turn toward language, culture, sites and spaces in poststructural social theory, and the associated interest beyond traditional social scientific analytic categories associated with 'big' social forces like class, gender and race. Linked with the rise of poststructural theory is an interest in the importance of different variables and sites in social formation and transformation such as the body, space and objects. These approaches don't ignore social-structural dimensions; however they do consider them in a contextualised, grounded way. As well as interpretive and textual work in the humanities and cultural anthropology (such as Clifford Geertz), the work of Foucault has been of major importance in this development, for it takes social scientists away from studying traditional macro, structural patterns and directs their interest to discourses, technologies and strategies that are applied at the level of ideas, the body, time and space, as techniques for social governance. While Foucault generally ignores questions of meaning and interpretation that are the central focus of the current work, he has made us aware that it is through the microphysics of temporal and spatial organisation that social power and control is both established and challenged. Objects such as the guillotine, the uniform, the timetable, the school writing desk, or the panopticon – which is the central motif in his work *Discipline and Punish* – are important material tools in the establishment of such capillaries of power, rather than mere 'props' or environmental filler.

How can objects be 'cultural'? A selection of case studies

Having made some preliminary progress, the best way to proceed is to think about objects and culture through practical applications and exemplar cases. This section emphasises the varied capacities of objects to do cultural and social work. In particular, the following case studies demonstrate the diverse capacities of objects to afford meaning, perform relations of power, and construct selfhood. The three sections show how objects can be (i) used as markers of value, (ii) used as markers of identity and (iii) encapsulations of networks of cultural and political power.

Objects as social markers

It is in Bourdieu's (1984) writing on taste that the idea of objects as markers of aesthetic and cultural value is most thoroughly developed. Bourdieu emphasises the role of aesthetic choice – one's tastes – in reproducing social inequality. Bourdieu usurped the (Kantian) idea that judgements of taste are based upon objective and absolute criteria by showing that particular social and class fractions tended to have distinctive taste preferences, which amounts to professing a liking for certain objects over others. Moreover, dominant social groups have the authority to define the parameters of cultural value (e.g. notions of what is 'highbrow' and 'lowbrow' culture), thus devaluing working class modes of judgement as 'unaesthetic'. In consumer societies where taste becomes a highly visible marker of difference, such judgements are implicated in structures of social position and status. Importantly, aesthetic choice is so thoroughly learnt and ingrained that class markers are expressed in the body, self-presentation and performance. Simple learning of cultural and aesthetic rules may not be enough, as one's demeanour and comportment ('bodily hexis', in Bourdieu's words) can seldom succeed in betraying one's class origins.

With this brief overview of Bourdieu's theory of aesthetic judgement in mind, one can progress to consider the following case studies where objects act as markers of aesthetic value and of self-identity. These cases were gathered as part of a larger project into the narrativisation of aesthetic judgement, which is more fully discussed elsewhere (see Woodward, 2001, 2003; Woodward and Emmison, 2001). Note that it is not just the actual objects these respondents choose to discuss which is important, but also the *content of their talk about the object*. The object is given meaning through the narrativisation of broader discourses of self, identity and biography, which link aesthetics to ethics of self, and social identity. So, when you read the following case studies, look not just at the *what* (i.e. the actual object), but the *why* and *how* (i.e. the narrative and performative accompaniment) of aesthetic judgement.

Helen

For Helen, a chair that sits in a corner of her main bedroom is an object which exemplifies her aesthetic taste. In the research interview, Helen interprets the chair through an aesthetic frame, reflecting on its style and design and how she feels this fits with her self-presentation. Throughout the interview, Helen portrays a high level of aesthetic competence – in Bourdieu's terms, she has mastered the 'symmetries and correspondences' (1984: 174) associated with her choices. As a result, she is able to contextualise her own choices within wider social and aesthetic trends with a degree of high cultural authority, bringing a range of cultural knowledges and expertise to bear on her discussion of the chair.

Helen is someone who places a high value on appropriate home styles and choices, to the extent that she works with an interior designer through important phases of home renovation. Helen and her partner are both professionals in high-salary positions. Helen lives in the inner north east of the city on top of a prominent hill with outstanding views to the city's east toward the ocean. In terms of questions of taste and style, Helen could be classified as 'modern classicist': one who is committed to traditional, classic notions of 'good taste' which are based on subtle colour combinations founded in whites and creams, with soft blues and greens as highlight colours. Helen's aesthetic choices are not directed towards the bright or ostentatious. Rather, decorative schemes are themed consistently through the house, employ neutral-based colours, and present an image of understatement and timelessness that are typically ascribed characteristics of classic 'good taste'. Asked during the interview to describe her own style, Helen responds:

> Pretty minimalist, without being minimalist in terms of futuristic minimalist. I certainly tend to be a … it's the same with the way I dress, fairly uncluttered, fairly simple, clean lines, certainly very neutral in colours, simple patterns, very classic I guess.

Helen has such a well developed conception of what constitutes her style that she is able to adroitly sum up her aesthetic values through the use of an exemplar object – a chair that stands in a prominent corner of the main bedroom. Helen uses the chair as a prop for her account. The chair – apart from its functional or use value which is not addressed by Helen – is an object that signifies, and summarises, the style of its owner and the desired ambience of the whole house. The chair's simplicity, neutrality and classical enduring style are instructive:

> I can't see myself ever really taking the plunge and going really bright with the upholstery. As I said, in the main bedroom, come in and I'll show you, it's probably the most recent. To me that chair, that sums up my idea. That's me, I love that. That sort of cream, neutral, New England look.

Helen's chair then sits as an example, reminding her of the bounds of her own aesthetic variance which she describes as: 'really simple patterns and simple colours and again very neutral'. There are no serious or problematic issues to be faced in the chair. For example, some may wonder whether investing such importance in this chair is trivial, or overly materialistic. The most challenging issue for Helen is the progressive 'modernisation' of her taste and the chance that the chair will no longer fit variations in her style. However, Helen feels that such variations are unlikely to challenge the basic, well-honed values of her modern, classic aesthetic: 'I don't think I'll ever be ultra-modern, but I think I'll go a little less cottagey'. One of the impressive, important aspects of Helen's aesthetic value system is the degree to which it is a finely tuned, almost 'technical' (Bennett et al., 1999: 56), scheme of knowledge. Its basis is so thoroughly realised in Helen that the nuanced distinctions she makes of shade and style in this piece of material culture are rendered entirely natural.

Christina

The following section turns to a different case altogether, using interview data from the same research project. Christina lives in the same suburb as Helen, though with a less prestigious view, and is approximately the same age (early to mid-30s). However, her aesthetic choices and the reasoning and narrativisation that accompany them, are widely different. Christina has lived in this house, originally the family home, for over 25 years. Now without both parents, the house belongs to Christina and her sister. The house is an architect-designed bungalow built in the late 1940s. Christina's family was originally from a farming region, and Christina retains a strong affinity for the country despite her privileged private school education, which she now rails against. Christina sets apart her own identity from what she sees as the snob-based culture of most in her suburb to the extent that she has now centred important aspects of her life in different parts of the city:

Christina (C):   I live my social life in other suburbs, I certainly started off doing the old 'creek' 'hammo' [*Landmark local pubs frequented by upwardly mobile, socially conservative young people*] sort of deal ... because I went to St Margaret's, and most of the people were private school around here – we had Churchie boys, we had Grammar next door, we had Churchie [*these names refer to elite, 'private' secondary schools*] down the road, Ascot state school was about as state school as it got ... everyone went to Ascot 'til grade seven and then went off to their private schools at enormous expense ... um, that was when I first started but then it didn't really suit me very much so I sort of moved on to different sorts of people so I hang out at Mansfield [*a middle-class, rather unmarkable suburb in the mid to outer zone of the city*] suburb these days to tell you the truth ...

Interviewer (I): So you have friends out there?

C: yeah, yeah ...

I: So what sort of activities do you get into, what sort of lifestyle and leisure things do you like?

C: well ... I suppose pretty much the pub sort of scene really, just a few pubs, go to the football a bit, go to the races a bit, I don't go to the races as much as I used to, that's more for this sort of crowd. And I do a lot of things on my own really, I just go over there, I've got a boyfriend over there and spend a few nights and that's about it really ...

I: Were your parents more into this scene?

C: Well, it was a single parent family and mother actually came from out west, but that's probably why we didn't jump straight into this, she knew a few people who had country links but she didn't really know this sort of snob value group here ...

This is important contextual material for the aesthetic stance maintained by Christina, which is relatively hostile to conventional concerns about colour, design and style:

C: I've always been totally disinterested in décor, I don't care as long as there's a seat, a kitchen and a bed, that's all I really care about

I: so you don't have an interest in it?

C: no, don't care, really don't care ... I like clean, I like neat, but I don't care if it sort of clashes or whatever.

Christina moves to distance herself from mainstream ideas about taste and style, on the basis of its elitist nature, its lack of person-centred authenticity, and its perceived lack of relevance to her key leisure interests: cable television, pub culture, football and clothes shopping. This anti-style position is reflected in one of the objects Christina chooses to discuss in the interview – what she calls the 'wartishog':

I'm a bit of a wood girl, and I can show you another piece that I like I'll bring it to you ... I got this over in Africa for $50, and one of my friends did it up for me ... I like the warthog, my cousin's been living in Africa for about seven years, we just went over there I think it was two years ago and did a driving holiday around South Africa and it was just in one of those reserves, it's really a game park, a lot of them carve them, but he was just a really good piece ... but not finished, totally unfinished, that sheen, the finish has been done since I've been back, which has made it come up a whole lot better ... he's just unique, everyone goes 'ughhh ... what's that!!!' ... wartishog ... I sort of like oddities I suppose, something that no one else has got that's a bit weird you know ... not because it's really expensive but because it's a bit weird ... it's unique, you're not going to find things like that in many houses in Hamilton, are you?

As an object the 'wartishog' seems to have been chosen partly for its perceived lack of conventional beauty or fashionability – for its aggressively anti-style position. Seen in this context, Christina adopts a strongly political attitude toward conventional prescriptions of taste, which has its origins in an anti-fashion outlook. At the same time, Christina's stance is display-oriented, because of its emphasis on the shock-value of the object, manifested through its perceived strangeness or quirkiness. The sign-value of the object for Christina is thus not based in conventional standards of beauty or taste. Its value lies in the same domain as other status objects, but obtains its currency through different signifiers: physically shocking rather than refined and understated, provocative rather than calming, aggressive rather than peaceful. In addition, it is apparent that the wartishog is strongly associated with Christina's experiences of travel, family and friends. It is an exotic object (Riggins, 1994), linked to a specific touring experience and the contacts with friends and family involved in such travel. These two cases show how people attach various meanings to commonplace objects, using them to think through and account for aspects of self and society more broadly.

Objects as markers of identity

As the previous examples show, separating aesthetic claims from narratives or claims about self-identity in the study of objects is somewhat futile, for in everyday talk – and especially within the artificial setting of a research interview – a personal aesthetic choice is generally required to be accompanied by a justification. Such justifications – which sociologists might classify as being a matter of 'aesthetics' – are rarely couched in purely aesthetic terms, but associated with matters of self-identity and a range of external factors (such as, for example, monetary cost or needs associated with one's life stage). So, while it is rare for respondents to ignore matters of identity in relation to possessions (even when they are 'aesthetic' possessions), the following case looks at a very private object with a high degree of personal meaning and a very strong association with personal identity – a bible. The bible – like any sacred religious text – is perhaps the ultimate case of a mass-produced object retaining a powerful aura. Even though it is an important spiritual text, it is also an object of mass production with a vast circulation. At odds with the status of a sacred text, a bible originates from nowhere special, essentially having the same qualities as any other mass-produced textbook or magazine. Yet, it manages to retain an aura of authority. The following case is not just about *any* bible, for example, the sort you may find in a bedside table draw when staying at a hotel, but a highly personalised, customised object.

A bible is an object that is not generally displayed or carried in public, but reserved for particular occasions and rituals. It may symbolise deeply held, cherished values for Christians, and may be respected by people as a possible legitimate moral code whether or not they are Christian. Yet, depending on your attitude to religion, the bible can also be an object with particular stigmas attached – for example, its association with Christianity as a form of moral imperialism and entrepreneurship, morally and socially conservative values generally, and adherence to strict or anachronistic moral codes. This said, the bible may seem an entirely appropriate accoutrement for a conservative Christian to carry or exhibit, but what about a university student majoring in philosophy and sociology? The following case study considers university student Sarah, through her own words, who nominates her bible as a focal object for understanding her identity.

Sarah

For Sarah, her Christian faith is a crucial aspect of her identity which defines her life's direction and meaning. She wishes to live her life consistent with Christian beliefs and perceives a significant difference between her life choices and the life choices those of those who do not have such beliefs. Her bible is symbolic of her beliefs and, she says, offers her a way of 'fighting' the social pressures that could pull her away from such beliefs:

My bible comes to represent my identity, and to shape it. When I say that it represents me I do not mean that it is simply any bible that can express my identity. It is with the book that I saved to pay for, that I hand covered, and that I have spent hours poring over, and sometimes crying over, that I identify.

Sarah's bible represents her decision to identify with the Christian beliefs as defining parts of her personal search for direction and meaning. Yet, she cannot control the way the bible is perceived by others, and recognises that some people may perceive it with suspicion. Hence, she reports some anxiety about how the object is perceived by others, especially amongst young people and particularly her peers at university – 'my nervousness about carrying the bible in public … can in some ways be seen to indicate the pressure I feel to conform to a more secular lifestyle'. While the bible carries special, significant meanings for her, she also recognises that it may signify conservative, restrictive values to others. Her response is to customise the bible, transforming it from a mass-produced object into a personalised object that serves to deconstruct typical notions of how a bible (and a Christian) should appear. One might say the pressures she feels relate to (apparently) contradictory roles or membership category locations – sociology and philosophy student, Christian, alternative university student, member of a youth sub-culture. Sarah has customised a young person's bible:

> My fear of being misunderstood can be seen in the way I adorn my bible. I am aware of the hypocrisy of many people who share my belief in God and choose not to live a life that exemplifies this, and so I wrap my bible in corduroy and fill it with poetry so that an observer can see that it is something I treasure. I want people to see that it is interpolated into my life, and that it interacts with other parts of my identity … It is because I am afraid of being seen as a traditional rule-focused Christian that I need to cover my bible and fill its pockets with other identity markers.

Sarah's bible is then a marker of who 'Sarah' is, both in terms of her social identity and for Sarah herself. Furthermore, its meaning is mediated through popular and contradictory discourses related to Christianity, youth and being a university student that Sarah has to negotiate as she reflexively monitors her identity. Her bible thus retains its core meaning to her as a spiritual guide, but, in its customised form, helps Sarah to socially mediate aspects of her identity, given the multiple social locations her identity intersects (youth, alternative lifestyles, Christian, university student).

Objects as sites of cultural and political power

In this oeuvre, which emerged from new theorisations of the relations between people and technology, objects are constructed by particular power relations, and in turn also actively construct such relations. In this tradition, known as actant-network theory, objects are produced by particular networks of cultural and political discourses and, in conjunction with humans, act to reproduce such relations. So, the discourses and networks which connect people to objects are not only inextricable as if they are one actor, but may in fact be 'made of the same stuff' (MacKenzie and Wajcman, 1999: 25). Arising from work in the sociology of science and technology, actant-network theory tends to focus on new technology objects such as mobile telephones, machinery which 'acts for' people such as remote controls, speed-bumps or door-grooms, and 'technological network' objects like aeroplanes, buildings and motor vehicles. The next section discusses Foucault's famous example of the panopticon to explain how objects are at the centre of discourses and networks of power, and how they 'act' to influence human action. Since Foucault died before the current research on 'actant-networks' arose he is not identified with that field. However, his work can be seen as developing some important themes taken up by the current group of actant-network scholars.

Foucault's genealogical studies of the prison, the hospital and the asylum plot the emergence of historical discourses which condition the formation of social institutions and practical knowledges. They might be said to be historical studies, but first and foremost chart a genealogical history of the present. Therefore, *Discipline and Punish* is not a history of punishment and incarceration. Rather, it is a history of oscillating historical discourses surrounding punishment. The conclusion it reaches has implications more far-reaching than understanding the history of incarceration. The corpus of work is to be found in the case studies presented by Foucault in the book's opening chapter which deals with how the body of the condemned prisoner is treated. In these, he juxtaposes the story of Damiens, guilty of regicide and committed to make the *amende honorable*, with the rules drawn up by Faucher for a house of young prisoners in Paris. Drawn from newspaper sources, the story of Damiens' execution is entirely gory and sanguineous, with the body's destruction the focus of the state's brutal revenge. This account contrasts starkly with Faucher's rules for prisoners which emphasise routines, classifications and timetables which serve to discipline the prisoner's body, or make it docile. Only 80 years separates these divergent penal styles. Both strategies focus on the body. However, one makes a spectacle of bodily humiliation, the other takes place out of public view and touches the body lightly, and only to direct its routines on a spatial and temporal plane.

This novel penology forms the basis of new economies of power which play on the body and soul in various subtle but highly efficient ways. It is this new mode of power, generalised throughout society, which Foucault heralds as paradigmatic of disciplinary society. While the emblem of the classical age of punishment was public torture and spectacle, Foucault argues that modernity has abandoned this for the architectonic configuration of the panopticon (first proposed by the utilitarian philosopher Jeremy Bentham). The panopticon is thus a product of emergent discourses about the nature of punishment, and its relation to the body and soul. Without the existence of ideas about discipline and surveillance, it cannot exist. But more than this, the panopticon as an object of technology *acts for* people. The insidious elegance of the panopticon's design (through the use of lighting and architectural form) is that it allows for the efficient surveillance of a prison population, for prisoners cannot tell with certainty if they are being surveilled or not. Faced with this ambiguity, and their relative powerlessness as prisoners, they are encouraged to self-monitor their behaviour under the assumption that they are under surveillance at all times.

The panopticon is thus an object which is the product of historical changes in discourses about punishment, and which – although 'inanimate' – as a product of its design 'acts' to achieve political and organisational ends. In this way, the distinctions between the discourses about punishment, the panopticon as material object and the human actors involved (in the first instance prisoners and guards) can be seen to result from a network of understandings and relations – as 'enactments of strategic logics' (Law, 2002: 92) – about punishment and control of the body. Furthermore, the distinction between the panopticon as merely an 'object' and the humans who designed and inhabit it is of minor importance, as the object and human actors perform in concert to achieve certain ends.

Defining 'material culture'

Having presented introductory material and considered a range of cases that fuse with selected theoretical ideas which give a flavour for how objects can carry cultural meanings, the final section of the chapter defines the key terminology of material culture studies. Studies of material culture have as their primary concern the mutual relations between people and objects. In particular, studies of material culture are concerned with what uses people put objects to and what objects do for, and to, people. Furthermore, scholars working in the field of material culture studies aim to analyse how these relations are one of the important ways in which culture – and the meanings upon which culture is based – are transmitted, received and produced. Readers will observe from the previous case studies that objects have various symbolic meanings for people, as much as their physical presence is important in structuring the pragmatic aspects of social life. In its popular scholarly usage, the term 'material culture' is generally taken to refer to any material object (e.g. shoes, cup, pen) or network of material objects (e.g. house, car, shopping mall) that people perceive, touch, use and handle, carry out social activities within, use or contemplate.

Material culture is, chiefly, something portable and perceptible by touch and therefore has a physical, material existence that is one component of human cultural practice. Moreover, consistent with contemporary work in consumption studies that emphasises the mental or ideational aspects of consumption desires which are mobilised through media and advertising, material culture also includes things perceptible by sight. This ability to visualise material culture allows it to enter the imaginary realm of fantasy and desire, so that objects are also acted upon in the mind as 'dreams and pleasurable dramas' which are the basis of ongoing desires for objects of consumption (Campbell, 1987: 90). Having made this point, it is important to note that in everyday practice this distinction between discrete physical, embodied and ideational elements of material culture is indistinguishable and artificial – objects are culturally powerful because *in practice they connect physical and mental manipulation*.

What term is best to describe the 'material' component of material culture studies? The term 'material culture' is often used in conjunction with 'things', 'objects', 'artefacts', 'goods', 'commodities' and, more recently, 'actants'. These terms (with the exception of the last) are, for most purposes, used interchangeably. There are, however, some important nuances in the meaning of each term, which help to demarcate the context in which it should be used. We can begin with the most general term and move to the most specific. 'Things' have a concrete and real material existence but the word 'thing' suggests an inanimate or inert quality, requiring that actors bring things to life through imagination or physical activity. 'Objects' are discrete components of material culture that are perceptible by touch or sight. 'Artefacts' are the physical products or traces of human activity. Like objects, they have importance because of their materiality or concreteness, and become the subject of retrospective interpretation and ordering. Artefacts are generally regarded as symbolic of some prior aspect of cultural or social activity. 'Goods' are objects that are produced under specific market relations, typically assumed to be capitalism, where they are assigned value within a system of exchange. The word 'commodity' is a technical expression related to the concept of a 'good'. Similarly, a commodity is something that can be exchanged. Objects enter into and out of spheres of commoditisation, so that an object that is now a commodity might not always remain a commodity due to its incorporation into private or ritual worlds of individuals, families and cultures. 'Actant' is a term developed from recent approaches in the sociology of science and technology which refers to entities – both human and non-human – which have the ability to 'act' socially. By dissolving the boundary between people who 'act' and objects which are seen as inanimate or 'outside', the term 'actant' is designed to overcome any a priori distinction between the social, technological and natural worlds, and emphasises the inextricable links between humans and material things.

When using any of these terms there is a danger of reification – that is, of imagining that objects are simply there for human actors to engage with or use up, as though they exist apart from cultural and social history, narrative and codes. Kopytoff (1986) points out that in western thought a mythic dichotomy exists between the notion of 'individualised' persons and 'commoditised' things which has constructed an inflexible and limiting binary for understanding the relations between persons and things. What's more, there is a danger in pursuing a hard distinction between objects as part of an artefactual world and the other natural world (Miller, 1994: 407). As Miller argues, we should take care to recognise that 'the

continual process by which meaning is giving to things is the same
process by which meaning is given to lives' (1994: 417).What's more, some
theorists are of the opinion it may be of greater use to collapse such distinctions and see a radical dissolution of the human/non-human distinction, as suggested by actor, or 'actant', network theory. According to this
theory, objects are not only defined by their material quality, but by their
location within systems of narrative and logic laid out by social discourses related to technology, culture, economy and politics. Objects exist
within networks of relations that serve to define, mediate and order them,
and which in turn are 'acted upon' by such objects and human subjects,
affording them purpose and meaning within a system of social relations
(Law, 2002: 91–2). In other words, objects exist because social, cultural and
political forces define them as objects within systems of relations with
other objects.

Whatever term one chooses to apply in a given context – whether it is
objects, actants, material culture, things or goods – one needs only look to
their immediate surroundings to find examples. It is this endless diversity
and ordinariness of subjects for study that makes material culture studies
fascinating and fundamental to understanding culture.

SUGGESTED FURTHER READING

Lury's *Consumer Culture* (1996) is a concise and interesting critical review of a
range of literatures within the related field of consumption studies. Particularly
useful is Chapter 2 of this work, which investigates the link between consumer
culture and material culture. Douglas and Isherwood's *The World of Goods*
([1996]1979) is a foundational work, uniquely combining insights from the
disciplines of economics and anthropology. Much of what Douglas and Isherwood
say about the uses of material culture has since become elemental to contemporary studies of material culture. The principle ideas of the work are expressed in
Chapters 3 and 4. Kopytoff's (1986) essay is also important to defining the current
field and requires some close reading. This essay on the cultural biography of
things explains how objects have biographies and discusses the way objects
are commoditised and 'singularised' – personalised or given special or sacred
meaning within a culture – in capitalist societies. Chapter 1 of Dittmar's *The Social
Psychology of Material Possessions* (1992) is a lucid introduction to consumption
and material culture studies from a social psychological perspective. In addition,
consider reading small-scale empirical studies which engage with material culture
perspectives in relation to identity-based consumption in a way accessible to the
beginning reader – see Miles (1996) on youth and the use of sneakers in construction of a symbolic universe, Lupton and Noble (2002) on the customisation of
personal computers within the workplace, and Woodward (2001, 2003) on narratives of identity construction using domestic material culture.

TWO

Studying Material Culture. Origins and Premises

SUMMARY OF CHAPTER CONTENTS

This chapter has two main sections which:

- review the interdisciplinary origins of material culture studies
- summarise the basic premises of the material culture approach.

The nature and growth of material culture studies

This chapter introduces the most important disciplinary influences in the formation of what is understood as the material culture perspective. Studies of material culture have a multidisciplinary history, and their origins can be traced to a range of theoretical literatures and research traditions, some of which have faded in their popularity and others which are burgeoning. The fields of research discussed are: (i) evolutionary anthropology, (ii) modern sociology and social theory, (iii) marketing and psychological approaches to consumer behaviour, (iv) consumption studies within sociology, and (v) the new anthropologies of consumption and economic behaviour.

Evolutionary anthropology and the exhibition of cultural difference

Early studies of material culture had a relatively narrow focus and existed within anthropology to document and categorise the material expressions of diverse human cultures. The first studies of material culture catalogued and described objects, generally of non-western or, more specifically, non-European origin. These were often objects and technologies such as spears, knives or shields. The manifest goal of these studies was to use such artefacts as a means for retrospectively understanding human behaviour and culture. However, the latent effect was to objectify, hierarchicalise and marginalise the cultural expressions of non-western cultures. During the zenith period for museum collecting – the 'museum age', formally between 1880–1920 (Jacknis, 1985: 75) – such displays of material culture performed a perverse educative role by demonstrating evolutionary stages and models of cultural development, and implicitly communicating the superiority of western culture.

A novel way of ordering material culture for viewers' gaze that performed an educative role was pioneered by Franz Boas at the beginning of the twentieth century. Termed the 'life group' arrangement, the idea was to build a realistic, scale model which scenically represented some aspect of social life as it was supposed to have been practised (Jacknis, 1985). Models were dressed appropriately, within particular social contexts, and were typically depicted engaging in some aspect of work or art production. A savvy cultural audience might now read with some irony Boas' accompanying captions, which allow us to visualise the style of these displays: 'A woman is seen making a cedar-bark mat, rocking her infant, which is bedded in cedar-bark, the cradle being moved by means of a cedar-bark rope attached to her toe' (Boas, cited in Jacknis, 1985: 100).

There was a strong preoccupation in these early manifestations of material culture studies with ordering and arranging collections of the artefacts of 'others'. Consequently, debates ensued over the principles of organising presentations of such artefacts that centred upon either evolutionary or comparative, and geographic principles. An intriguing example was Pitt Rivers (a.k.a. A.H. Lane-Fox Pitt Rivers) who first became interested in the progression of rifle and musket models as a result of his time as a British military officer (Chapman, 1985). Rivers could be characterised as a keen, even obsessive, amateur collector who had academic tendencies. He possessed an apparent heroic desire to provide public instruction and articulate a type of universal material order through the objects he assembled. Rivers' overseas military career afforded him the perfect opportunity to amass a variety of artefacts and his burgeoning collection began to attract interest from academic ethnographers and museums. His collection was eventually to be housed in a newly built annex of Oxford University Museum in 1884. Rivers' interests were evolutionary and ethnological – using material culture to 'trace all mankind back to a single source and to reconstruct the history of human racial differentiation and interconnection' (Chapman, 1985: 39).

Over time, the ethnological principle that informed the basis of such collections aroused suspicion, and was increasingly interpreted as problematic for it implicitly attached a hierarchical ordering of value to the artefacts of other cultures. Moreover, the emptiness and isolation of objects presented apart from their original cultural and spatial contexts was seen as unsatisfactory. Rather than developing as a discrete discipline of inquiry, material culture became integrated into anthropological inquiry generally, with objects used principally for evidence and illustrative purposes related to larger anthropological themes and narratives. No specific interest in the sub-discipline of material culture studies endured. Up until the 1960s and 1970s the field was predominantly colonised by archaeologists who had a specific interest in the analysis of materials, and by museum scholars and practitioners whose task it was to document and present cultural artefacts. Readers interested in contemporary debates on the meanings of material culture in museum contexts should consult the numerous very useful works by Susan M. Pearce.

Sociological theories of modernity: commodities and the values of modern society

A central theme within classical political economy, sociology and cultural theory from the eighteenth to twentieth centuries concerns the contradictory effects of the great productive capacities of burgeoning capitalist economies. In this body of literature capitalism is acknowledged to have an immense capacity to produce a surfeit of consumption objects. However, there is an underlying suspicion about what such excesses of consumer objects could do to individuals, and society generally. Within these discourses it is not the actual objects or consumption practices of actors that theorists are concerned with. Rather, these literatures are really discourses on the ethics and ideologies of consumption objects, and the burgeoning culture of materialism more broadly.

Adam Smith saw the tendency to admire and strive for the vices, follies and fashions of the wealthy, as goals which lead to the sacrifice of wisdom and virtue, and ultimately as 'the universal cause of the corruption of our moral sentiments' (Smith, 1969[1759]: 84). While it is Marx who represents the most radical manifestation of this line of thought, such sentiments also find unique, sometimes more or less subtly cultural expressions, in a number of other works. These include Veblen's acerbic critique of the pecuniary nature of taste judgements (1899[1934]), Simmel (1904[1957]) on fashion and style (1997a, 1997b) within modern contexts, Bataille (1985) on abundance and the expenditure of 'useless splendours' that define capitalism, and Sombart's (1967[1913]) analysis of the role of luxury goods in the genesis of capitalism.

Later chapters will focus on these authors in more detail. However, in introducing their ideas as part of this group of classical modern writers concerned with material culture, we can turn to Simmel and Marx to briefly distinguish two dominant threads in classical analyses of material culture. First, to Karl Marx's writing on the commodity as a symbol of estranged labour. Marx acknowledged that the wealth of capitalist societies was based on their ability to accumulate capital through producing an immense array of commodity objects. For Marx, one of the principal characteristics of being human is to fashion an objective world. It is by understanding the objective world of things or objects that humans can understand themselves: 'man reproduces himself not only intellectually, in his consciousness, but actively and actually, and he can therefore contemplate himself in a world he himself has created' (Marx, 1975: 329). As the fundamental objective unit of production and consumption, the commodity object symbolises both the glorious success and the exploitative basis of capitalism. The political economy of production also entails a significant loss for workers. Capitalism 'produces marvels for the rich, but it produces privation for the worker. It produces palaces, but hovels for the worker' (Marx, 1975: 325). As later chapters of this work show, Marx had a deep suspicion – bordering on outright hostility – toward the objects of capitalist economic production, and saw objects of consumption as the embodiment of exploitative capitalist relations.

Of the classical sociologists who charted early forms of modernity and capitalism, it is Georg Simmel who had the most explicit interest in how material culture defined the nature of modern experience. A foundational element of Simmel's work was the insight that the modern economy precipitated an unprecedented multiplication in the numbers of things, objects and materials. In recognising this Simmel makes a similar observation to Marx, yet he goes further in exploring the cultural and experiential implications of this observation. His fundamental claim is that this ever-growing body of things becomes increasingly important in the mediation and experience of modern life. In particular, as objects multiply in style and type they are appropriated by individuals to differentiate themselves. Further, objects perform a tragic role by creating a distance between the human sphere and the sphere of material things, which is increasingly out of the grasp of people. This becomes the basis of modern reification and alienation.

Simmel's sociological interests were diverse, to the extent that his work was considered by some as brittle and shallow (see Frisby, 1992: 68–101). Furthermore, he did not pursue any methodologically formal analysis of material culture as understood by anthropologists of the day. But despite this apparent diversity and – perhaps – superficiality, much of his work is centrally about the dialectical, contradictory forces that propelled modernity – the problem of individual differentiation within the context of the peculiarly modern trajectory of uniformity and solidarity. Simmel was interested in understanding the nature of relations between individuals, which he termed 'forms of sociation'. Crucially, objects played a significant part in mediating these forms of sociation. Simmel's interest in objects can be partly understood as an element of his overarching concern with the role of the senses on social life – particularly the sense of sight – and with the experience of metropolitan life in the burgeoning cities of Europe. Both of these interrelated elements privilege the role of objects in mediating forms of sociation.

It is not just the objects of money and fashion that Simmel writes about, he also has essays on the symbolic capacities of objects such as bridges, doors, handles, picture frames and domestic interiors. His masterly analysis of fashion and style is essentially an attempt to understand processes that propelled modernity, and in turn their impact on the psycho-social development of the modern person. Fashion and style represented much more than merely clothes, home decoration or manners; they were fundamental processes of modern social life, in fact, 'a universal phenomenon in the history of our race' (Simmel, [1904]1957: 53). Processes of conflict, compromise, elevation and adaption, all serve the basic Simmelian dialectic: generality/uniformity versus individuality/ differentiation. The clarity of Simmel's understanding means that even though his analysis of fashion and style are arguably flawed and anachronistic in some ways, much of what he says provokes interest and rings true for present-day lay and specialist readers alike.

Marketing and psychological approaches to consumer behaviour

There are some excellent research contributions within this oeuvre that genuinely advance knowledge on matters of consumption and the nature and meaning of human–object relations, whatever discipline or approach one identifies with. Those with more of a cultural interest may not take to the psychological, positivist flavour of much of this research, in its attempt to develop clear measures and means for studying people–object relations. However, this research approach has some advantages over other styles. Take work by Belk (1985, 1988, 1995; Belk et al., 1989), Wallendorf (Walendorf and Arnould, 1988) and Kleine and Kernan (1991) (also Kleine et al., 1995) in the field of marketing and consumer research, and Csikszentmihalyi and Rochberg-Halton (1981) and Schultz et al. (1989) within the field of psychology, as examples of such universally excellent research. These are, however, high profile and exceptional exemplars. A significant amount of research in this field is indeed unsatisfying from a cultural perspective, leaving the work of major research figures within the fields of sociology of consumption and cultural anthropology, particularly European and British scholars, unconsidered. By focusing predominantly on the psychological elements of human–object relations this work precludes understanding consumption and materialism as cultural practices and values that generate social inequality and difference. Yet, these types of studies do succeed in an important way, for while sociologists and social theorists have persistently referred to the salience of identity management in contemporary consumption processes without attention to empirical settings and processes, these studies have fostered advances by empirically exploring the way self-identities are generated by processes of attachment to, integration of, and individuation, based on relations with material culture (e.g. Schultz et al., 1989). Their high level of conceptual clarification and specification, and attention to empirical detail, gives such psychological studies advantages.

For example, in a unique study Wallendorf and Arnould (1988) use a triangulated methodology with samples of respondents from USA and

Niger to explore the notion of favourite objects. Their theoretical premise is that objects serve a fundamental psychological function by providing a material site for attachment of meaning. Following Douglas and Isherwood ([1996]1979), they assert that rather than being about materialism, acquisition is about meaning making and intelligibility of one's cultural universe. Their key findings are as follows: the US sample is more instrumental and materialistic in their focus on possessions as a key goal of consumption; females select biographical and family-based items while males select objects to reflect mastery and accomplishment; and young people's consumption is pleasure-based compared to older respondents who emphasise intergenerational bonds.

   Much of this genre of research is associated with marketing, business and consumer research studies, most strongly developed in North America, whose main aim is to apply scientific research techniques in order to understand consumer behaviour. The ultimate goal is to market and sell products more effectively. The end result of such research is not *necessarily* to understand patterns of consumption or materialism (let alone to challenge them as core cultural values), but to actually advance materialist values by generating more accurate, and ultimately strategic, understandings of consumer behaviour. As Rose points out concerning the government of consumption: 'It is the expertise of market research, of promotion and communication, underpinned by the knowledges and techniques of subjectivity, that provide the relays through which the aspirations of ministers, the ambitions of business and the dreams of consumers achieve mutual translatability' (Rose, 1992: 155). What is interesting about this research is that it seems to thrive in North America, where consumerist and materialist values reign, and suggests an association between thriving marketing faculties and materialist societies. This speculation aside, through careful selection, scholars of material culture could make profitable use of such literatures – paying limited attention to those which are most strongly empirically abstracted and acultural, but engaging with those which make genuine connections between consumer psychology and cultural narrative and forms.

Consumption studies within sociology

Attention to objects as rudimentary elements of consumer culture has acquired renewed status in socio-cultural accounts of consumption processes in late-modern societies. While sociologists and political economists have historically had an enduring concern for the material constituents of culture and consumption broadly (Goffman, 1951; Marx, (1954[1867]); Simmel, 1904[1957]; Sombart, 1967[1913]; Veblen, 1899[1934]), the recent interest in the material objects of consumption has developed in the context of prominent socio-cultural accounts of contemporary consumerism and, in turn, the emphasis these have given to the material basis of consumption processes (Appadurai, 1986; Douglas and Isherwood,

[1996] 1979; Miller, 1987; Riggins, 1994). Moreover, the optimism generated by the emergent material culture perspective within sociological studies of consumption seems in part a reaction to the excesses of prominent celebratory accounts of postmodern consumption. Such accounts embraced the expressive, astructural and aesthetic possibilities of particular types of consumption, and associated them theoretically with identity-maintenance, choice and freedom, and reflexivity. Emerging from some of the key texts in European and British social theory and cultural studies published from the 1970s onward, these accounts located consumption at the core of contemporary processes of social change and introduced a variety of concepts which were theoretically rich and novel. However, it could be argued that they were also generally without systematic empirical warrant or methodological sophistication, and have latterly been seen to place too much emphasis on the expressive and identity aspects of consumption. They were successful in narrating the apparent tempo of the era and sketching macro scale social changes, but often inadequate in specifying, measuring and empirically tempering the claims they established.

The gist of the postmodern claim is that consumption has been aestheticised and semioticised by recent processes of hyper-commodification (Featherstone, 1991; Jameson, 1991[1984]; Lash and Urry, 1994). The contrast made commonplace in commentary on consumption processes is that if consumption could ever be characterised in historical perspective as typically utilitarian – that is, being essentially a question of utility in use – then by contrast it is now characteristically constructive: identity-forming, reflexive, expressive and even playful.

Featherstone's account of the contours of contemporary consumer culture is principally indebted to the theoretical work established by Jameson (1991[1984]), Lash and Urry (1987) and Harvey (1989) and the semiotic analyses of Baudrillard ([1996]1968) and Barthes, (1967, 1993[1957]), who established new ground by the application of semiotic techniques to everyday consumer culture. Featherstone's analysis of the move to a postmodern consumer culture finds the concept of lifestyle to have particular salience in a postmodern regime of consumption. Of the three approaches to consumer culture Featherstone (1990) outlines, he chooses to emphasise the role of pleasure and desire in framing recent consumption practices. The development of a postmodern consumer culture rests on an assumption about the use of goods as communicators, not just utilities. Featherstone sees this trend as a component of what he has labelled 'the aestheticization of everyday life' (1992), for in a society where the commodity sign dominates, by default each person must be a symbolic specialist.

There are two relevant applications of Featherstone's (1991) discussion of aestheticisation which are applicable to consumer culture, or at least some social fractions of it. The first is where life is conceptualised as a project of style, where originality, taste and aesthetic competence are measures of success and superiority (1991: 67), and thus become important motivators for social action. This is a style project that is not merely accomplished by the outlay of sheer sums of disposable income. While Featherstone assigns the avant-garde and intellectuals an important role in the dissemination of new consumption ideas – and he also endorses Bourdieu's (1984) emphasis on the new middle classes as the fiscal backbone of the consumer economy – *all* classes are held to approach the project of lifestyle with an outlook Featherstone labels 'calculating hedonism, a calculus of stylistic effect and an emotional economy' (1991: 86). The notion of lifestyle is particularly useful for Featherstone's formulation of consumer culture, because it suggests how people act as postmodern symbol processors through the coherent and meaningful deployment of symbols that exist within 'economies' of commodity objects:

> Rather than unreflexively adopting a lifestyle, through tradition or habit, the new heroes of consumer culture make lifestyle a life project and display their individuality and sense of style in the particularity of the assemblage of goods, clothes, practices, experiences, appearance and bodily dispositions they design together into a lifestyle. The modern individual within consumer culture is made conscious that he speaks not only with his clothes, but with his home, furnishings, decoration, car and other activities which are to be read in terms of the presence and absence of taste. (Featherstone, 1991: 86)

The cultural and postmodern turn in consumption studies rests substantially on a scepticism concerning the totalising claims of the critical or neo-Marxist approach to consumption which has stressed the manipulative, ideological nature of consumer capitalism (for example, Horkheimer and Adorno, 1987[1944]; Marcuse, 1976 [1964]). The logic behind this flight from critical versions of consumption theory is built in part on the substantial body of literature that has recently emerged concerning social and economic processes of spatialisation and semioticisation associated with what have been labelled 'late' (Jameson, 1991) forms of capitalism (see also Beck, 1992; Harvey, 1989; Lash and Urry, 1987, 1994). The groundwork of this approach rests on the identification of a variety of fundamental transformations in the circulation of global capital, and an array of associated cultural changes (tellingly understood as a mere 'dependent variable'), which generally include shifts in the way consumer objects are produced and consumed. A principal claim advanced in this literature is that the nature of consumption has changed as capitalism spatialises and semioticises in unique ways at an accelerated pace; and as a corollary, consumption is commonly theorised as an important sphere for reflexively monitoring self-trajectories and for generating a social identity. As part of their theorisation of flexible flows of capital and signs, Lash and Urry exemplify this view in their description of the consumption component of these regimes of reflexive accumulation:

> What is more important is the process of *Enttraditionalisierung*, of the decline of tradition which opens up a process of *individualization* in which structures

such as the family, corporate groups and even social class location, no longer
determine consumption decisions for individuals. Whole areas of lifestyle and
consumer choice are freed up and individuals are forced to decide, to take
risks, to bear responsibilities, to be actively involved in the construction of
their own identities for themselves, to be enterprising consumers. (Lash and
Urry, 1994: 61)

The new anthropologies of consumption and economic behaviour

It is from within the discipline of anthropology that some of the most
influential recent works on the cultural aspects of consumption have
emerged. These new approaches are distinguished by the application of
anthropological concepts and methodologies to contemporary consumption settings and practices, such as shopping, fashion and home decoration. While there are strong and influential bodies of related work within
sociology, North American consumer research, anthropology, psychology
and sociology which deal with objects have already been highlighted
(and), contemporary manifestations of material culture studies have principally been drawn around the work of Daniel Miller. Miller's status as a
virtual one-person industry in material culture studies is based mainly on
the groundbreaking achievements of his work *Material Culture and Mass
Consumption* (1987) and the large volume of work published since then. Its
principal accomplishment was to show how material culture studies
could be profitably applied to studies of contemporary consumption,
using concepts from across the disciplines of anthropology, philosophy
and sociology. Though in this work Miller deals primarily with the
abstract and philosophical dimensions of objects as material culture,
throughout it he retains an interest in modern life and its fundamental
processes as they were understood in classical social theory: individuali-
sation, materialism, alienation and objectification. In prefacing this work
Miller suggested that the re-emergence of the field of material culture
studies may give hitherto unconnected threads in an otherwise homeless
and residual field of inquiry 'a new integrity as a basis for tackling topics
such as mass consumption' (1987: vii). Judged against this goal, the success of *Material Culture and Mass Consumption* is undisputed, as this aspiration has been substantially realised. In 1996, Miller and Tilley became
the founding editors of the *Journal of Material Culture*, whose broad concern they defined as interdisciplinary research dealing with 'the ways in
which artefacts are implicated in the construction, maintenance and transformation of social identities' (Miller and Tilley, 1996: 5).

The other significant accomplishment of *Material Culture and Mass
Consumption* was to provide a new analytic focal point for studies of consumption and to actually name the framework of 'material culture' as a
field for common inquiry. Mary Douglas and Baron Isherwood
([1996]1979) may have managed the same some years earlier had they
used something other than the term 'goods' to proclaim their interest in

anthropological accounts of contemporary consumption. This disciplinary defining aspect of Miller's success must be understood within the evolution of the field of consumption studies. Consumption studies within sociology and cultural studies flourished in the 1980s via emerging accounts of postmodernity and its basis in expressive, consumption-based reflexivities and identities. But in the 1990s fresh empirical accounts and re-evaluations by leading scholars surfaced that questioned some of the extravagant and unfounded claims in the literature. These criticisms were based particularly around the focus on particular forms of consumption as the foundation for generalising postmodern accounts. In contrast, by emphasising the transformative capacities people possess when they deal with objects, the material culture approach had the advantage of encouraging a grounded, empirical focus that addresses mutual relations between people and consumer objects.

Material culture studies may once have had a coherent basis within the discipline of anthropology, as a strand of evolutionary anthropology. However contemporary studies of material culture have developed a strongly interdisciplinary nature. Various disciplines have as their concern aspects of material culture: art history, design and fashion studies, architecture and landscape design, consumer research and marketing studies. All of these disciplines deal with aspects of material culture as their principal empirical focus. However, with the exception of consumer research and marketing studies, they are not centrally connected to the current scholarship associated with the growth of material culture studies, nor would they necessarily identify themselves as practising material culture studies. Likewise, there are various sub-disciplinary concerns within sociology that commonly deal with material culture as part of their inquiry, for example, studies of the body and body modification, urban and spatial studies, and technology studies. Few scholars within this field would be likely to explicitly identify themselves as doing material culture studies, though within the field of technology studies Michael (2000: 3) is one who has explicitly identified studies of mundane technologies and their role in mediating everyday life as part of material culture studies. Despite the tendency to celebrate the inclusiveness of an interdisciplinary approach, there is some danger in including all and sundry accounts of material objects within the field of material culture studies, simply because they study objects or artefacts in some way.

Basic premises of the material culture approach

Having surveyed various disciplinary bases and origins of theory and research into material culture, the next section generalises about the common assumptions of these diverse approaches. Such principles are not necessarily directly manifest in each of the individual approaches previously discussed, nor are they an attempt to constitute a type of mantra on how to practise legitimate material culture studies. Rather, the following principles provide the rationale and foundational assumptions that underpin these diverse approaches to accounting for objects.

Interdisciplinary and cross-disciplinary inquiry

The first characteristic that defines the contemporary field of material culture studies is its interdisciplinary approach and cross-disciplinary focus. Interdisciplinarity refers to studies of material culture that make use of multiple disciplines – for example, sociology, history, anthropology and psychology – as complementary elements of their explanation. In this interdisciplinary model, no discipline is given authority over explanations of material culture as each is seen to enhance the insights of the other. This is important because no object has a single interpretation – objects are always polysemous and capable of transformations of meaning across time and space contexts. For example, in his important examination of the process of commoditisation of objects, Kopytoff (1986) intertwines history, philosophy, anthropology and sociology to show how objects undergo changes in status and meaning over time, and across cultural spaces. Furthermore, there is an inherent diversity of analytic methodologies deployed within material culture studies, broadly ranging from formal structuralism and semiotic interpretations, to ethnography, interviewing and observational studies.

The idea of cross-disciplinarity is quite different. The cross-disciplinary nature of material culture studies means that discrete studies of material culture are undertaken across multiple disciplines, but do not necessarily make use of interdisciplinary approaches. For example, the North American tradition of consumer research and business studies is generally, though not exclusively, associated with psychological, positivist approaches to studying human–object relations (the work of Belk and Wallendorf are prominent exceptions to this generalisation). The restrictive and exclusive focus of this style of research means that one generally does not find reference to important sociological or anthropological traditions within it, even to those one might consider being amongst the most important and influential – including Baudrillard, Bourdieu, Mauss or Simmel. Yet, on the other hand, many important questions are addressed within this broadly positivist oeuvre using well-conceptualised, novel empirical approaches that build upon accumulated research findings from within the restricted field. To date, both approaches have tended to largely ignore each other's work. It is also accurate to say that the discipline-bounded focus of much psychological research into material culture has been generally overlooked by sociologists and anthropologists, save a few prominent exceptions such as Csikszentmihalyi and Rochberg-Halton (1981) and the work of Belk on collectorship (1995) and materialism (1985, 1995).

Objects matter

The fundamental conviction of material culture studies is that objects do matter for culture and society, and that social analysis should take account of objects in theorising culture and how it works. Even though the tradition of studying elements of material culture is relatively long, like theorists who have argued that social theory has too long ignored space, emotions, or the body, theorists of material culture are attempting to 're-materialise' social theory through an attunement to people–object relations. This is precisely the agenda that underlies Daniel Miller's case for studying material culture. He notes the contradiction that 'academic study of the specific nature of the material artefact produced in society has been remarkably neglected ... This lack of concern with the nature of the artefact appears to have emerged simultaneously with the quantitative rise in the production and mass distribution of material goods' (Miller, 1987: 3). But why are objects held to matter? The answer is not just because they are more plentiful or ubiquitous, but because they are involved in social representation or symbolisation, and are recognised as containing important meanings for social action. Thus, as semiotic studies of objects illustrate, objects represent or symbolise some aspect of culture, and have cultural resonance because they are recognised by members of a society or social group. So, objects represent and are recognised within society.

Not only do we constantly engage with objects in a direct, material way we also live in a world where objects are represented as images and have global mobility. This means that understanding the 'social lives' (Appadurai, 1986; Kopytoff, 1986) of objects is one of the keys to understanding culture. In his efforts to develop an alternative political economy that understands the processes which underpin people–object relations, Baudrillard (1981, 1996[1968]) writes persuasively in favour of a social theory that takes account of objects, which up until now had 'only a walk-on role in sociological research' (1981: 31). Baudrillard expresses a desire to see objects in terms of their general structure of social behaviour, and 'as the scaffolding for a global structure of the environment' (1981: 36). More recently, Miller (1998b) has asserted that, in the first instance, things or objects – rather than people alone – do matter in studies of culture. By focusing on objects in a way that is inclusive of the subjects who use them and of their motives and meanings, such approaches avoid fetishisation of material culture. In showing how objects matter, Harré (2002) suggests that all objects belong to material and expressive orders. The former relates to their practical utility, and the latter component to their role in helping to create social hierarchies of honour and status. He usefully reminds the reader that social life can be seen to be made up of a series of symbolic exchanges which construct and manage meanings (ie. 'culture'), and that such exchanges cannot be accomplished without the help of material things. What's more, this means that the narrative – storylines, talk, conversation and interaction – and the material orders cannot be separated, for to 'become relevant to human life material beings must be interpreted for them to play a part in human narrative' (Harré, 2002: 32).

A concern with the cultural efficacy of objects has enduring salience within sociology and anthropology, and includes some of the foundational statements within each discipline by, for example, Marx, Durkheim, Simmel, Malinowski, Mauss and Veblen. While these texts are not always, and not principally, concerned with objects or material culture directly as are today's studies, objects do play an important role in these canonical analyses of society and culture. What distinguishes these classical, modern studies of society from current material culture studies is that current studies have a direct interest in people–object relations as the prime motive and aim of their analytical work. For example, Marx spoke of objects within his larger theory of capitalist development, Durkheim of objects as representations of fundamental classes of things as either sacred or profane, and Veblen of the ability of objects to show off luxury and beauty. In current studies of material culture the object-person relation is the direct focus of inquiry, and taken to be a matter of interest in its own right. This means there is a greater potential for material culture to be theorised and conceptualised in more sophisticated ways, made central to the theoretical narratives and arguments of researchers, and become more pivotally imbricated in the articulation of social actions and outcomes.

Objects have social lives

One of the basic insights of recent conceptualisations of material culture studies has been the idea that objects have 'social lives' (Appadurai, 1986) or 'biographies' (Kopytoff, 1986). Essentially, this means that in modern societies, where meanings and interpretations attached to images are relatively flexible and fluid, objects have careers or trajectories whereby their meaning for consumers changes over time and space. As Kopytoff (1986) points out, this may involve objects shifting in and out of commodity status. That is, at some stage of their lives, objects are primarily defined by their relation to a monetary or exchange value which defines them as 'commodities', while at other times, generally some time after an economic exchange has taken place, they become 'de-commodified' as they are incorporated – or 'subjectified' (Miller, 1987) and 'singularised' (Kopytoff, 1986) – by people according to personal meanings, relationships or rituals. For example, Corrigan (1997) uses the example of a pet, such as a cat, to illustrate this distinction. When the cat is encaged in a pet store it is primarily a commodity, yet when its future owner exchanges cash for it and brings it home, its commodity status dissipates and the pet is primarily defined by its relations to its new owners and 'family'. Kopytoff (1986) also gives the case of art to explain this process. An iconic piece of modern art is principally defined by its commodity status when it enters the market for sale, for example when it is displayed in an auctioneer's room in preparation for sale. Yet, once purchased, it re-enters the sphere of 'art' once more, and is presumably put on display as a symbol of beauty, status or the good aesthetic taste of its new owner.

The trajectories and biographies of objects are not just related to their commodity status, but to more complex meanings and interpretations given to them by individuals, restricted taste communities (such as those who appreciate avant-garde, or fans of a particular pop group or television show) and larger social groups (such as social classes, or 'tribes', see Maffessoli, 1996). The underlying assumption of this argument is that in complex, differentiated, pluralistic societies inhabited by omnivorous, knowledgeable and flexible consumers, the rules or criteria for discriminating and classifying the worth of material culture are diffuse and variable. As Kopytoff states (1986: 78–9):

> ...the public culture offers discriminating classifications here no less than it does in small scale societies. But these must constantly compete with classifications by individuals and by small networks, whose members also belong to other networks expounding yet other value systems. The discriminating criteria that each individual or network can bring to the task of classification are extremely varied. Not only is every individual's or network's version of exchange spheres idiosyncratic and different from those of others, but it also shifts contextually and biographically as the originators perspectives, affiliations and interests shift. The result is a debate not only between people and groups, but within each person as well.

Hebdige's (1988) essay on the networks of production and consumption meanings and discourses which construct the life of the Italian scooter is a seminal illustration of how commodities have such trajectories. The 'scooter' is, of course, a small wheeled, low-capacity cycle with a flat, open platform and engine mounted over the rear wheel. The first scooters were the 'Vespa', manufactured by Piaggio in 1946, and the 'Lambretta', produced by Innocenti in 1947. The scooters were originally targeted to continental women, and youths in general, who were the new, emergent consumers of the era. The scooters offered mobility and freedom, and were marketed as an object that carried possible emancipatory effects for young women. In 1950s Britain, the scooter acquired a strong association with 'Italianness' and continental style and sophistication, which for design and aesthetics conscious British consumers symbolised 'everything that was chic and modern' (Hebdige, 1988: 106). In the late 1950s and 1960s the scooter was appropriated by Mod youth as an identity marker which fitted their sartorial and musical preferences and aspirations. Customisation and accessorisation of the scooter followed, as did the establishment of rules for scooter wear, and an associated 'correct' way of riding.

Turning to more recent phases in the biography of the scooter, what can be noted is that scooters remain associated with youth, and particularly inner-city consumers due to their economy, size and mobility. Readers may be familiar with the image of celebrity chef Jamie Oliver scooting in and out of East London laneways on his way to find the 'freshest seafood', 'most pungent herbs' and 'matured cheeses'. Once again, the scooter is a lifestyle accessory, appropriated to suit the gentrified, inner-city market. Just as Hebdige has written the biography of the scooter, so other pop culture objects spring to mind as having their own careers: the Doc Marten boot which was once skinhead wear, became a mass youth brand somewhere in the 1980s or early 1990s, and is now being challenged by the 'sneaker' market; the 'Ben Sherman' and 'Fred Perry' shirts, again associated with skinhead and mod sub-cultures in Britain, then latterly inner-city, 'cool' consumers, and now are emerging as mass brands whose mainstream success have the potential to alienate their loyal base of original consumers. In these cases, the objects become saturated with meaning for particular sub-cultural groups, or 'tribes' (Maffesoli, 1996), and as they circulate amongst and throughout these cultures – often as a result of fashions – they are seen to have a trajectory or 'social life'.

SUGGESTED FURTHER READING

Slater's *Consumer Culture and Modernity* (1997) is an authoritative contextualisation of consumption cultures within social theory. See especially Chapters 5 and 6 of this work which look at the meaning and uses of things. The Editorial essay by Miller and Tilley (1996) which introduces the first edition of the *Journal of Material Culture* modestly develops a manifesto for contemporary studies of material culture, drawing together various strands and traditions of intellectual engagement with objects. Hebdige's (1988) essay on the trajectory of the Italian scooter (described above) within popular culture makes interesting reading and deftly illustrates the way commodities have cultural trajectories. I would also recommend consulting the first few chapters from Baudrillard's *For a Critique of the Political Economy of the Sign* (1981). Though it may sometimes be difficult to grasp the historical and intellectual context of Baudrillard's writing (given his engagement with intellectual traditions including structuralism, Marxism and semiotics), this is an ambitious, unique and readable work that takes up the case for studying objects as part of social life. For a design perspective on material culture, see works by Attfield (2000) and Heskett (2002). For a social psychological perspective on people–object relations, consult the works by Csikszentmihalyi and Rochberg-Halton (1981) and Lunt and Livingstone (1992).

PART II

THEORETICAL APPROACHES TO STUDYING MATERIAL CULTURE

THREE

The Deceptive, Suspicious Object. Marxist and Critical Approaches

SUMMARY OF CHAPTER CONTENTS

This chapter reviews the work of key authors who adopt a critical approach to theorising material culture. It has four main sections:

- Marx and the theorisation of objects as commodities
- Lukács on the links between commodification and reification
- The Frankfurt School authors, including Horkheimer and Adorno, Marcuse and Fromm who link commodity culture to social psychopathology
- popular criticism of commodity culture in liberal economics and new social movements.

The wealth of those societies in which the capitalist mode of production pre-vails, presents itself as 'an immense accumulation of commodities', its unit being a single commodity. Our investigation must therefore begin with the analysis of a commodity. (Marx, *Capital*, 1954[1867]: 43)

Marx: the commodity object as congealed labour

In the introduction to *Capital* Marx makes the point that the commodity – which we could understand as a technical category of 'material culture' – must be the starting point for an analysis of society. Reading this tract, one is likely to deduce that, at least at one level, Marx was centrally interested in questions of material culture and objects. Indeed, a survey of either of Marx's key works – *Capital* or *Economic and Philosophical Manuscripts* – will give one the impression that objects are the fundamental unit in his analysis of capitalist society. Moreover, one would understand from Marx that being able to grasp the 'true' nature of objects is crucial to comprehending the totality of human existence. Such an inference would be correct, but only in so far as these objects were to be understood as 'commodities'. By commodity, Marx was referring to material culture that is defined by a specific relation generated within a system of monetary exchange and produced in capitalist social relations.

Despite such exhortations to study material culture in the form of the commodity, one could not assert that Marx was interested in material culture *per se*. That is, he is not interested in the nature of objects as material elements of culture, the relations between people and objects, and the cultural uses of objects. Objects are important for Marx because they are the unit representations of fundamental processes of capitalist society: alienation, exploitation and estrangement. So, even though in *Capital* Marx develops a formidable model of the materialist, class basis of capitalist society that begins with the commodity as its fundamental unit for analytic focus, he does so in a way that completely obliterates the possibility for an interpretive or cultural account of the meaning of objects. The intellectual legacy of Marxist accounts of the commodity has been to focus on the relations and means of production, at the expense of consumption. And, when consumption was studied, the scholarly accounts developed were generally reductive and deterministic. Such studies tended to view consumption practice and the commodity culture upon which it is based with scepticism and disdain, seeing it as evidence of ideological manipulation, the generation of false consciousness, and as degrading to authentic human values.

The following section examines more closely the role of the commodity within Marx's account of capitalism. Objects perform two principal functions in Marx's analysis of capitalism. First, because they are products of human labour organised within capitalism, they embody exploitative capitalist labour relations. Furthermore, objects engender a false consciousness within exploited social classes who focus on the lure of commodity jewels, and in doing so overlook their exploited status within the capitalist system. The closest Marx gets to an anthropological or deeply 'cultural' understanding of material culture is his admission that people learn about themselves and broader humanity by contemplating the objective world they have created. The highest form of this learning would be to develop a consciousness of their alienation and how material culture, as commodity, embodies such alienation.

Marx's materialist methodology leads him to conclude that what matters is not merely the intellectual world, but the objective or material world. Further, he urges people to realise that they are the creators of such an objective world – including the everyday objects of consumption they engage with – rather than taking it for granted or assuming they hold no individual responsibility for it:

> It is therefore in his fashioning of the objective that man really proves himself ... for man reproduces himself not only intellectually, in his consciousness, but actively and actually, and he can therefore contemplate himself in a world he himself has created. (Marx, 1975: 329)

The integral unit of Marx's analysis of the objective world is the commodity form. To understand capitalism, one must understand the commodity. By commodity, Marx had quite a special meaning in mind. One could not simply substitute 'object', 'thing' or 'material culture' to capture Marx's meaning, as is popular in current discussions about objects. In the first case Marx uses the term commodity to refer to objects that are assigned a monetary value and are exchangeable. Additionally, Marx seems to imagine the commodity as being a material container or expression of the history of capitalist relations – the exploitation, alienation and oppression of the working class is implicit in its material form. He points out in the introductory sections of *Capital* that in the first instance commodities must satisfy human wants, however, 'the nature of such wants, whether, for instance, they spring from the stomach or from fancy, makes no difference. Neither are we here concerned to know how the object satisfies these wants' (1975: 43). In other words, he makes clear his treatise is not about economic, cultural or philosophical questions of satisfaction, utility or value – the type of questions a treatise on modern consumption would be expected to develop. Rather, it is with the commodity as an object of ideological obfuscation or trickery. For this reason Marx's account of the commodity can never really be the basis for an adequate theory of material culture for he is not concerned with a subjective interpretation of the commodity, the cultural work objects afford, or the reasons why and how people give it value and consume it.

Marx develops his theory of the commodity by arguing that the object of consumption within capitalism is not as it seems. At first glance, the commodity may appear 'a very trivial thing, and easily understood. Its analysis shows that it is, in reality, a very queer thing, abounding in metaphysical subtleties and theological niceties' (Marx, 1954[1867]: 76). The queerness of the object is that it is a material embodiment of exploited human labour. Once one understands this historical fact, according to Marxist doctrine, one is likely never to see consumption objects in the same light. For Marx, the link between the object of consumption and its origin within capitalist labour relations was clear:

> commodities come into the world in the shape of use-values, articles, or goods, such as iron, linen, corn etc. This is their plain, homely, bodily form … (however) they acquire this reality only in so far as they are expressions or embodiments of one identical social substance, human labour. (Marx, 1954[1867]: 76)

The case of sports shoes and fashion clothing is apt here. Critics point out that if western consumers realised many of the expensive brands they wear are produced at very cheap rates by lowly paid labour in third world countries, or sweatshops within their own country, they may be convinced to change their consumption habits. Especially within the sports fashion market dominated by iconic global brands, such changes seem some way off, despite the existence of a developing critical awareness fostered by popular works like Naomi Klein's *No Logo*.

Looking further into the detail of Marx's analysis, we can see that it is by distinguishing between use-value and exchange-value that Marx has the technical–theoretical means for expressing his deep mistrust of the objects of capitalist economic production. Marx theorised that material objects have a range of palpable use values – to feed, clothe, entertain or give satisfaction and pleasure. However, objects of consumption also embodied a specific set of exploitative social relations. In fact, they are quantities of 'congealed labour time' (Marx, 1954[1867]: 30) which are material crystallisations of the sweat, blood and energy of workers. The product of labouring is a double-edged alienation – from one's own labour activity which Marx saw as a tragic activity ultimately directed against itself, from other workers, and from the product of one's labour, which was the objective world of consumption objects. The more the worker produces, the more he is alienated from the objects of his production. This means that the objects workers produce shall ultimately confront them as something hostile and alienating, symbolising their estrangement (Marx, 1975: 326). In developing such a powerful theory of alienation and exploitation, Marx laid down perhaps the most influential framework for understanding commodity objects. His analysis intersected in minor ways with some of the concerns expressed by earlier moral philosophers such as Adam Smith, and served as the groundwork and inspiration for later lines of commodity criticism in works by Lukács, Horkheimer and Adorno, Fromm and Marcuse, and in an indirect way through the writings of foundational postmodernists such as Jameson (1991[1984]). It is to the twentieth century descendants of the Marxian view on material culture as commodity that the remainder of this chapter turns.

Lukács, reification and the commodity form

Writing in the tradition of Marx over the first three decades of the twentieth century, Lukács' work can be seen as a response to the failure of Marx's materialist account to explain the continued advancement and colonisation of capitalism. The problem, for Lukács, was to explain why it was that the exploited classes did not rise up in revolt to liberate themselves, as predicted by Marx's scientific, materialist dissection of the laws of capitalism. Lukács' explanatory solution was to begin looking toward the realm of culture and non-economic dimensions of social life for blockages to capitalism's downfall. He concluded that culture – defined in this tradition as the values held by citizens that were identified as an impediment to radical social and economic change – existed as a form of ideology. Like Marx, Lukács' analysis begins with the commodity form. However, in contrast to Marx who focused on processes of labour exploitation and the expropriation of value from workers and its embodiment in the commodity, the body of Lukács' explanation centred on the processes of commodification and reification which were identified as entrenched cultural impediments to radical social change. He also identified that society-wide rationalisation processes ushered in changing forms of consciousness which encouraged exploited classes to take current social arrangements for granted.

Lukács begins the essay 'Reification and the consciousness of the proletariat' from his best known work *History and Class Consciousness* (which compiles political essays written between the years 1918 and 1930) at the same point Marx begins *Capital* – with an assertion of the universality of the commodity form and an entreaty to understand the commodity as the basic component of capitalist social relations. Like Marx, Lukács saw the bedrock of capitalism as the commodity form. In holding a commodity in one's hands, wearing a commodity on one's feet or one's back, purchasing or producing a commodity, one held the nucleus of capitalism and the key to understanding the exploitative and despairing nature of contemporary society (that is, if only one could realise it). The commodity is the holy grail of such Marxist accounts. Lukács pronounces that 'there is no problem that does not ultimately lead back to an analysis of commodities' and that the secret to understanding capitalist society is to be 'found in the solution to the riddle of the commodity-*structure*' (Lukács, 1971: 83).

In Lukács' vision, the commodity object is also magically deceptive. In people's everyday subjective contemplation and use, the object seems rational and transparent enough. However, in reality it has acquired a 'phantom objectivity' which serves to hide its true nature from those unaware or ignorant (1971: 83). So, par for the course in this genre, we see that Lukács believes that to see behind the commodity is to understand capitalism. Furthermore, by implication, to consume goods and services without regard for the structural conditions of their production (that is, relations of capitalist production) is to overlook a basic fact of social existence – commodity objects embody a set of exploitative relations connecting people within capitalism: the bourgeoisie (owners of the means of production) and proletariat (those who only have their labour to sell to the bourgeois capitalists).

The object thus performs an ideological function. By posing deceptively as a prop on the stage where social activity is enacted, its everyday or 'use value' masks a menacing ideological content. The result is that the relations of production which combined to produce the thing go unobserved to the social actor, and the social structure is ultimately unchallenged – the basis for Lukács' master process of reification:

> The commodity becomes crucial for the subjugation of men's consciousness and for their attempts to comprehend the process or to rebel against its disastrous effects and liberate themselves. (Lukács, 1971: 86)

Lukács ventures a bleak vision, for in the end, people cannot exist without commodification touching their existence. Moreover, they have no way of living without the increasing penetration of reifying processes into their psyche. To disrupt and overcome reification would involve 'constant and constantly renewing' revolutionary efforts. This was unlikely however, since such radical sentiments were bound to be extinguished by the growth of status-consciousness which was an increasingly prominent feature of modern society at the expense of a revolutionary class-consciousness. One might suggest that shopping – as symbolic of the pleasures of commodity culture broadly – won out over revolutionary values.

The Frankfurt School and commodity culture

The Frankfurt School is the name given to a group of scholars working in an updated Marxist tradition often characterised as 'critical theory' (hereafter referred to as CT). The label 'Frankfurt School' could be considered a misnomer as the writers included beneath such a banner may not necessarily be considered a cohesive 'school' or tradition of scholarship and were not only based in Frankfurt. The most well known central figures of the Frankfurt School were Max Horkheimer, Herbert Marcuse, Theodor Adorno and Erich Fromm. There are two key focal points for the development of the Frankfurt or critical tradition: the first was the body of work emerging from the Frankfurt School of Social Research established in 1923, and second, Max Horkheimer's influential manifesto 'Traditional and Critical Theory', published in 1937, Horkheimer (1982).

Kellner (1989a: 2) identifies the development of CT as associated with crises of both capitalism and Marxism. The crisis of capitalism is associated with the doomed modern goal of building a rational society based on technological, scientific and economic advancement. The crisis of Marxism is associated with the failure of Marxist theory to foster the concrete existence of socialist republics, given that its central premises were based upon such an event. Further, it became recognised that the scientistic basis of orthodox Marxism was conceptually rigid and altogether too heavily based upon Enlightenment-style premises. CT was established on a programme of interdisciplinary, Marxist-oriented social research. At its philosophical core was a belief that traditional social science approaches treated human beings as mere objects within mechanical schemes of understanding. Furthermore, the consequence of traditional social science approaches was to operate as if social scientific facts could be separated from social values. CT could be seen as a re-appraised form of Marxist theory – members of the Frankfurt Institute remained committed to working in the Marxian tradition and identified with much of its analytic premises and approaches, but went beyond much of its anachronistic classical vocabulary and conceptual core (Kellner, 1989a: 12). A primary assertion of CT was that contemporary Marxism was best served by the development of an interdisciplinary research programme that gave importance not only to the economic bases of social organisation, but to matters of socio-psychological integration and the capitalist contours of culture. This unique blend of Marxism which considers culture and psychology (rather than just economy) can be identified in the way Frankfurt scholars understood the rapidly developing consumerist commodity culture of the twentieth century.

Horkheimer and Adorno: dominating objects and the psychopathology of modern life

Horkheimer and Adorno begin *Dialectic of Enlightenment* (1987[1944]) by contending that objects of Enlightenment (the philosophy underpinning modern social life) are endowed with a mythical element that promises utopian liberation – but delivers domination, ossification and, finally, psychopathology. Reading this text, one could get the impression that a person might unwittingly fall prey to such things by going to the movies, listening to pop music and reading newspapers and magazines – or so Horkheimer and Adorno warned.

Horkheimer and Adorno's goal was to expose enlightenment philosophy as bankrupt: 'the fully enlightened earth radiates disaster triumphant' (1987[1944]: 3) is one of the stirring opening sentences from their treatise on Enlightenment ideology. Their focus in the early parts of *Dialectic of Enlightenment* is on the philosophical basis of enlightenment traditions, and they argue that what supersedes old forms of social domination, such as language and military power, is technology. Technology then becomes the object of their interest and symbolic of a master narrative of modern life, which is highly understandable given the era in which they were writing. The reason for CT's concern with technology is interesting, and can illuminate a crucial aspect of their theoretical outlook. CT scholars are not interested in technology because of how it mediates or enables everyday life, or how people interact with it and use it to suit their own ends, but how it signifies a hollow promise and a technique of subjugation. Technology is thus ideological (based on false ideas that are enmeshed within systems of social power) and material (because it becomes the physical means for controlling bodies).

Horkheimer and Adorno draw attention to key technological advances associated with the growth of modern societies, or what they called the Enlightenment project. These were objects such as those Francis Bacon identified like the printing press, military artillery and the mariner's needle. According to modern Enlightenment philosophy each of these things promised control, productivity and rationality: printing presses allowed for widespread communication and the promotion of democratic ideals, artillery allowed nations to protect their citizenry and for citizens to protect their private property, while the mariner's needle (compass) allowed for effective navigation and the discovery (invasion) of new lands and their resources. Yet, despite their liberatory promise, such objects are resources for powerful social groups to enslave those with less social power – rather than liberation, such elements of material culture are the wherewithal for social exploitation. They become technologies of exploitation and enslavement.

But, for Adorno and Horkheimer, the problem with modern objects extends deeper than this, and it is this point that distinguishes them from earlier materialist Marxist positions because of its emphasis on the psycho-cultural component of social progress. The trouble with objects in modernity is not only that such objects materially exploit people and nature (as Marx first pointed out), but that they psychologically enslave those who own, possess or use them. This is the sinister flipside of Enlightenment progress – its 'negative dialectic' in Horkheimer and Adorno's terminology – which links to the Marxist idea that objects or commodities are not as they routinely appear. The suggestion is that people are mistaken to believe that an object (for example, such as a motor vehicle, a business suit, a computer or a mobile telephone) is positive in its implications for social progress and individual betterment, or at best neutral in its effects. In deploying such objects, people actually mentally enslave themselves, becoming victims of the ideology which is embodied in the objects of modernity they mistakenly believe liberate them:

> Men [*sic*] pay for the increase of their power with alienation from that over which they exercise their power. Enlightenment behaves towards things as a dictator toward men. He knows them in so far as he can manipulate them. The man of science knows things in so far as he can make them. (Horkheimer and Adorno, 1987[1944]: 9)

The ultimate downside of the Enlightenment philosophy is that people become alienated from the things that they produce, and the effect of using (perhaps considered 'worshipping' in the language of Horkheimer and Adorno) such objects is that the organic quality of social relations become compromised – with the assistance of objects and technologies of modern life, social relations become ossified, empty and mechanical in nature. The bottom line is that material culture becomes a mere carrier of capitalist or Enlightenment ideology. People lose sight of the things that matter in life (presumably some type of authentic human relations, though this is not entirely clear), worshipping the power of new technologies, which in turn order relations between people to the extent that organic relations are impossible, and an arthritic influence is extended over all aspects of human relations.

Horkheimer and Adorno point out that whereas in traditional societies objects were 'spiritualised', in modern industrial societies they are 'fetishised' (1987[1944]: 28). Though it was not around in Horkheimer and Adorno's day, the computer would be a good case to consider here which one could take to either prove or disprove their assertion. The computer (including the software within it and its components such as mouse and monitor) is indeed something that orders the daily existence of a good percentage of the global population. Furthermore, it is a powerful – seemingly indispensable – machine for ordering, calculating and measuring bits of existence. Currently, it is perhaps the ultimate mass-owned symbol of progress and achievement (perhaps the mobile telephone carries similar status for particular social groups). What's more, it allows us to virtually travel the globe, communicate effectively with connected others afar, and to sustain personal and professional networks. It is also an object of leisure and shopping as much as it is a tool of modern life – through that box on your desk what can't you buy over the internet? Yet, it is something that we may be conned into using (and upgrading) by marketers and corporate giants – as if it is the ultimate object for our personal and professional advancement. Moreover, it may be that far from making our lives easier, the computer complicates our tasks and disciplines us, molding our consciousness into something akin to an Excel spreadsheet.

Horkheimer and Adorno (and Adorno alone in the essays collected in *The Culture Industry* (1991)) reserve their most trenchant criticism of modern life for the emerging culture industries of their time. Though their fascination for 'new' cultural targets seem somewhat antiquated and old-fashioned now – cinema, radio, television – their message remains powerful to the extent that (somewhat) refined versions of such a perspective are commonly promulgated in contemporary critical cultural and consumption studies. In addition, for those currently concerned about the dross of mass cultural forms from manufactured pop music to glossy magazines to fashion sneakers, their message has a stirring ring of truth: culture is now a commodity like any other and is produced according to the same degrading logic of exploitation, appropriation and standardisation.

What has happened to the possibility of (sub-)cultural authenticity, you may ask? Well, in the CT theoretical schema it is available to be purchased in a range of subtly differentiated forms, so varieties of style have been catered to match one's identity preference: 'something is provided for all so that no one may escape; the distinctions are emphasized and extended' (Horkheimer and Adorno, 1987[1944]: 123). Horkheimer and Adorno link with lines of theory in classical sociology (particularly Weber and Durkheim) by pointing out that modern social progress rationalises and demystifies phenomena (including cultural, artistic and religious forms, but generally involving the loss of traditional social arrangements based around community and locality), and that master narratives of social life are now provided for by commodity-producing cultural industries which provide a (commodity-based) filter for everyday experience.

Horkheimer and Adorno give a couple of examples to illustrate their argument. They suggest that radio broadcasts are packaged forms of entertainment that are standardised and massified. This results in the denial of human agency and creativity in the engagement with culture, to the extent that participants become mere 'listeners' who are simply channels for the consumption of controlled and managed broadcasts promoting commercial interests. Similarly, in the case of the motor vehicle, they claim that consumers are conned into believing that subtle differences in mass-produced automobiles are meaningful and important. For example, in today's car market hardly a model is released without a range of options available, as the following niche market dichotomies illustrate: economy/luxury, city/country, sporty/thrifty, young person/family, and so on, depending on whether you're trying to sell a sedan, off-road vehicle, city runabout, luxury or sports model. Baudrillard, in *The System of Objects* (1996[1968]), apparently reworking some ideas of the CT tradition, wrote about this aspect of marketing through the idea of 'models' and 'series', suggesting that a car cannot readily be differentiated on the basis of its basic technical function, but on its inessential aspects (like tail fins). Baudrillard wittily sums up this aspect of 'packaging individuality' that Horkheimer and Adorno railed against:

> The most insignificant object must be marked off by some distinguishing feature – a colour, an accessory, a detail of one sort or another. Such a detail is always presented as specific: 'This dustbin is absolutely original – Gilac Décor has decked it with flowers for you!' 'A revolution in refrigeration – complete with brand-new freezer compartment and butter softener!' 'An electric razor on the cutting edge of progress – hexagonal, antimagnetic!'. (Baudrillard, 1996 [1968]): 141–2)

Horkheimer and Adorno's ultimate fear seems to be the psychological degradation of people and the collapse of meaning and value in western society. The fusion of mindless entertainment with culture is perfected by the culture industries. Furthermore, the triumph of rationality and progress embodied in faith in science and technology become pathological features of western societies, deceiving and stultifying the individual. Moreover, culture industries inhibit the development of a revolutionary class consciousness, and become a prevailing instrument of social control. Capitalist commodity culture becomes a dead hand guiding every aspect of social life – the ultimate denial of human agency and the victory of commodified culture is the only possibility in such a schema. As Horkheimer and Adorno (1987[1944]: 127) tellingly put it: 'The might of industrial society is lodged in men's [*sic*] minds'. The next section of this chapter considers the work of Fromm and Marcuse, who develop this notion further.

The psychic effects of commodity culture: Fromm, Marcuse and humanistic Marxist psychoanalysis

The work of Erich Fromm and Herbert Marcuse is often credited with developing a psychoanalytic – or at least strongly psychological – form of Marxism. Both writers were interested in the effect of capitalist society on the psychological traits and outlooks of individuals. We have seen that in the work of Horkheimer and Adorno the notion of a psychopathology generated by capitalist social relations was developed to some degree, but we must look to Marcuse and particularly Fromm for a fuller development of such an idea. It is as if Marxist critics of the era realised that the fight for people's consciousness in the factory and workplace was lost, and that the terrain of criticism must move to other sites – to the consumption of culture industry goods and new technologies, and the psychic make-up of people. Thus, the birth of a radical humanist, Marxian-inspired social psychology that attempted to explain how commodity culture impacted on the nature of human beings and their psychological make-up.

In *The Sane Society* (1955) Fromm states that the psycho-social problems he sets out to analyse constitute a 'pathology of normalcy' – a sickness associated with the nature of humans arising from their modes of everyday living in capitalist society. This central thesis of the work may have been more accurately signalled by titling the work *The 'Insane' Society*, for Fromm views the values propagated by western capitalism as psychologically inhibiting and ultimately degrading to the realisation of authentic human ethics. What values does he criticise? Materialism, acquisitiveness and hyper-individualism constitute his main targets, and it is the relation of these dispositions to the prevailing commodity culture (which is identified as the cause of these pathological values) that makes Fromm's ideas important. On middle-class prosperity in western capitalist societies, Fromm points out that although capitalism fulfils our basic needs more than satisfactorily, the human want to possess wealth and objects of desire 'fails to satisfy profound needs in man [*sic*]' (1955: 11). This leaves people with feelings of persistent emptiness and boredom despite their consumption expenditures and accumulation of objects, eventually stunting their psychic development as human beings.

Fromm associates such a pathology with wider neuroses in western culture, arguing that western society as a whole suffers from a deceptive condition of 'consensual validation' of its organising principles: 'the fact that millions of people share the same forms of mental pathology does not make these people sane' (1955: 15). Fromm labels the pathology a 'socially patterned defect', and while he points out that it is possible for individuals to live with such defects without becoming seriously mentally ill, the final result of the illness is that they fail to actualise a genuine expression of self. What stops such pathologies from becoming manifestly neurotic and troubling people to the extent that they can no longer function in their everyday lives? Escapist forms of consumption – especially within the realm of culture such as movies or popular magazines – assuage such pathologies, keeping them at bay by generating temporary feelings of happiness, satisfaction and self-efficacy. Fromm contends that the core feature of social existence within capitalist society is alienation from work, consumption and one's fellow citizens. The problem is not so much consumption *per se* – for Fromm saw that it could be a 'meaningful, human, productive experience' (pp. 133–4) – but *the way people consume*, pursuing needs that are frivolous, excessive and undertaken for the wrong reasons, as he notes:

> If I have the money, I can acquire an exquisite painting, even though I may not have an appreciation for art; I can buy the best phonograph, even though I have no musical taste; I can buy a library, although I only use it for the purpose of ostentation. I can buy an education, even though I have no use for it except as an additional social asset. (Fromm, 1955: 131)

The main problem Fromm saw with consumption is that it was estranged from human needs, and put to perverse and socially divisive uses, such as ostentation and social distinction. Acquisition of goods becomes a goal in itself, effectively displacing genuine human needs – relatedness, creativity, brotherliness, individuality and reason – with the empty promises of material goods. Fromm developed these ideas further in his tellingly titled work *To Have or To Be* (1976), which was an inquiry into the character structure of citizenry in western societies who are exposed to the hegemonic acquisitive culture promoted by capitalism. Fromm distinguished between two modes of living: 'having' and 'being'; the former centred upon materialism and the latter around people and relationships. In the mode of having, desire to accumulate and acquire goods becomes pathological to the extent that actualisation of identity is inhibited:

> Consuming has ambiguous qualities: It relieves anxiety, because what one has cannot be taken away; but it also requires one to consume even more, because previous consumption soon loses its satisfactory character. Modern consumers may identify themselves by the formula: *I am = what I have and what I consume*. (Fromm, 1976: 27)

Fromm notes similarities between western consumers and Freud's characteristation of the anal personality, suggesting that accumulation of consumer objects becomes a strategy for displacing painful questions related to identity and sexuality, resulting in stunted psychological development. The anal character is a person whose main energy in life is directed toward having, saving and hoarding things (objects), and Fromm concludes that since most members of western society are anal in the sense that they live to acquire, society at large must be sick. Fromm uses the example of car ownership (1976: 72–3) to explicate the links between the capitalist system of production that encourages periodic replacement of personal automobiles through obsolescence, and the accompanying psychology of personal ownership, which instills in people the idea that owning a 'new' car is important. Fromm suggests that purchasing and owning a new car serves a variety of purposes for one's personal psychology: it is a symbol of social status, it is a symbolic extension of one's ego, it enhances an individuals' sense of personal efficacy by demonstrating one's ability to 'make a deal', and finally, the very fact that the car is *new* is important in itself. In consumer societies, people have a constant need to experience the consumption of new objects 'because the old stimuli are flat and exhausted' (Fromm, 1976: 73).

Marcuse's *One Dimensional Man* (1976[1964]) is another work in the post-Freudian Marxist psychology tradition that, at its core, addresses the question of integration of the exploited working classes into capitalism. The essential problem relates to the potential for development of a revolutionary consciousness within the exploited working classes – now bought out by the spoils and lures offered by modern western economies and the ideological promises made in the name of increased rationality and freedom. Like Fromm, Marcuse's goal was to uncover the ideological basis of capitalist society. Marcuse exposes what he sees as new forms of control ('totalitarianism') – the ideology of 'scientism' embodied in positivist scientific values, technical forms of knowledge and instrumental forms of reasons and association, is at the heart of capitalist domination. Class is arguably less important as a form of exploitation and social control in latter day capitalism, and has been replaced by science and technology. Technological rationality is the contemporary substitute for political forms of rationality, and becomes a new form of social control. Marcuse argues that advanced capitalism is a dressed-up form of totalitarianism. Framed by the overarching ideology of the free market, attainment of technological superiority and differentiated forms of abstract knowledge become social goals in themselves, and in addition they order the material and psychological existence of people.

Marcuse's 'one-dimensional' society is one where ideas, aspirations and broader social objectives are framed in terms of the limits presented by advanced capitalism. People believe they are free in capitalist society, but Marcuse points out that what they have is only freedom of the market. Therefore, there is freedom to consume (as Bauman puts it a couple of decades later in *Freedom*), but this is generated by the creation of false human needs through marketing and advertising. As Marcuse notes:

> ... liberty can be made into a powerful instrument of domination. The range of choice open to the individual is not the decisive factor in determining the degree of human freedom, but *what* can be chosen and what *is* chosen by the individual. (Marcuse, 1976[1964]: 21)

Marcuse distinguishes between 'true' and 'false' needs. True needs are those such as nourishment, clothing, lodging and culture, and are consumed in accordance with the individual's own judgement of his/her requirements free from coercion by marketing pressure. The question of what constitutes a fair determination of one's requirements can only be made in a truly free society, without the assistance of 'need creating' industries and ideologies. Advanced industrial society is one that specialises in engineering such false needs – Marcuse sees this as the basis of its totalitarianism. Marcuse observes that individuals' psychologies are now incorporated into capitalism, rather than just factories and technologies being the focus of productive activity. The individual becomes the expression of capitalist processes, and is simultaneously its agent. False needs bind people to the existing social order, restricting their freedoms, their search for happiness, fulfillment and community. Such false needs become 'ways of life' (1976[1964]: 24) through which an individual – whose psycho-social development is now pathologically circumscribed by capitalistic urges – vainly searches for an authentic and viable self-identity:

> The people recognize themselves in their commodities; they find their soul in their automobile, hi-fi set, split-level home, kitchen equipment. The very mechanism which ties the individual to society has changed, and social control is anchored in the new needs which it has produced ... Mass production and mass consumption claim the entire individual, and industrial psychology has long since ceased to be confined to the factory. (Marcuse, 1976[1964]: 22–3)

What can we make of such claims: rants against capitalism, or deeply felt, valid criticisms of western culture? Given the cultural turn in social theory and consumption studies in the last couple of decades, such views seem like outdated and limiting rhetoric. What's more, they don't seem to fit with what we now know about how and why people consume objects. Yet, one should not discard critical approaches, but perhaps seek to find new ways of developing and applying them using careful empirical approaches and novel theoretical frameworks. An innovative, non-reductive empirical investigation into the 'productive' elements of advertising that mobilise new kinds of psychological outlooks or subjectivities, and generate relations between people and commodities is offered by Miller and Rose (1997). Commencing with Marcuse's insight that advertising now incorporates individuals by transforming them into everyday agents for capitalist innovation through the commodity sphere, Miller and Rose make a divergent case by pointing out that studies of the relationship between advertising, consumption and agency have typically tended to assume consumers are, at best, passive and robotic in their actions, or, at worst, irrational or foolish. Marcuse's analysis of one-dimensionality created by culture industries manages to forcefully combine both points of view, which is a problem with his approach if one wishes to explore the meaning of human–object relations. Yet, Marcuse did manage to see that new industries were increasingly using scientific techniques of calculation and measurement to map consumer desires. In their study, Miller and Rose use archival material from research conducted at the Tavistock Institute of Human Relations, which undertook paid work on behalf of advertisers in the period after the Second World War for corporations selling a range of products as diverse as ice cream, beer, petrol and chocolate. Miller and Rose show how consumers were 'mobilised' – their subjectivities assembled – by techniques that offered individuals opportunities for self-gratification without breaching civilities, modes of negotiating tribulations and challenges of everyday life through the deployment of consumer goods, and new ethics and techniques for living (1997: 32). Rather than merely reiterating an account where powerful corporate interests manipulate consumer desires, these constitute technologies that assemble spaces and modes of action, establishing regimes of governance for the consuming passions that are mobilised within individuals:

> This was not a matter of the unscrupulous manipulation of passive consumers: technologies of consumption depended upon fabricating delicate affiliations between the active choices of potential consumers and the qualities, pleasures and satisfactions represented in the product, organized in part through the practices of advertising and marketing, and always undertaken in the light of particular beliefs about the nature of human subjectivity. (Miller and Rose, 1997: 31)

Popular criticisms of commodity culture

A number of works surfaced in the decades after the Second World War that considered the basis and ethics of consumer society and had an impact by bridging public and scholarly consciousness. Broadly, we could distinguish between criticisms of commodity culture and consumer society emerging from liberal criticism in economics and public policy, and those emerging from the new social movements, especially environmentalism.

John Kenneth Galbraith's *The Affluent Society* (1987[1958]) is perhaps the best example of liberal criticism from within an American institutionalist tradition (see also Vance Packard's *The Hidden Persuaders*, 1957, or *The Status Seekers*, 1959). In *The Affluent Society* Galbraith highlights the rather perverse situation achieved by western economies that had solved the 'problem of production', but were beset by other fundamental public sector problems. They were able to provide employment and rising incomes for their citizenry, thereby escaping the risk of poverty (for most citizens) that had plagued pre-modern societies. Yet, the values of this 'affluent society' were problematic, for they emphasised and held in esteem the achievement of private wealth, rather than public wealth or the public good. The irony of the affluent society was that increasing wealth did not build up a stock of public (civic) affluence, but only encouraged the expression of new consumer wants whose necessity was questionable. So, for example, rather than satisfying hunger and shelter, excellent roads and public hospitals, contemporary economic activity satisfies desires for shiny new luxury cars, silk shirts, kitchenware, glossy magazines, soft drinks and so on. Galbraith diagnosed a 'dependence effect' by which new wants are created by the very process of production that satisfies them: the producers of goods are able to synthesise new desires within consumers. Typically, and problematically from Galbraith's perspective, economic theory has been reluctant to judge, let alone consider, the moral nature of consumer wants, and whether they could be classified as frivolous or essential. More than anything, Galbraith urges us to consider whether the contrivance by producers of consumer demand for non-essential or luxury goods should be considered valuable and viable from economic and social perspectives:

> As a society becomes increasingly affluent, wants are increasingly created by the process by which they are satisfied. This may operate passively. Increases in consumption, the counterpart of increases in production, act by suggestion or emulation to create wants. Expectation rises with attainment. Or producers may proceed actively to create wants through advertising and salesmanship. Wants thus come to depend on output … The higher level of production has, merely, a higher level of want creation necessitating a higher level of want satisfaction. (Galbraith, 1987[1958]: 148)

Galbraith's critique came from within a liberal economic tradition but around the same time environmental critiques of capitalist consumer culture were also emerging. In 1973 E.F. Schumacher published a manifesto for 'Buddhist economics' that was widely influential and popular – *Small is Beautiful*. Schumacher's work can be seen in the same context as popular environmentalist critiques of western society, such as Rachel Carson's landmark work *Silent Spring* (1962). Schumacher offered an analysis of western society and its economic principles 'as if people mattered'. He was critical of the western value of profits and progress as they were embodied in the search for 'bigger and better' technologies and economic efficiencies. Schumacher opposed degrading technologies and workplaces, and exploitative, dehumanising economic principles that ignored 'real' human needs. Like Galbraith, Schumacher criticised the discipline of economics for making people believe that the problem of production had been solved. He pointed out that though western societies appear to be materially better off, this is an illusion that masks the great damage done to the environment and the human soul in the name of such material advancement. Schumacher argued for an incorporation of the Buddhist point of view into western values: to make work more meaningful and fulfilling, to focus on the local and small-scale in terms of technologies and programmes of economic growth, to work with the environment rather than seek to dominate it, and to pursue the acquisition of wealth and commodities keeping in mind the principle that consumption wants should be satisfied 'to attain given ends with the minimum means' (1973: 48).

Selling 'good' forms of consumption: ethical toiletries and anti-materialist über-designers

The success of environmental and social critics like Schumacher and Galbraith in encouraging people to question the extent of their consumption and materialist values has been cleverly incorporated into marketing. The fact that in many markets' consumers are increasingly educated, and anxious, about the ethical standards companies adhere to has meant a change in the way corporate ethical standards are presented, if not practised. Marketing for some products encourages consumers to look for goods that are environmentally friendly (e.g. safe domestic pesticides, plastic shopping bags, reduced use of aerosols) and produced according to ethical principles (e.g. animal products such as eggs and meat, fashion and sports wear). Presuming one consumes the 'right' goods, personal acquisition can be seen to service a more just society and improved environment.

Anita and Gordon Roddick's 'Body Shop' philosophy is a good example here. The Body Shop began trading in 1976 with the core goal of delivering profits to investors, and luxury toiletry and cosmetic goods to customers (much the same goals as typical corporations). Yet, The Body Shop also strives to promote social and environmental responsibility and change. The Body Shop has developed and promoted a statement of its 'Values Mission' to define its ethical approach to business practice. These statements offer good public relations for the company, advertise the company's stock to the growing ethical investment industry, and encourage consumers to 'feel good' about buying their products, perhaps alleviating feelings of guilt some may have about the origin and testing of toiletry products they purchase. The core principles of The Body Shop's ethical approach are: Defend Human Rights, Protect our Planet, Support Community Trade, Activate Self-Esteem and Against Animal Testing.

Just as Schumacher proposed 'Buddhist economics', is it possible to have Buddhist consumerism? The Body Shop is one way to think about such a possibility. French designer Philippe Starck's postmodern pitch to assuage consumerist excess is another. In The Body Shop case what was being encouraged was environmentally and ethically responsible consumption. In the case of marketing for the design products made by Philippe Starck, we can see a curious pitch to alleviate any guilt associated with fitting out one's household top to bottom in Starck designer gear. Starck's designs have acquired a ubiquity in the aspirational middle-class household, and have made him one of the most creative and interesting designers of the last half-century. When one thinks of modern design, masters such as Arne Jacobsen, Charles and Ray Eames, Le Corbusier, Mies van de Rohe and Verner Panton come to mind. In Starck, we see not just the objects of design, but the apotheosis of designer as brand and celebrity. What is important is not just the objects that Starck designs, but Starck's aura as a designer.

Starck's persona is managed through the dissemination of ludic imagery: Starck as provocateur or clown who creates objects and spaces of play, fantasy, irony and childish pleasures. In Starck's designs for domestic objects we can see a postmodern concoction of irony, humour and irreverence coupled with the residual modern desire to sell 'good design' to the aesthetically impoverished masses: think of his range of playful oral hygiene products (the toothbrush named 'Dr Kiss' and the toothpick set named 'Dr Kleen'), or his famous toilet brush and flyswatter (named 'Dr Skud'). Though he has designed and decorated a massive range of objects, scapes and environments including hotels, airport control towers, waste recycling plants, motorcycles, boutiques, breweries and bookstores, Starck is known to most consumers for his range of mundane household goods that allow those with relatively small amounts of spare cash to buy into the design market and the Starck brand cachet.

One of the downsides for Starck is that his designs have become associated with a period of luxury and excess in the 1980s and 1990s. Thus, Starck was the perfect designer for cash-rich 'yuppies' and wannabe design aficionados. Yet, understandably, this is not the legacy Starck wishes to cultivate. Hence his range of 'Good Goods' promoted in the late 1990s advertised as: 'The Catalogue of Non-Products for the Non-Consumer for the Next Moral Market' (see Sweet, 1999). Attempting to make a stand against the acquisitive values of consumerism and materialism – that, ironically, his empire of designer goods is built upon – Starck proclaims that from now on he shall produce 'non-products':

It is a global proposal, my last major work, and It is about the equipment of life – about food, washing powder, clothes, music, books, transport, furniture, toys. I call these the 'No Products'. They are No Products because they are not created by marketing or advertising or by greedy people wanting to make piles of money. These are the basics of life made to fulfill a function with respect, fantasy, creativity, tenderness, humour and love. (Starck, in Sweet, 1999: 9)

It is difficult to judge the sincerity of Starck's anti-materialist manifesto, though it appears to be somewhat disingenuous given the personal profit he derives from the design industry. What the Starck case illustrates is how the consumption of design is framed by the consumer's anxiety not to be seen as 'too materialistic', or obsessed with the acquisition of frivolous or fanciful objects. Enthusiastic consumers are caught between establishing what is seen as an authentic or 'real' self-identity in the eyes of others, and the pressure to accumulate the 'right' collection of household designer objects necessary to establish themselves as a person of taste or good judgement (see Woodward, 2003). Starck's marketing strategy is to offer them a tactic for easing any anxiety – his design pieces distinguish the purchaser as a person of aesthetic integrity, but are amusing, ironic and serve to deconstruct themselves. A further matter for Starck relates to whether the integrity of his designs are challenged by the fact that the Starck brand is associated with such a wide range of design products, becoming synonymous with consumerist desire for objects with design cachet. Before concluding this chapter, let's return briefly to ponder Starck's postmodern manifesto for the consumers of his design objects:

Less is more. In the past five years I have changed completely. I am not the same man – now I am far more well tuned. Our civilization is based on the idea of making progress, so I cannot stop – I have to make things better, it is poetic. It is not enough to make things of beauty, however. They must also be good. The beautiful object was the product of a particular cultural regime, a regime obsessed with aesthetics. The problem with this is that the regime was ruled by the laws of taste, by what is in fashion and what is out of fashion. These laws are some of the most important levers of consumerism and lead to over-consumption. (Starck, in Sweet, 1999: 15)

Conclusion: evaluating critical approaches to the commodity object

Before proceeding to evaluate the critical perspective, consider the following recap of the general features of the critical account of material culture:

- Marx's materialist analysis of capitalism offers a production-based, rather than a consumption-based, account of human relations. Material culture is seen as something that relates principally to the sphere of economic production, rather than transformed through its appropriation in the act of consumption. Marx focused on how the workers who produce commodities (in an exploitative workplace) must then face these commodities in another social sphere (the marketplace). This is the basis for false consciousness of the working class, as workers do not recognise the way their labour has been exploited in the process of producing the commodity objects they desire and purchase. In Marx's analysis of capitalism, the commodified material culture that we use in everyday life is the material expression of exploited labour, embodying the sweat, blood and energy of workers.
- Consumers encounter material culture as something that is 'external' to them, as if it magically appears on shop shelves, rather than having a history. People uncritically accept material culture as autonomous, ahistorical and separate from social relations. Developing the ideological implications of Marx's thesis, Lukács referred to this as 'reification'. Reification ultimately directs consumer's attention away from a critical understanding of the 'truth' about the origin of the objects they consume.
- As a corollary, Lukács argued that consumer objects are carriers of capitalist ideology. By engaging in the act of purchase and use of consumer objects, consumers are really purchasing an embodiment of bourgeois ideology, thus reproducing capitalist relations.
- The Frankfurt School scholars emphasised how material and consumer culture suppresses, and eventually deadens, people's critical and aesthetic faculties. New forms of social control develop based around the mapping (and creation) of consumer desire through marketing

industries, and people become psychologically enslaved by the objects they consume – mindlessly entertained by frivolous goods to the extent that such consumption ultimately undermined their 'authentic' human needs for community, creativity and reason. For Fromm and Marcuse – scholars who developed a Marxist inspired form of psychoanalysis – this symbolised a pathological social system where people strive for acquisition of goods (what Fromm called the dominant social mode of 'having') as a substitute for the development of genuine, authentic human traits based on the mode of 'being'.

To what extent does Marxism and critical theory offer viable theoretical models for understanding material culture? The following arguments can be made in favour of such theoretical models:

- Critical accounts of the commodity object remind us that the objects we consume have to be made and distributed by someone, somewhere in the world. Most often, the people involved 'on the ground' in the production process in factories are far less privileged than we who do the consuming. Thus, critical accounts remind us that there are likely to be a set of unequal structural conditions that exist behind regimes of production and consumption.
- Critical accounts also suggest to us that we could do an ethical audit of the nature and origin of our personal consumption. Therefore, it points out that things such as global and regional economic and social inequalities, environmental damage, and harm to animals, should all play a part in determining the ethical standards we follow in our consumption practice.
- Critical theory allows us to reflect on how our own consumption practices might be fetishistic. This would be where our acquisition of consumer objects is undertaken for acquisitive or obsessive reasons, without any reflexive engagement as to how such consumption is linked to the positive development of self-image and self-efficacy. For example, a collector of shoes might question why they need so many pairs, or a fashion enthusiast might reflect on why they feel compelled to constantly be 'in fashion'.

Critical and Marxist accounts have generally fallen out of favour in studies of consumption and material culture. The following are commonly identified as their major flaws:

- Critical and Marxist accounts are generally about *materialism* and are *materialist* in analytic style, rather than having an interest in *materiality*. For this reason they offer inadequate models for understanding the relations between people and objects. Accounts of *materialism* focus on social modes of acquisition, and the associated ideology of consumerism where people become motivated to acquire consumer objects as the dominant mode of lifestyle. *Materialist* accounts focus on the material relations between owners of means of production and workers, producers and consumers, arguing that such categories give rise to basic social inequalities. On the other hand, critical and Marxist accounts neglect *materiality* – the most crucial dimension in understandings of material culture – which refers to the relations between people and objects, especially the way in which social life is inherently structured by everyday dealings with objects, such as technology or objects of memory.

* The most serious objection to critical and Marxist accounts is that they undertheorise agency in their conception of the relation between people and objects. Having agency in dealings with material culture doesn't just mean that people can experience pleasure or freedom when they engage with material culture, but that their engagements with material culture can possibly be subversive. Critical and Marxist accounts do not conceive that relations between people and material items of consumer culture can be creative, liberatory, constructive, expressive and emotional. Rather, they simply posit a reductive and determinist model that says all commodity objects embody exploitation, and that commodities serve ideological interests. The most sophisticated theoretical critique of such accounts is developed by Miller (1987), who argues that the work the consumer does after purchasing a good defines the essence of the consumption act:

> consumption as work may be defined as that which translates the object from an alienable to an inalienable condition; that is, from being a symbol of estrangement and price value to being an artefact invested with particular inseparable connotations. (Miller, 1987: 190)

Miller's point is that rather than dismiss mass-produced consumer goods as facile or irrelevant, we must understand them as crucial elements of culture. Not only do mass produced goods constitute the material environment we traverse, but they are integral to the process of objectification through which we establish our identities, affiliations and practices in everyday life (Miller, 1987: 215).

* Critical and Marxist accounts are uncertain about what recommendations to make to address the problems they diagnose. Even if the commodity objects people deal with in everyday life do embody exploitation and deaden consumer's critical faculties, what steps might be taken to change this, given people generally desire more goods and the rising standards of living often associated with them? Further, is there such a thing as an 'authentic' good serving a 'real' need? Who could arbitrate such a thing? (Miller, 1987: 188).

SUGGESTED FURTHER READING

The introductory tracts of Marx's *Capital* constitute bedrock statements on how and why material culture should be understood, first and foremost, as a commodity object. The early pages should be readily understandable to intermediate undergraduate students and beyond. Likewise, if one can overcome (or overlook) the arcane technical language, Lukács essay 'Reification and the consciousness of the proletariat' (in Lukács, 1971) and Horkheimer and Adorno's introductory essay in *Dialectic of Enlightenment* (1987[1944]), offer definitive post-Marxian statements on the deleterious effects of commodity culture. See also Erich Fromm's *To Have or to Be?* (1976) if you sometimes feel you are too acquisitive in your own consumption patterns and require conversion to a simpler life. While these books will not use the term 'material culture', one can infer how these authors understand the place of material culture in society. For a comprehensive and informed introduction to critical theory and its relation to Marxism, see Douglas Kellner's *Critical Theory, Marxism and Modernity* (1989a). Also in this vein, see David Held's *Introduction to Critical Theory* (1980). For a contemporary, reasoned discussion of personal and ethical problems related to consumerism, seek out Juliet B. Schor's research, starting with *Do Americans Shop Too Much?* (2000) before progressing to some of her journal papers. The work by Taylor and Tilford (in Schor and Holt's *The Consumer Society Reader* (2000)) puts the ecological case against ever-increasing patterns of consumption. Though it recites familiar arguments, at least it does so using contemporary data.

FOUR

The Object as Symbolic Code.
Structural and Semiotic Approaches

SUMMARY OF CHAPTER CONTENTS

This chapter reviews the work of key authors who adopt a semiotic and structural approach to theorising material culture, and commodity culture broadly. It has four main sections:

- an introduction to structuralism and Saussure's groundwork for a semiotics of everyday culture
- an examination of Lévi-Strauss' structuralist program for studying cultural objects
- an examination of Barthes' and Baudrillard's work on consumer societies and material culture
- a summary of Hebdige's work on sub-cultures which draws upon the structuralist semiotic tradition and critical sub-cultural theory.

...being in their place is what makes them sacred for if they were taken out of their place, even in thought, the entire order of the universe would be destroyed. Sacred objects therefore contribute to the maintenance of order in the universe by occupying the places allocated to them. They ... concern to assign every single creature, object or feature to a place within a class. (Lévi-Strauss, 1966[1962]: 10)

Structuralism, semiotics and reading material culture

The essential principle of the semiotic approach to studying material culture is that objects are signs referring to something other than themselves. As Eco (1976) beguilingly put it – the sign is intrinsically a lie. That is, an object is held to be a 'sign' of something else, a proxy for some other social meaning. For example, an object might refer to a category of social status like a person's occupation, their religion or gender. Or, an object might refer to a particular feature of a person's self-identity related to their affiliations and associations. Thus, according to the semiotic approach, material culture is said to be a 'signifier' that communicates things to others, accomplishing some king of social 'work'.

Consider a couple of introductory examples, the first of which was used by the semiotician Roland Barthes in his book *Mythologies* (1993[1957]). Barthes pointed out that a bunch of red roses is not merely an aesthetic and olfactory delight, but a cultural symbol of romance and love. Likewise, the wedding ring is a powerful traditional symbol of romantic love. Similarly, think of the necktie worn by a businessman. It should be obvious that people do not generally wear a necktie for the sake of comfort. Rather, they wear a necktie for a variety of other possible reasons, including symbolising their status as someone of importance, to abide by the dress conventions of a particular workplace, or to demonstrate to others that they perceive a social situation as formal. Or, consider a person who owns and drives a Rolls Royce motorcar. What would this communicate to you? There is no certainty about such matters of judgement, but it would likely indicate that the person is wealthy. It might also suggest something about the owner's broader social values. For example, it may suggest that they are from an 'old money' family background – or that they are trying to be perceived in such a way – or, that they are socially conservative.

Reading material culture

Being able to 'read' material culture in terms of its cultural meaning is an indispensable – yet somewhat problematic – social skill that is integral to our commonsense everyday interpretations. This is especially the case in large metropolitan centres, where potential for visual contact amongst citizenry is high, yet the probability of personal interaction is low. Such 'readings' of visible material culture afford rapid social communication without the need for speech. This allows people to make speedy judgements about social situations and others as they enter their visual field within various urban scenes. Yet, conversely, this skill also forms the basis for making hasty, stereotypical or discriminatory judgements based on incorrect classifications of people or things as dangerous, or a threat to social order. For example, a youth carrying a skateboard in a shopping mall, or other privatised public space, may be identified by local security as potentially troublesome. The skateboard has the capacity to symbolise social threat or danger within this consumption context.

In addition to the possibility for social and cultural discrimination based on making such generalised readings of material culture, there is a further fundamental risk associated with our search for social and cultural meanings through attendance to bits of everyday material culture. The idea that there could be unanimously correct, universally available readings of the meanings of material culture is problematic for three important reasons. In the first instance, we do not always have access to another individual's intended meaning for wearing, possessing or displaying some item of material culture. In fact, it may be that an individual claims or feels no meaning should be attached to their use or display of an object. Secondly, sometimes we simply do not have the cultural skills or 'capital' required to interpret the meaning of objects. This is the case if our interpretations of things – like items of clothing or shoes – rely on possessing specialist cultural knowledges, or cultural nuances, of which we are unaware. Thirdly, the use of material culture is always contextualised within particular time and space settings where social conventions of appropriateness and consideration are mobilised. When certain pieces of material culture are viewed outside the boundaries of time and space that define their meaning, they can appear incongruous, inconsistent or even disturbing.

Reflect on a couple of examples which illustrate some of the complexities and nuances of reading material culture. First, consider what you might wear to a dance party or nightclub. You would be unlikely to choose the same outfit to wear to a relative's marriage, or in turn, a funeral. This would be a *faux pas* – literally a 'false step' – wrong move, or social gaffe. Your relatives are likely to consider your dance party attire inappropriate or insensitive for the mood of solemnity at a funeral, just as it is likely to be unsuitable for the ambience of elegance desired at most weddings. To take a second example, wearing a cross around one's neck is potentially ambiguous in its message, though again this depends on time and space contexts, and other information we can gather about the wearer of the cross. Wearing a cross can display a person's commitment to Christianity – a visible symbol for self and others displaying the key symbolic act in Christian mythology. Alternately, wearing a cross is also associated with the dress and musical styles of gothic sub-cultures. Is it possible to confuse a 'goth' with a Christian church-goer on the basis that both are wearing a cross? One would have to admit this is possible, but not likely. This is not just because many goths tend to follow alternative spiritual beliefs and would rail against mainstream Christianity, but because we can use other material cues to help us make likely classifications. As most of us know, goths are also likely to wear black clothing, with signature items such as dark overcoats and black leather boots, have dark hair, body piercing, pale skin and extravagant jewellery. This is not an expected mode of self-presentation for committed Christians, who we would generally presume to be more moderate and conservative in their presentation of self, exhibited by softer colours, more modest clothing styles and conservatively styled hair.

Finally, to take another example which illustrates the complexities of making readings of material culture, think about the proliferation of fashion sneakers in recent years. For the last decade or so, sneakers, or trainers, have become the choice of footwear amongst fashion conscious urban youth (see Miles, 1996). Sneakers often borrow their design and aesthetic features from sportswear of earlier eras, appropriating fashions and trends of the 1970s and 1980s. Thus, some of the most popular sneakers today produced by mainstream sports brands such as Puma or Adidas reproduce sneaker models from the 1970s that were originally designed for basketball players, tennis players or even wrestlers. Does the contemporary wearer of such sneakers signal a direct association with basketball, tennis or wrestling by wearing such shoes? Generally, the answer is no. A knowledge of the history of the shoe design may be important to the wearer as a form of distinctive cultural capital. However, the meaning of the sneaker must be seen in temporal context, using nuanced forms of cultural capital, often dosed heavily with irony. Some decades on, these types of models are now strictly fashion objects, completely stripped of utility related to their original designed purpose, and appropriated within fashion logics where they are free to signify multiple, contradictory, conflicting messages, at the whim of the wearer who attempts to master the game of fashion through wearing such objects. Those ill-equipped with the cultural skills to engage in ironic, ludic readings may see such models of sneakers as bizarre, eccentric or plain inappropriate.

The point of these examples is that we cannot always assume a social message is directly or simply coded in an object, as if there is universal or perfect social knowledge of the manifold codes that frame material culture (see Campbell, 1995a, 1996). Yet, some of the most important contributions to understanding how people use material culture are substantially predicated upon the understanding that material culture is put to social work by actors to communicate a social message, including the work of Veblen, Goffman and Bourdieu. Though such authors have developed original contributions to understanding consumption and the social use of material culture that do not make formal use of semiotic analysis, their theories do rely to some degree on a model of 'semiosis' – or social recognition of the value and meaning of items of material culture – where consumption is assumed to convey certain social messages within networks of relational meaning. Before considering such theories in later chapters, we must first examine how the field of social semiotics we know today emerged from the theoretical tradition known as structuralism.

Structuralism as a general model for understanding culture

Smith (2001) gives an effective outline of the core features of the structuralist approach to analysing culture by pointing to five tenets.

- First, though the 'surface' of social life appears complicated, diverse and unpredictable, there are generative processes beneath it that guide the playing out of such minutiae. Thus, in order to come to grips with all that we identify at the face of social life, we need to look to deeper, constructive processes.

- These deeper constructive processes are relationally patterned, and they are also limited in number. So, a relatively small number of fundamental generative cultural schemes are present within a society, and these can be recombined in various ways. Lévi-Strauss (1966[1962]) referred to this process as 'systems of transformations'.
- The analyst of this structuralist generative scheme is objective. There are deep generative principles to be discovered; however everyday social actors who are immersed in them take them for granted, along with most aspects and events in social life. Consequently, they are not able to identify such structures. The patterns that these structures create on the surface of cultural life can be best observed and analysed by detached scientific investigation that employs a structuralist analytic approach.
- While early structuralism developed around the turn of the twentieth century from linguistic origins in the theories of Peirce and Saussure, later developments by Barthes and Lévi-Strauss in the middle of the twentieth century extended the analogies between language and culture, arguing that aspects of culture such as food, cuisine or motor vehicles could be analysed through structuralist methods. For example, foods or cuisine can be understood according to rules associated with cultural preferences for hot and cold, raw or cooked. Consequently, cultural objects can be decoded using a structuralist approach, as if they were a language.
- Finally, structural approaches tend to negate the role of the human subject. The focus of structuralist analysis is the working of the 'language of culture', according to systematic rules at the heart of social life. This was in contrast to approaches that emphasised the agency of the human subject in enacting or mediating such rules. It should be noted that such agentic approaches in sociological theory were substantially developed after the birth of linguistic structuralism.

Saussure and systems of linguistic communication

Largely, the genesis of the principles Smith (2001) outlines can be identified in the work of the founder of structural linguistics, Ferdinand de Saussure. Saussure's *Course in General Linguistics* (1966[1916]) was published posthumously, compiled from lecture notes gathered over the period 1907–11 from consecutive cohorts of his students at the University of Geneva. Saussure's great contribution was to conceptualise the systemic structures of language, making his work foundational to the development of linguistics. One might ask why Saussure's ideas on language are seminal, and more importantly, one may ask what linguistics has to do with studies of material culture? The answer to this is that the authority and elegance of Saussure's conceptualisation of linguistic structures meant that the mode of analysis Saussure developed to examine language could be used to investigate the structures of culture more broadly, including systems of objects as diverse as clothing, technological objects, food, the built environment and motor vehicles. This is why it is important to know about Saussure's theories. In the following section his influential ideas are elaborated.

An important feature of Saussure's approach was his interest in synchronic, rather than diachronic, studies of language. Previous scholarship within the field of linguistics had focused primarily on the historical evolution of language systems over time – their diachronic features. Saussure argued that at any particular point in time, language must exist as a system – a series of related parts that are inseparable and form a system of linguistic communication. This system was not necessarily closed, inviolable or inflexible, for as we know, language conventions change over time. Yet, at any point in time language could be analysed as a communicative system. Accordingly, rather than attending to the proliferation of 'speech acts' – words, sounds, sound images and alphabetic texts – Saussure argued that scholars must understand these linguistic structures as: (i) irreducibly psychological, (ii) intrinsically contoured by social-communal codes, and above all, (iii) as a system. Thus, language is a social institution whose structures must be understood on their own terms – 'in itself', and as a system of relations (Saussure, 1966[1916]: 16). Language then, conceptualised through Saussure's systemic perspective, becomes a 'self-contained whole and a principle of classification' (1966[1916]: 9) – a system of signs (1966[1916]: 15).

The 'systemness' of linguistic phenomena is further emphasised by Saussure's important distinction between 'langue' and 'parole'. In shorthand, one might think of langue as referring to language, while parole refers to speech. To elaborate, langue refers to the underlying rules and principles that govern the use of language and is used by Saussure to refer to its systemic quality, for example, the order in which we combine words to make sense. On the other hand, parole refers to the phonic and psychological manifestations of language – talk, utterances and sounds – that comprise the surface of language. These are the innumerable speech acts that humans proliferate each day.

Rather than the busy surface of speech facts that comprises the parole, Saussure's interest was in the generative capacity of the langue, which he identified as 'a well-defined object in the heterogeneous mass of speech facts' (Saussure, 1966[1916]: 14). A crucial element of the langue was that it could be understood as a system of relational differences, meaning that something can only be understood in structural relation to other things from which it is different: thus, 'where there is meaning ... there is structure' (Pettit, 1975: 3). For example, as a category of domestic companion, we understand 'cat' to be different to 'dog', 'parrot' or 'duck'. Similarly, we understand the meaning of 'green' within a system of colours by its difference to 'red', 'yellow' and 'blue'. Likewise, to use a material culture example, we understand different categories of shoes, assigning them different roles according to their usages – sports shoes for tennis or running, sneakers for street wear, low-cut leather shoes for formal occasions, moccasins for domestic relaxation, and leather boots for late night, or glamorous occasions. We know one type of shoe from its difference to another – a different colour, shape, sole and so on. Thus, getting back to Saussure, what co-ordinates the proliferation of words in our language is a system of relational differences, where the meaning of one thing is understood in terms of its difference or opposition to others. In Saussure's words then, the langue is an 'inventory of distinctions which create signs and of rules of combination' (1966[1916]: 33).

The system of signs can be further understood with reference to Saussure's ideas of 'signifiers' and 'signified'. The 'sign' is the unity created by a concept and a sound-image. Within the linguistic system, there is an opposition between the signified, which is the concept, and the signifier, which is the sound-image or word that refers to it. Thus, we can think of a particular category of flora or vegetation through such signifiers, be it a category of flora such as 'tree', 'shrub' or 'succulent', which can be visually identified through images called forth, such as their distinctive shapes – called the 'signified'. For explanatory purposes, Saussure makes a preliminary delineation of these concepts as if they were separate, though he maintains that to acquire cultural meaning they can only exist as components of a single sign – 'the two elements (of the signifier and signified) are intimately united, and each recalls the other' (1966[1916]: 66). Such signs should be understood as the basic units of language. Importantly, Saussure argues that the sign is necessarily arbitrary in nature, which means that the sequence of sounds we use to sound a signifier ('tree', 'dog', 'yellow shoe') is arbitrary, and comes to be accepted through collective use by members of a community over time.

For scholars of material culture perhaps Saussure's most important contribution – though one he does little more than offer a preliminary suggestion for in *Course* – is the proposal for a more broadly conceived programme of a 'science that studies the life of signs within society' (1966[1916]: 16). Linguistics then forms only one part of the general science of 'semiology'. The task of the general science of semiology is to contribute to understanding the exchange of meanings in society, which function as signs. According to Saussure's structuralist approach, underlying codes, conventions and relations that function as sign systems must generate these signs. This programme is more than simply a science of language, but an application of semiology to other realms of culture. In Saussure's words:

Linguistics is only part of the general science of semiology, the laws discovered by semiology will be applicable to linguistics, and the latter will circumscribe a well-defined area within the mass of anthropological facts. This procedure will do more than to clarify the linguistic problem. By studying rites, customs etc. as signs, I believe that we shall throw new light on the facts and point up the need for including them in a science of semiology and explaining them by its laws. (1966[1916]: 16–7)

Thus, if we think about how to apply such a principle to studying material culture, we can say that material objects or things should not be seen as isolated, individual things but as part of a broader system of object signs. Now we can begin to identify some of the impact of Saussure's ideas on later developments in social and cultural theory. Cue Baudrillard's proto-structuralist study of consumer goods *The System of Objects* (1996[1968]), or Barthes' *The Fashion System* (1967) where the Saussaurian linguistic imperative drives an analysis of societies wherein objects exist in rare abundance. Saussure's theorisation also has important implications for twentieth-century structural anthropology, the burgeoning field of semiotics (no longer called 'semiology' as Saussure had originally named it), and recent accounts of systems of ordering and technology within science studies, where the notion of relational or cohered objects is crucial to understanding modern systems of order and fluidity.

Lévi-Strauss: cracking the code of (material) culture

It is in the anthropological studies of Claude Lévi-Strauss that we can identify one important line of influence for Saussure's structuralism. Lévi-Strauss' general approach is instructive and highly influential in laying the foundations of the structuralist theoretical scheme, which he applied with great intellectual skill and precision in anthropological studies of myth, kinship and consciousness. The powerful ambition of Lévi-Strauss' analytic model is apparent in the subtitle to his book *Myth and Meaning* (1979), 'Cracking the Code of Culture'. We can see from this subtitle that Lévi-Strauss' oeuvre is of no small ambition – to apply the structuralist model developed by Saussure to studies of culture in order to uncover the underlying laws: to 'crack its code'.

First, one should understand that Lévi-Strauss' ideas can be regarded as anti-phenomenological. He believed that self-understanding was contrary to scientific understandings, and so rejected the promise of a subjective basis for interpretation and meaning (see Pettit, 1975). This key principle of the structural approach is diametrically opposed to much contemporary work in material culture studies which – in its opposition to forms of Marxist determinism – gives priority to individual interpretation and narrative in a sphere of meaning generally divorced from structural relations of production and consumption. In his key works, Lévi-Strauss argued a line of structuralist determinism (Pettit, 1975), meaning that the expressions of the human mind are determined by linguistic laws and semiological systems which are not knowable to everyday actors or non-specialists.

It was Lévi-Strauss' intention to offer a scientific way of understanding the linguistic expressions of the mind: following the philosophers Haudricourt and Granai he believed uncovering these semiological systems was akin to the Copernican revolution, or to the revolutionary role of nuclear physics within the physical sciences (1968[1963]: 33). Structural linguistics conceived in the Lévi-Straussian tradition were likely to be the only 'social science' that could rightfully be called a science. Furthermore, it would have implications not only for understanding language, but for all forms of cultural communication: it offered diverse applications outside formal linguistics of speech, to fields of anthropology, sociology and psychology (1968[1963]: 31). From here, we can begin to make links to the field of material culture, and contemporary commodity culture. There is a surfeit of commodities in advanced society, but how can one make sense of them and their communicative capacities? Do they fit together into some form of understandable sequence or system? Are their meanings understandable at a systemic level as forms of cultural communication, using the scientific and linguistic model advocated by Lévi-Strauss?

In *The Savage Mind* (1966[1962]) Lévi-Strauss investigates the scientific practice of the 'primitives'. Resisting attempts to portray primitive thought as inferior (Smith, 2001: 105) as people in the west often assumed, he showed how primitive forms of classification and cultural ordering were akin to what we in western societies have called 'science'. In fact, the processes of primitive ordering were analogous to the processes of advanced 'science', having both practical and intellectual uses. Working with Saussure's fundamental principle of communicative systems in mind, Lévi-Strauss argued that the universe is ordered according to systems of classification and taxonomies. Thus, objects can be understood within particular contexts where systemic cultural rules and codes operate to inform and contextualise their meaning. Objects therefore have appropriate cultural places.

For example, think of a crucifix as a sacred object. If it were possible to empty our own cultural knowledge of the crucifix's meanings and associations, we could identify it quite simply as a piece of timber affixed to another piece at a point three quarters along its length forming a 90 degree angle. If however, you live in a country that identities Christianity as the predominant religion, then to many people the crucifix is much more than two pieces of wood. It carries great symbolic meaning to those who follow the Christian religion, and signifies a crucial element of the most important story of Christianity. The crucifix then has great symbolic potency in particular cultural contexts, which is acquired through the circulation of religious myths. On a contrasting plane – perhaps a profane plane depending on your perspective – think of the visual ensemble of dress deployed in British punk sub-culture of the 1970s. Take the example of the safety pin, which is a motif of punk style. Considered apart from punk style, the safety pin seems an innocuous enough object, its principal function being to temporarily affix clothing, for example when a button goes missing or a zip malfunctions. Yet, within the system of punk style the safety pin is reappropriated by being worn outside its normal conventions, appended to jackets or shirts, acquiring symbolic potency precisely because it is worn *outside of context*. As Hebdige points out in his classic study of the signifying styles of youth sub-cultures, rather than destroying conventions, the visual ensemble of punk actually disorients them:

> Safety pins were taken out of their domestic 'utility' context and worn as grue-
> some ornaments through the cheek, ear or lip ... The perverse and abnormal
> were valued instrinsically. (Hebdige, 1979: 107)

Returning to Lévi-Strauss, and keeping in mind the punk sub-culture example, we can understand that objects have symbolic potency because they have a place. They therefore also have a non-place: a place where they are out of context. To have a cultural place implies the existence of a larger scheme of classification, which Lévi-Strauss' science of structural linguistics was able to identify:

> being in their place is what makes them sacred for if they were taken out of
> their place, even in thought, the entire order of the universe would be
> destroyed. Sacred objects therefore contribute to the maintenance of order
> in the universe by occupying the place allocated to them. (Lévi-Strauss,
> 1966[1962]: 10)

In explaining the nature of mythical thought – how it came to build classifications, rituals and orders – Lévi-Strauss referred to the idea of the 'bricoleur'. Although Lévi-Strauss originally used the idea to describe an intellectual strategy, the term has applications to studying the way people interact with material objects, whether it is in the domains of dress and clothing, home decoration or collecting. The bricoleur is a kind of 'tinkerer', who is able to bring multiple creative tools and strategies to bear to solve material problems or create new structures. Using a host of materials lying around at various stages of construction or (dis)repair the bricoleur works by continuously responding to the ever-changing requirements of a task, as makeshift materials show themselves to be useful or not, to varying degrees. In this way, the bricoleur can be said to practise a 'science of the concrete', whereby totemic messages are encoded and re-coded within the simplest materials of the natural world. Although the medium may be through material objects, the bottom line is that the bricoleur works with signs.

A fascinating example of bricolage can be found in outback Australia, in the form of the indigenous bush mechanic, who because of geographical isolation (and also economic marginalisation) is unable to use professional help to fix their motor vehicle. They respond by ingeniously using various bits and pieces from the surrounding bush (wilderness) as substitutes for vehicle parts: replacing brake pads with pieces of wood, using branches as substitute drive shafts, affixing boomerangs as clutch plates, using old shirts as makeshift windscreen wipers. We can observe that rather than being restricted by the fixed, artefactual nature of the objects at hand, the bricoleur transcends such restrictions by regarding the object as fluid or malleable. As Lévi-Strauss puts it, the bricoleur does not directly link tasks to the availability of particular raw materials, for the bricoleur's means are not related to a certain order of projects (1966[1962]: 19). The bricoleur makes do, collecting and using objects in a variety of possible combinations. These combinations do not come from 'nowhere', nor are they conjured up on the spot: they are drawn from already existing linguistic structures. Objects can thus be arranged in a variety of combinations, but are derived from language structures that already exist. The bricoleur thus deploys particular practico-theoretical logics to enable systems of transformations, meaning objects can have fluid meanings within systems of classification and exchange. The bricoleur therefore does not merely *speak with* things, but speaks *through the medium of things* (Lévi-Strauss, 1966[1962]: 21).

In his study *Totemism*, Lévi-Strauss (1962) applies this principle that things are mediums in generating cultural understandings in order to grasp how systems of human meaning are attached to animals, celestial bodies and other natural phenomena (1966[1962]: 135). Working from the insights of the anthropologist Boas, Lévi-Strauss argues that totemistic beliefs do not constitute a unique or isolated practice of classification, but rather are a practice best understood within a general field of relations between humans and natural objects. So, totemism has nothing to do with classifying nature or people *per se* – rather it is centrally connected to the logical order of culture and civilisation. The totem object thus becomes a medium through which cultural myths explain facts, rather than being something which myths must account for (1966[1962]: 95).

Totemism is a cultural attempt to understand the world and its systemic organisation. It involves classifications of phenomena into their cultural place. This means that plants and animals must be treated as elements of a type of cultural message system, the signs and signatures of which (the 'logics') are not only discovered, but ordered, by human activity. The ends these objects are put to are not merely technical or utilitarian in any simple way, but are part of the cultural grammar. As Lévi-Strauss famously points out in a brief, yet widely quoted and instructive, section toward the end of his book *Totemism* (1962: 162) 'natural species are not chosen because they are "good to eat" but because they are "good to think"' ('*bonnes á penser*'). From this insight, we can conclude that a fundamental tenet of Lévi-Strauss' theoretical model is that material objects do not exist just to serve straightforward, utilitarian purposes. In fact, the more important, symbolic role of objects is to allow humans to construct and assign meanings within their cultural universe. Such a proposition is a – possibly *the* – bedrock assumption within material culture studies.

Barthes: exposing the ideological basis of bourgeois commodity symbols

An intriguing problem is whether the principle proposed by Lévi-Strauss that humans use objects to construct and assign meanings within their universe – developed through anthropological inquiry in non-western societies – still holds within advanced consumer societies where there is a surfeit of commodities, many seemingly meaningless or of little personal and cultural value. In this section we go on to consider a key author who dealt with this question through the application of a structural approach: Roland Barthes. The work of French semiotician Roland Barthes is important because he was the first to systematically consider the symbolic meaning of material culture within advanced consumer societies. Barthes' work on commodities is an exciting fusion of the structuralist programme of Saussure and Lévi-Strauss, with the critical power of Marxism. His work offered a new and compelling way of interpreting the proliferation of commodity objects within advanced societies of the twentieth century. My assessment, however, is that in emphasising the mythical meanings of goods, his theoretical position is ultimately unable to account for the highly charged personal meanings they offer to consumers, and therefore offers a partial theoretical scheme for understanding material culture.

In the preface to the 1970 edition of his key work *Mythologies* (1993[1957]), Barthes elaborates two key aims of the book, and his semiotic approach more broadly. The first is to make an ideological critique of mass culture. This critique was to concentrate on certain mythologies within mass culture, but its key was Barthes' focus on the commodity object. Barthes believed very strongly that the mythic quality of bourgeois culture could best be investigated by focusing on particular objects. Objects thus have a very powerful story to tell, offering an investigative path for an analyst (or in Barthes' terms a 'mythologist') to elucidate the widespread ideological myths of bourgeois culture. The commodity object was perfect for such an analytic move because it appeared natural, transparent and, seemingly, it just magically 'exists'. Yet – and we can see the affinities of this line of reasoning with Marx's dissection of the commodity outlined in the previous chapter – the commodity object was thoroughly rooted in the ideological basis of capitalism. It was capitalist mythology objectified, but cleverly disguised to consumers as a thing to impart any number of desirable traits such as emancipation, romance, potency or elegance. In making such a suggestion about the social and psychological capacities of commodities, Barthes clearly went well beyond the very technical – though impassioned – Marxian analysis of the commodity.

The second key aim of *Mythologies* was to realise Saussure's ambition of a science of semiology that moved beyond a narrowly conceived linguistics, by applying semiological analysis to uncover the 'language' of the ideological system of capitalism. Taking inspiration from Saussure's writings, Barthes advocated that one could best understand this ideological system by analysing it as a system of signs, with the commodity as a prime 'carrier' of such ideologies. Barthes believed that Saussure's rigorous structuralist methodology has the capacity to unmask and show the linguistic workings of the commodity-based ideological system, and – through the idea of 'myth' – to reveal how their basis in bourgeois culture becomes transformed into 'nature', as something that appears as natural, untouched by human influence. The ultimate goal of the work is summed up by Barthes in the word he uses to express his twin tasks of: (i) iconoclastically uncovering and denunciating bourgeois norms and (ii) applying the rigorous scientific, structural approach of Saussure. The neologism Barthes uses to combine these two ambitions is telling of his approach: 'semioclasm' (1993[1957]: 9).

What motivated Barthes' work in *Mythologies* was the goal of revealing the ideological basis of contemporary bourgeois culture. Barthes recognised this ideological system as being shaped by the false promises of consumerist objects. Newspapers, art, everyday or common sense beliefs, films, advertisements, consumer objects – all 'dress up' reality by giving it a glossy appearance that imitated something natural and transparent but was, in Barthes' view, clearly false, deceptive and implicitly ideological. Rather than the everyday, common sense order of things being natural, such relations hid ideological interests, primarily capitalist interests. Barthes reiterates that what he is trying to do is to uncover the 'natural' and show it to be intrinsically, deeply 'historical' – inextricably shaped by the forces of capitalism:

> I resented seeing Nature and History confused at every turn, and I wanted to track down, in the decorative display of what-goes-without-saying, the ideological abuse which, in my view, is hidden there. (Barthes, 1993[1957]: 11)

Barthes' idea was that capitalism works to deceive subjects through propagating myths, which are embodied within a multitude of everyday objects and experiences, from motor vehicles, to white goods, implements like cricket or baseball bats, to shoes and clothing. What exactly, in Barthes' terms, was a 'myth'? Barthes initially indicates that myth is a type of speech, which acts to mislead and obfuscate. As Culler represents it: 'myth means a delusion to be exposed' (Culler, 1983: 33). Barthes then clarifies his meaning by pointing out that myth is a system of communication, or message. It is thus more than merely a physical object, but is a mode of signification that is attached to objects (Barthes, 1993[1957]: 109). Myth thus adds a certain patina to objects, endowing them with special qualities and abilities: consider mythical objects like the bats of legendary sportspeople such as baseball star Joe Di Maggio or cricketer Don Bradman, the guitar of Hendrix or the trumpet of Miles Davis, the boxing gloves of Ali, the iconic white jump suit of late Presley, or a dress once worn by Monroe. Myth thus equals pure matter, plus ideology. Barthes identified myth as a second-order semiological system (1993[1957]: 114). The first order within any semiological system is language, and the second higher level is mythology, which functions like a meta-language by informing our interpretations of what might otherwise be considered a mundane object. Barthes calls mythology a form of 'depoliticised speech', because of the ability of myth to banish history – to do away with the material dialectics of the production of consumer objects, and so transform history into nature (1993[1957]: 142). Much like the classic Marxist analysis of the commodity, Barthes argues that commodity objects appear to have a blissful clarity and simplicity. Yet, if we scratch below the surface using the structuralist tools of the mythologist, we can identify that they merely disguise the brutal and exploitative context of their production by deploying the veil of certain mythologies. Objects within consumer societies are always political, it is just that the political intensity of objects fades once myth is attached to them:

> In passing from history to nature, myth acts economically: it abolishes the complexity of human acts, it gives them the simplicity of essences, it does away with all dialectics, with any going back beyond what is immediately visible, it organizes a world which is without contradictions because it is without depth, a world wide open and wallowing in the evident, it establishes a blissful clarity: things appear to mean something by themselves. (Barthes, 1993[1957]: 143)

There are two well-known works by Barthes which collect a series of short essays on various cultural myths: *Mythologies* (1993[1957]) and *The Eiffel Tower and Other Mythologies* (1979). Both collect popular essays in cultural criticism published in various forums in France, and illustrate the type of analysis Barthes had in mind for his critical semiotics. In these works, Barthes analyses a massive range of cultural objects, including images, texts, art, urban settings, commercial settings, events, sports, foods, books and more. To understand his methodology it is worthwhile looking at some examples of Barthes' analysis of the myths he sees embodied in diverse items of material culture.

The new Citroën

The first point Barthes makes is a more general one about motor vehicles, though clearly he has the new Citroën, model DS19 (referring to its 1.9 litre engine) in mind, when he says that: 'cars today are almost the exact equivalent of the great Gothic cathedrals' (1993[1957]: 88). By this he means that industrial commodity production has substituted commodities as the new things to worship. Not coincidentally, the 'DS' is short for 'Deesse', meaning Goddess in French. The model was first seen by Parisians at the 1955 Paris Motor Show. The DS is widely known amongst car enthusiasts and Francophiles, and frequently highly regarded for its novel, hydropneumatic suspension and its aerodynamic design, supposedly providing hitherto unknown levels of comfort without sacrificing performance. Barthes writes that the Citroën is a type of superlative object, something that appears to us as if it has magically fallen from the heavens. He adds that the DS19 is a perfected mass produced object that sits above nature because it combines a perfection of human input (design, finish, quality, shape, scale) with an apparent genuine absence of human input.

Barthes argues that a key aesthetic attraction of the DS19 is its apparent smoothness and roundedness. The car doesn't look as if it has been assembled through brute forces of industrial production. In fact, it suggests a feeling of lightness, speed and elegance rather than aggression. The sweeping curves of glass at the front and rear of the DS19 add to this feeling of light, air and space. Barthes sees this novel design as marking a shift: from industrial objects that betray their dirty and brutish production methods, to objects that are inviting and spiritual, now more attuned to new philosophies of post Second World War household luxury goods. The car now becomes an extension of comfortable domestic space. Here, Barthes may have picked up on an early trend toward extending the home and domestic technologies of comfort into other domains of life. Cue the contemporary fad for incorporating things such as cup holders, flower vases, DVD players, power outlets, and small refrigerators into motor vehicles. What is the ultimate conclusion to Barthes' analysis of the new Citroën? He posits a type of psychoanalytic analysis, suggesting that the car becomes an object of intense, amorous desire which displaces sexual urges: through the senses of sight and touch this technological object is appropriated and ultimately prostituted to serve people's desires.

After reading Barthes' essay on the Citroën, one is provoked to ask: what might be the current equivalent of the DS19? Well, this is a question for your private consideration and a matter determined by your own tastes, but a few suggestions are: a BMW 7 Series motor vehicle, an Apple iPod, a pair of Manolo Blahnik shoes, a Tiffany bracelet, an Eames chair. In their own way, each of these could be seen as a current embodiment of Barthes' Citroën DS19. No doubt, each reader could add their own 'DS19' to this list.

Toys

In this essay Barthes seems intent on reminding us that a child's toy is not an object of innocence, mere fantasy or play. Rather, toys encode various ideologies of the modern adult world. First, Barthes points out that toys – as miniatures of the adult world, allow us to objectify children as a unique self who is able to act autonomously in the world. Because toys commonly reproduce copies of the adult world in reduced form, they allow adults to identify children as 'small adults' who need to learn skills and attitudes, which toys can introduce. In doing so, toys serve an ideological purpose by embodying the myths and ideologies of the modern world, whether it be myths of war, transport, science, or fashion and hairstyles. One might think here of the debates about what constitute appropriate toys for children: is playing with a Barbie doll advisable for young girls? Should young boys play with toys that have strongly, stereotypically masculine codes, like toy soldiers, guns and swords? Barthes argues that toys also allow users to begin to identify themselves as objective actors in the world: 'owners', 'users' and 'doers', rather than creators. In doing so – and especially if the toys are made of plastic – they assist in creating a relation with the world that is disengaged from nature.

Plastic

This is an interesting essay, because Barthes doesn't focus on any particular object or class of objects, but rather on a class of material that was becoming ubiquitous in the era he was writing: plastic. Again emphasising the enchantedness of an object, Barthes states that plastic 'is the first magical substance which consents to be prosaic' (1993[1957]: 98). Plastic is spectacular not so much in its manifestation in any particular amazing object, but through its ubiquity and in the sheer range of its end products: 'it can become buckets as well as jewels' (1993[1957]: 97). Barthes suggests our amazement at plastic is at the sight of the way it proliferates within our mundane existence. Barthes puts it this way: plastic has a singular origin, but plural effects. Because of this, plastic becomes a ubiquitous material representing to us a triumph of modern production.

Yet, in typical Barthesian myth debunking mode, there must be a downside to plastic – a tragic counter code that Barthes identifies which allows us to see behind the myth of plastic to identify what plastic truly represents. Here, Barthes says that despite the magic of plastic – its durability and sturdiness – the price we pay is to be found in the way plastic becomes a cold, alienating material whose primary virtue is (mere) resistance. Hardly the stuff of an heroic, beautiful material like gold! The ultimate tragedy with plastic is that in becoming ubiquitous, it virtually abolishes hierarchies of substances. With plastic, Barthes suggests, we no longer need silver, gold, aluminium or zinc: 'the whole world can be plasticized' ([1993]1957: 98).

Given Barthes' analysis, we may want to ask a few questions in response. First, is it possible to use plastic to build high status objects which betray the status of plastic as a common, popular material used for mass production? One example of this is to be found within furniture and design, where plasticised forms can be highly valued. Second, one might suggest that given the whole world was becoming 'plasticised' as Barthes suggested, would there not arise counter discourses that devalued plastic in favour of higher status materials like woods? A good example is to be found in the production of luxury motor vehicles, which frequently have wood panelling liberally splashed on their dashes and fittings to give their interiors a feeling of warmth and quality. Ironically – at the lower end of the luxury market and in some motor vehicle brands attempting to suggest status – plastic material is produced in such a way as to imitate walnut wood panelling. This is indeed something Barthes would have enjoyed analysing.

The Eiffel Tower

In this piece, Barthes deploys a narrative device he uses frequently in the essays on mythologies: the ubiquity of an object and the paradox of its mythical quality. Put differently, he asks how an object can be so mundane, yet so culturally powerful? He adopts this analytic mode in his essay on the Parisian icon, the Eiffel Tower. The Eiffel Tower is 'there', Barthes argues (1979: 3). It has a 'factness' that is incontestable and hence entirely mundane: 'like a rock or the river, it is as literal as a phenomenon of nature whose meaning can be questioned to infinity but whose existence is incontestable' (1979: 3). Barthes points out that the Eiffel Tower iconic status is acquired on a number of levels. The Tower functions as a symbol for Parisians: allowing them to orient themselves within the city, and to have a collective gaze upon it. For those within the metropolis, it is a centre. For the world, the Eiffel Tower is a universal symbol of travel, reproduced in thousands of tourist photographs which are taken home to relatives who may marvel at the towering structure which constitutes the symbolic centre of Paris. Barthes also states that the tower is a universal symbol of modernity, communication, science and cosmopolitan travel. For Barthes, what is paradoxical and somewhat farcical here – but in the end crucial for the Tower's signifying capacity – is that the Tower itself is a useless structure. As he says, it is nothing, a 'zero monument' (1979: 7) and can ultimately live on itself. Its utter lack of function is in inverse proportion to its capacity to act as a lightning rod for infinite mythological meanings. As an 'empty signifier', the Tower is all the more open to attract meanings.

Baudrillard's structural analysis of consumer objects

In his early career writings of the late 1960s and early 1970s, Baudrillard was essentially trying to come to grips with the burgeoning consumer society of the time and whether Marxism could offer a viable framework for understanding a society where consumer objects proliferate in exceptional abundance. Inspired by the structuralist vision of Lévi-Strauss and the antecedent grand ambitions of Saussure's linguistic model, Barthes on the mythologies embodied in everyday objects, and also (in a less direct way) the critical theorist's writings on commodification, Baudrillard's first two books (*The System of Objects*, 1996[1968], and *The Consumer Society*, 1998[1970]) dealt squarely with important questions related to consumption, material culture and the broader cultures of consumption that were beginning to characterise western cultures in the latter half of the twentieth century. Despite what we may know, or think, about Baudrillard's recent writing, these are singular works in his oeuvre. As Rex Butler (1999: 5) points out, these books and the couple that followed them, were directly sociological in nature: 'observational, empirical, scientific', compared to those which Baudrillard published post-1977. They are of significant interest to those who study material culture, and at turns are accessible and complex, brilliant and foggy. Reading them can be a confusing journey of reconciling Marxism and critical theory, structural semiotics and psychoanalysis. Nevertheless, because Baudrillard tries to come to grips with the special problems associated with abundance, excess, signification and structure, these works constitute some of the most interesting and valuable studies of material culture within consumer societies.

Let's look at what Baudrillard has to say about material culture. Baudrillard's goal in these early works is to develop a systematic study of consumption (perhaps we could go so far as to call it a 'sociology of consumption') that is not so much consumer-centred, but object-centred. Consistent with the structuralist ambition, Baudrillard is attempting to undertake an analysis of the 'architecture' of contemporary material culture: that is, how it fits together into an overarching structure of meanings and codes. The downside of this resolute structuralism is that Baudrillard's analysis is relatively agentless, in the sense that he ignores the discourses and practices of actors. Yet, Baudrillard's approach is consistent with one of the central tenets in material culture studies: to study the objects themselves.

Baudrillard's analysis of objects combines a powerful structuralist technique with an updated version of critical theory. His goal is ambitious in the best Lévi-Straussian tradition: it is no less than to incorporate objects into a general theory of communicative behaviour. At the base of his analysis, Baudrillard is determined to take consumption seriously. Rather than consider consumption autonomously, as a site where individual needs are pursued and gratified, Baudrillard asserts that consumption must be considered an important social institution where social forces such as class, status and prestige are measured and played out. As such, his work is an important precursor to the postmodern writings of the 1980s and 1990s on consumption, and can be seen as a (somewhat eccentric) companion text to Bourdieu's *Distinction*. Dual principles drive Baudrillard's analysis: (i) a focus on objects as the irreducible elements of the act of consumption, and (ii) a commitment to conceptualising objects as having symbolic value, rather than a use value or exchange value. In terms of Baudrillard's first axiom, his goal is consistent with developing a strong programme in material culture studies: objects should be identified in terms of their place in the 'general structure of social behaviour' (1981: 35). An adequate theory of objects is important in sociology, though to date, notes Baudrillard, they have only had a 'walk-on role in sociological research' (1981: 34). Moreover, the sociological concern with identifying objects as indices of social membership is merely a preliminary task, much more vital is to consider objects as the scaffolding for a global structure of the environment (1981: 35). His major concern then is with the processes that exist between people and objects, and the systems of behaviour and relationships that result from them. Echoing a robustly cultural sentiment in the tradition of Lévi-Strauss, he asserts that objects are all in perpetual flight from technical structure towards their secondary meanings, from the technological system towards a cultural system (Baudrillard, 1996[1968]: 8).

Baudrillard's second axiom is that all objects should be studied in terms of their sign value, rather than their use or exchange value. Objects may well have a pragmatic, utilitarian component – that which Baudrillard dismisses somewhat freely as an 'empiricist hypothesis' – but this is little more than a practical 'guarantee' of lesser interest (1981: 29). What is far more important is the symbolic value of objects. Baudrillard writes: 'objects never exhaust themselves in the functions they serve' (1981: 32), meaning that, above all else, objects serve as symbolic markers of class, status and prestige. So, we can begin to see how Baudrillard comes to give Marxism a consumption orientation. In fact, in contrast to other Marxist interpretations, Baudrillard makes the radical proposal that it is only through studying *the opposite of production* that we can understand contemporary capitalism. So, he says, an accurate theory of objects must take into account social 'prestations' (meaning symbolic displays of status and prestige) and social signification: objects as signifiers have a significant role to play in reproducing relations of social power. To consume an object is to engage with a system of cultural signs: 'the fundamental conceptual hypothesis for a sociological analysis of "consumption" in *not* use value, the relation to needs, but *symbolic* exchange value, the value of social prestation, of rivalry and, at the limit, of class discriminants' (Baudrillard, 1981: 30). These are strong sentiments, but herein lies the seed of Baudrillard's eventual departure from these more sociological early writings. In staunchly emphasising the sign values of objects within cultural systems of prestige and display, Baudrillard laid his analysis open to substantial revision in the wake of emergent poststructural critiques which would come to radically break the relationship between sign and signifier, which Baudrillard's model was seemingly based upon.

In *The System of Objects* (1996[1968]) Baudrillard identifies the modern consumer citizen as someone who plays with signs as an integral part of their identity. There is no greater evidence of this than within the domain of interior design, he suggests, wherein modern objects have undergone a process of 'liberalization'. No longer required to symbolically service the requirements of moral constraints, such as for example, proper familial lineage, religious and moral uprightness, or dedicated cultural learning, the domestic setting is free to represent the whims of its inhabitants: 'the substance and form of the old furniture have been abandoned for good, in favour of an extremely free game of function' (1996[1968]: 21). Modern living spaces, and the objects that sit within them, are problematic not for their moral quotient, but for questions of desired ambience, design and atmosphere: for example, coolness, warmth, colour, spontaneity, order (1996[1968]: 30). Baudrillard highlights glass as a modern *décor par excellence*, for its coolness, transparency, lightness, freedom and affordance of an uninterrupted view. The larger meaning of this engagement with objects and materials, Baudrillard argues, is that the modern homeowner has become a type of symbolic technician – one who dominates, controls and orders objects. Consumption then is about weaving objects into a coherent signifying fabric:

> consumption is the virtual totality of all objects and messages ready-
> constituted as a more or less coherent discourse. If it has any meaning at all,
> consumption means an activity consisting of the systematic manipulation of
> signs. (Baudrillard, 1996[1968]: 200)

Baudrillard calls his theory of material culture, a theory of 'object signs'. Reworking the Saussurian model of *langue* and *parole* to show how every object of consumption must be seen as part of a larger system of object language, Baudrillard argues that consumption is defined by its status as a system of exchange, difference and signification: 'the generalized exchange of signs' (1981: 87). Baudrillard develops a four-stage historical model to show the evolution toward the contemporary logic of sign value. His four stages are as follows:

1 The logic of utility, labelled its *'functional logic'*. This refers to the capacity of an object to perform a functional need. It is equivalent to Marx's notion of use-value. For example, the purpose of a biro is for writing, a motor vehicle is 'to get from point A to point B', a cup is to hold liquid, or a chair is for supporting one's body in an upright position.
2 The logic of the market, labelled its *'exchange value'*. This refers to the capacity of an object to measure value. Thus, a biro may be roughly equivalent in value to an orange, a computer equal to the whole of a month's salary, and an ounce of gold can be exchanged for a number of hundred US dollars. In a market economy, barter is a relatively marginal activity, as we use money as a means of measuring universal value.
3 The logic of the gift, labelled its *'symbolic exchange value'*. This refers to the value of an object in relation to a subject. For example, a diamond ring is a gift given to symbolise love and commitment toward another, a bunch of red roses may be given to another to symbolise romantic feelings, and a bottle of champagne given to signal success or congratulations.
4 The logic of status, labelled its *'sign value'*. Value here is symbolic and, because of this, intrinsically relational. This means that a particular object has value only in relation to other objects, which are used as points of comparison. For example, a Mercedes might be roughly equivalent in status value to a BMW of the same size, but each have a higher status than a Chrysler, Honda and Hyundai. Writing with a Mont Blanc pen might signify success – or one's aspiration for success – and will likely have higher status than a generic biro. Having a signed, limited edition of an art print will have higher status than a poster. A Rolex watch is likely to be perceived as having higher status than a Seiko. As a challenge to Baudrillard's position, it is worth noting that this type of hierarchical logic of status value has to some degree been challenged by cultural practices including the growing deployment of irony in judging cultural goods, the growing popularity of kitsch, and the embracing of punk and trash cultures. This makes it possible that in some circles what was once thought to be cheap, lowbrow or trashy could have the highest symbolic value.

The works by Baudrillard discussed here are generally taken to be his most concrete, empirical and straightforwardly sociological. They are substantial intellectual labours of quite a traditional nature. What followed were periods of work devoted to simulation and the hyperreal, a series of auto-biographical reflections including the postmodern travelogue *America*, as well as a series of works on popular political and cultural topics like the Gulf War and the iconography of Princess Diana. In these works, the analytic and political purchase of Baudrillard's early works is replaced by a sort of resigned flattening out of critical consciousness. As Bryan Turner points out, Baudrillard's writing 'simulates the condition it wishes to convey rather than producing a critical style in opposition to postmodern culture' (1993: 85). While this air of acquiescence may be characteristic of Baudrillard's later works, it is not the case for those referred to here. For Marxists, Baudrillard's writing – even the intellectually disciplined early works – represent a failure to offer a compelling development of contemporary Marxism. Moreover, he is often served with rendering social agents politically impotent. For more inclusive sociologists who are likely to embrace some of the innovations coming from continental theory and cultural studies, Baudrillard's work is provocative, suggestive and valuable. How far one wishes to travel with him into the self-referential world of simulations and simulacrum seems to be the most important question one needs to consider.

Hebdige and the codes of sub-cultural fashions

One of the strong principles in the structural approach to objects emphasises coherence, relationality and semiotic order. The corollary of this principle is that any individual object obtains its capacity to signify through its relational difference to other objects within a broader discursive field. Objects, as Lévi-Strauss says, have places. One way of knowing their place is recognising when they are out of place, when the semiotic order is breached. Being 'out of place' – consequently disturbing semiotic coherence and the 'natural order' of things – thus gives an object cultural power. Hebdige's (1979) analysis of the meanings of youth sub-cultural style illustrates this central premise of culture most vividly.

In this analysis Hebdige addresses two questions. First, how is sense-making within sub-cultural groups enabled through various types of signifiers, for example, dress, self-presentation, musical preferences and various other accoutrements. Second, how can sub-cultures (particularly punk) cohere around a central belief in 'disorder'? Hebdige pinpoints 'style' as a type of cultural weaponry of sub-cultural groups – conceptualising it is a technique of 'intentional communication' that functions for both members within the group, and for those in the general mass of 'straight' or conventional culture. 'Sub-cultural style' refers to the bundle of features that comprise one's self-presentation. For the sub-cultural groups Hebdige considered – principally youth sub-cultures centred around music and fashion – style is an 'emphatic combination' of dress, dance, argot, musical preference, hair colour and style, and accoutrements like hair combs, bracelets, earrings or watch chains. Hebdige asserts that the key to understanding sub-cultural style is that it is intentionally, consciously *constructed*, in contrast to conventional style which he sees as less consciously constructed. Punk style, for example, is assembled according to principles of drama and spectacle. 'Straight' or mass style is seen as drawing upon contrasting cultural codes and practices. In this sense, it too is a type of intentional communication, but the communicative intent is to be 'appropriate', 'modest' and to 'fit in'. Dominant cultural discourses encourage us to identify straight or conventional style not so much in terms of a particular assemblage of ideological codes and symbols, but as something that is entirely natural and without 'history' in Barthes' sense – something that is without ideology. This view of straight style as *the* 'natural' way of presenting self is, of course, plainly wrong.

The power of sub-cultural communication comes from its ability to strategically draw upon the symbolic grammar of 'straight' style and to subvert it through various subtle, and not so subtle, ways. Hebdige follows a Saussurian line of reasoning here and also injects his own interest in cultural power and social stratification, to suggest that any ensemble has its place within an internal system of differences, and each sub-cultural variation must position itself in relation to 'conventional' modes of sartorial discourse. He argues that spectacular sub-cultures have a visual ensemble that is obviously fabricated, so that symbolic power is accumulated through consciously *using and abusing* the conventional rules of self-presentation. In this sense, spectacular sub-cultures go against nature by rendering 'the world of objects to new and covertly oppositional readings' (1979: 102). Applying Lévi-Strauss' idea of the *bricoleur*, who is seen to continually alter and extend the meanings of objects through a process called 'systems of transformation', Hebdige suggests that the members of sub-cultures are a type of bricoleur who transforms the meaning of objects by recontextualising them. Here, we can see affinities with important early twentieth-century art movements, including dada and surrealism. Artists such as Duchamp, Dali, Breton and Ernst played around with objects and their appropriate cultural places by *de* and *re*-contextualising everyday objects to twist their meanings. Duchamp for example presented a bicycle wheel, a signed urinal, a snow shovel, a bottlerack and a side table as art. The important question one is prompted to ask is, is this art? Moreover, what makes art, one may ask, apart from a theory of interpretation to define it? Drawing upon the work of Saussure and Lévi-Strauss, the semiotician can explain why Duchamp's readymade sculpture of found objects might have been considered so culturally provocative.

The data for Hebdige's analysis comes from a close reading of the materials deployed by various youth sub-cultures, principally from Britain in the 1960s and 1970s. His discussion of Mods and – especially – Punks have great illustrative value in understanding semiotic approaches to material culture. The Mods (also see Cohen's (1972) book *Folk Devils and Moral Panics*) appropriated commodities by placing them in a symbolic ensemble which served to erase or alter their original, 'straight' meaning. The motor scooter is a great example discussed by Hebdige. The scooter was originally a benign response to inner city transport needs of the young and the working class, but was turned into 'a menacing symbol of group solidarity' by the Mods (Hebdige, 1979: 104) who customised and fetishised their machines with various decorations and enhancements, often riding in packs to enhance the apparent 'menace quotient' of what is otherwise a low-powered – though economically and environmentally rational – runabout. Mods also appropriated the conventional insignia of the middle-class business world, such as suits, collared shirts, ties and short hair, but stripped them of their meaning, transforming them into empty fetishes: 'objects to be desired, fondled and valued in their own right' (1979: 105). It is ironic that in some markets around the world, the brands that Mods valued are now undergoing their own transformation. A great example of this is of two brands of shirts: Fred Perry and Ben Sherman. Both are 'old school' London Mod attire that were extensively worn by Mods in the 1960s to the extent that they became an iconic part of their wardrobe. These days, both brands remain popular with Mods, but both brands have also expanded into mainstream markets. The dilemma is: how can the 'old school' interpretation of the Mods be reconciled with extension of the brand in to new, mainstream markets? This is something of a problem for the brands (who wish to retain loyalty from old customers while generating new markets), and the fans of the brand (who wish to hang onto emotional attachments to old brand certainties). Part of the solution seems to be that shirt production is differentiated according to different markets: unique shapes (the original design is a tighter fitting 'slim fit' style, compared to the recently produced shirt), a range of colours and patterns (the newer ones appealing to mainstream tastes with conventional checks or stripes). For some consumers, such a change in production may cause the brand to lose its aura.

It is within punk sub-culture that the 'collage aesthetic' is most clearly identified. Hebdige shows how the punk aesthetic disrupts meanings through re-appropriating and reorganising meanings. Hebdige describes how this is carried out through the use of 'cut ups'. This process allows the most mundane and unremarkable objects to take on a forceful new meaning through recontextualisation which relied upon rupturing 'natural' contexts with 'constructed' contexts. Just as the coherent 'naturalness' of conventional dress standards (termed their 'homological coherence') afforded symbolic authority, the punk style accrued power through expressing its complete opposites so that 'the perverse and the abnormal were valued intrinsically' (Hebdige, 1979: 107). Some of the binary opposites that punk promoted over conventional style are summarised below, beginning with Hebdige's 'master' discourse.

natural ——— constructed
conventional ——— unconventional
sexually respectable ——— sexually deviant
appropriate ——— out of context
refined ——— garish
quiet ——— loud
soft ——— sharp
good taste ——— kitsch/inappropriate
professional ——— amateur
harmony ——— cacophony
order ——— chaos

The binary codes of punk style (after Hebdige, 1979)

Evaluating the structural approach to material culture

Before proceeding to evaluate the structural perspective, consider the following recap of the general features of the structural and semiotic account of material culture:

- The fundamental principle of the structural approach to material culture is that any object derives its meaning from a semiotic relation to another object. That is, objects have meanings that are *relational* and *contextualised*. Saussure's groundbreaking work in structural linguistics established this. So, we can understand the meaning of an object by *reading* it in relation to its *difference* from other objects, of the same or different class. For example, a Ford motor vehicle is distinguishable from other motor vehicles (Honda, BMW, Chrysler) in terms of size, shape, quality, brand association and so on. The point is that we only know what a 'Ford' motor vehicle is because of how we perceive its differences in relation to other motor vehicle types.
- The structural tradition recommends that analysts focus on studying the *langue* plane of material culture, rather than its *parole* plane. This recommendation is drawn from Saussure's distinction between the surface of language (*parole*) and its deep, generative structure (*langue*). The point structuralists make is that only by studying these *langue* elements can we begin to understand the generative forces of culture.
- Structuralism has its origins in Saussure's theory of structural linguistics but, as Saussure noted, other aspects of culture have 'language-like' qualities in the sense that they have their own internal, systemic structure associated with codes, narratives and symbols. Thus, any aspect of culture, or social life broadly, can be studied along these lines in terms of their systemic associations: food, clothing, alcoholic drinks, the built environment and so on. Lévi-Strauss, who wrote on the practice of *bricolage* and objects as 'resources for thinking', was a forceful

advocate of this principle. In the context of consumer cultures this idea was developed first, and possibly best, by Roland Barthes in his influential work *Mythologies* (1993[1957]).

To what extent does structuralism and semiotics offer a viable set of theoretical resources for understanding material culture? The following arguments can be made in favour of such theoretical models.

- The key strength of this approach is that it offers what has been labelled a 'strong' or 'autonomous' approach to studying culture (Alexander, 2003). That is, in seeking to dissect the codes and symbols that inform our everyday interpretations and actions, the approach need not rely on materialist, economic or other extraneous factors in explaining the practices and processes of culture. Rather, culture is something thoroughly shot through all aspects of daily life whether they be related to inequality, family life, relationships, fashion or educational learning. All aspects of our lives owe something to systems of culture. In offering us resources to understand this in the form of narratives, codes and symbols – which can be conceptualised unhinged from 'last instance' materialist arguments, or 'bottom line' contingencies of class or gender – the structuralist intellectual toolkit is a rich one. It does not suggest that there are no inequalities or social differences, only that we can fully understand such dimensions when we uncover the cultural codes and processes that inform them.
- A corollary of this point is that semiotics offers cultural researchers a type of methodological and conceptual toolkit for analysing diverse aspects of culture. In its latter form, the strength of the approach is to be found in the way elements of understanding ('hermeneutics') are forged with elements of cultural structure, so that the analyst can move between questions of meaning and structure.

The following arguments are commonly used criticisms of the semiotic, structural approach:

- The major potential flaw of the structural approach, especially in its more pure form as advocated by Saussure, Lévi-Strauss and Barthes, is that questions of actors and their agency are not considered. So, we may appreciate the interpretations of authors like Lévi-Strauss and Barthes who are masterly writers on culture and cultural things, however, in the end – to some degree – we must trust their interpretations, which are often unqualified by actors' own accounts or interpretations. For example, Barthes tells us that people regard the Citroën as a contemporary gothic cathedral and that it is the ultimate symbol of advancement for the petit bourgeois class. From a social scientific perspective, this may be regarded in its most positive light as a plausible (though somewhat bold) hypothesis, or, in its worst light, as fanciful literary speculation. Likewise, what do iconic architectural structures like the Eiffel Tower which Barthes wrote about, or for that matter the Golden Gate Bridge, or the Sydney Opera House, really mean to people? In some versions of cultural studies such theorising, unhinged from reality and from the voices and minds of actors, can reach its most fanciful and unproductive heights. Such heretical questioning of virtuoso readings of sites and objects by celebrated scholars may be regarded as theoretically mean-spirited by some. To a certain extent we need imaginative analysts like Barthes to offer interpretations of these symbols, but in the end we also need to ask whether there is any empirical basis for the claims they make. Here, classic middle-level sociological approaches, which take regard of strong theoretical claims (such as that proposed by Barthes) but temper and modify them as required through nuanced empirical approaches, have an important role to play.

- An allied criticism of this approach is that in emphasising the textual and linguistic properties of social life, real actors and the hard social strains that hinder them in social life are relatively under-theorised, possibly even ignored. So, this criticism could be summarised by the slogan 'the world is not a text'. The counter point here is that, yes the world is not a text, but it has textual qualities: talk and discourse, narrative, expressivity and emotion are important aspects of social life. Moreover, these textual qualities – expressed through the codes, narratives and discourses of cultural life – can play an important role in political struggle and emancipation, just as they play a role in limiting and restricting free agents.

- The final critique comes from the poststructuralist camp. They claim that the old certainties established by classical structural approaches, represented by the work of Saussure, Lévi-Strauss and the early works of Barthes and Baudrillard no longer hold. Specifically, we cannot assume a direct, straightforward relationship between sign and signified, as suggested by foundational structural linguistics. In fact, in a world overloaded with signs, what is signified by which sign is no longer clear. Meaning in this context is then up for grabs, and any assurance that meaning is structured by a set of language-like relationships is challenged. One of the most extreme forms of this contestation of the real is found in the later works of Baudrillard, who – as we saw earlier in this chapter – was once the champion of a Lévi-Straussian structuralism. Baudrillard's argument is that the established meanings of sign and signifier can no longer be trusted, and that in a consumer, mass-mediated culture such relationships are reduced to play and gesture, such that distinguishing between reality and simulation becomes difficult or even, in fact, an outmoded and impotent defense.

SUGGESTED FURTHER READING

Roland Barthes' essays in his companion works *Mythologies* (1993[1957]), and *The Eiffel Tower* (1979), are a terrific place to start to understand some of the principles of the structural approach, especially in the context of how such principles play out in the context of a consumer society. The essays are generally no more than 2–5 pages each. Then try to consider the theoretical piece at the end of *Mythologies* that lays the groundwork for Barthes' critical-structuralist vision of semiotics. Also, the collection of Lévi-Strauss' interviews on Canadian radio published in *Myth and Meaning* (1979) are valuable distillations of his thinking and his vision for, and commitment to, structuralist analysis. I have discussed Dick Hebdige's work on youth sub-cultures in his book *Subculture, The Meaning of Style* (1979) which fuses structuralist principles with critical insights. Also try his book *Hiding in the Light* (1988), especially the section on the trajectory or biography of the Italian motor scooter.

FIVE

The Material Representing the Cultural Universe. Objects, Symbols and Cultural Categories

---

SUMMARY OF CHAPTER CONTENTS

This chapter reviews 'cultural' theories of material culture. These approaches are not formally semiotic or structural like the models considered in the previous chapter, however they situate objects as crucial to the practice and processes of culture. There are five main sections:

- an outline of the way tastes and preferences for particular objects and things are linked to cultural narratives
- a review of the foundational work of Durkheim and Mauss on culture and classification, showing its relevance to material culture studies
- a discussion of how contemporary scholars have applied, refined and developed the Durkheimian tradition in studies of technological objects
- a review of the work of Mary Douglas and Daniel Miller, who are centrally responsible for asserting a place of meaning and culture at the core of people–object relations, and consumption practice broadly
- a consideration of the way objects are transformed within culture, and how their meanings change, depending on time–space contexts.

The whole world seems populated with forces that in reality exist only in our minds. We know what the flag is for the soldier, but in itself it is only a bit of cloth … A cancelled postage stamp may be worth a fortune, but obviously that value is in no way entailed by its natural properties. But collective representations often impute to the things to which they refer properties that do not exist in them … The soldier who falls defending his flag certainly does not believe he has sacrificed himself to a piece of cloth … to express our own ideas even to ourselves, we need to attach those ideas to material things that symbolize them. (Durkheim, 1995[1912]: 228–9)

Recapping approaches to studying objects

This chapter begins with a brief review. The previous chapters surveyed two fundamental theoretical traditions for the interpretation of objects. The first theoretical tradition derives from Marxist and critical approaches (Chapter 3). Two general points can be made about this perspective. First, this tradition establishes the thesis that objects are the material embodiment of the human labour that produced them and, in the last instance, any object – as commodity – represents exploited human capacity and the ultimate degradation of human creativity and identity. Second – and this comes from authors who refined and developed Marx's work into the twentieth century – objects that exist in abundance in consumer societies actually do a type of psychological and emotional harm to citizens: they deaden creativity, exploit emotional needs, and encourage bogus developments of self which defy authentic human needs. In this tradition then, objects are capitalist objects first and foremost. The possibility that they can have positive, constructive meanings within culture is circumscribed by their status as commodities. The second theoretical field discussed (in Chapter 4) is associated with structural and semiotic approaches. Again, a couple of fundamental threads in this tradition can be discerned. First, we can say that this tradition is concerned with the symbolic meaning of objects, as opposed to Marxist and critical approaches where meaning is subsumed under a political economy framework. Moreover, objects are accounted for within an autonomous theoretical framework, indebted principally from Saussure's programme for structural linguistics, that is, objects have meanings that are established 'relationally' through a broader field of object associations, understood through the analytic model of signs and signifiers developed by Saussure. Further, as shown by Barthes, the language of objects speaks at another, meta level – the myth. Thus, an object first refers to something other than itself. At another level it signifies broader cultural myths or discourses, for example, about success, status, masculinity, individualism or even larger questions about social consensus and dominant belief systems.

In the current chapter, the third and final major theoretical platform for understanding material culture will be considered. It can be labelled a 'cultural' approach to understanding material culture. While it has more in common with the semiotic, structural tradition than the critical approach, it also has some differences. The semiotic and structural tradition, developed by Saussure and most forcefully advocated and applied in Lévi-Strauss' work, insists on the relationality of objects within a system of semiotic codes. What can be called the 'cultural' approach to material culture is less committed to this strong model of linguistic structuralism and a semiotic methodology. It does insist however, that objects have important cultural meanings and that they frequently do some sort of 'cultural work' related to representing the contours of culture, including matters of social difference, establishing social identity or managing social status. Much of the recent work in cultural anthropology has drawn attention to this culturally embedded nature of consumption objects; that is, the social, cultural and emotive capacities of objects that people acquire and use (Douglas and Isherwood, [1996]1979; Kopytoff, 1986; Miller, 1987). It is this work that the current chapter will consider.

The universe in an object: objects and classifications of the 'good' and 'bad'

This preliminary section considers the repertoires people deploy to make judgements about objects through the concept of taste. It is through such classificatory judgements that people come to define the boundaries of culture. Everyday notions of 'taste' provide a sociological context for the analysis and discussion of the material possessions people have, and the possible reasons for their choices. The concept of taste allows us to link material culture to individual choice and the discourses that situate and express it (that is, 'what I like and why I like it'), and in turn an individual's cultural location (that is, 'how my choices are different or similar to others').

An argument can also be made that when people make such choices broader issues are actually at stake, and that there is a grander, cultural narrative at work in the presentation and justification of material culture. At a literal level one's taste is about such things as: matching colours, appropriate skirt lengths or shoe heel sizes, the optimal way to spend leisure time, the ways one should greet others, one's choice in lounge coverings, preferences for antique or new furniture, how one's kitchen renovation was planned, and the search for beautiful things to fill one's house or cover one's body. At a more abstract, grand level, what can our tastes, and the objects we possess, tell us about the particular contours or discourses of contemporary culture?

The elementary place to start is with ideas of good and bad, inherently cultural notions in the sense that these two seemingly simple words assign value to things. We can think about ideas of worth philosophically as well as sociologically. Notions of what is good and bad have troubled generations of philosophers from The Ancients to Moderns. To judge something or someone as good or bad is a philosophical problem of some substance for it involves a series of thought processes which subsume notions of desirability, needs and wants, satisfaction, rightness, efficiency, pleasure and obligation (Sparshott, 1958). At the same time, from a sociological point of view, judgements of what is good and bad for us, others, groups or societies would seem to be routine, frequent and taken for granted elements of everyday life. However philosophically foggy and misplaced everyday evaluations of 'good' and 'bad' may be, they seem an inescapable component of social existence and can be found in myriad mundane feelings such as: 'eating something would be good', 'physical exercise would be good for me', 'to finish project x would be good', 'to buy a new shirt would be good', 'person x is not my type of person'.

The British philosopher Francis Sparshott (1958: 122) outlines the simple meaning of 'good' to be that which 'is such to satisfy the wants of the person or persons concerned'. While Sparshott does not concern himself with notions of bad things, it is reasonable to assume that bad things fail to satisfy wants, or at least people believe that they will fail to satisfy particular wants. It seems likely that everyday notions of what is perceived as likely to satisfy, and what is perceived as likely to fail to satisfy, are reflective of almost universal human habits and traits of judgement or evaluation. Such notions of satisfaction invariably carry references to a state of incompleteness, equivalent to Baudrillard's (1996[1968]) idea of 'lack', because there is an implied reference to a hitherto lacking desirable 'good' or undesirable 'bad' object or person which has potential to satiate desire. Sparshott puts it this way in his philosophical inquiry into goodness: 'desires and needs are alike deficiencies, and carry a reference to a perfected or completed somewhat' (1958: 133). Judging the ability of a thing or person to complete or satisfy seems an essential element of our culture – it is the basis of the act of consumption, and is a mandatory routine of our lives that involves navigating myriad options in order to weigh value, to find merits or deficiencies, and to decide in favour or against something (Sparshott, 1958: 128). As Sparshott points out, we live in a culture of evaluation, and the notion of good, and by implication also the notion of bad, are key operators in these everyday judgements: 'such arguments tend to present themselves in the form: good or bad?' (Sparshott, 1958: 128).

Moving from the philosophical dimensions of 'good' and 'bad', an argument can be made that notions of good and bad are universal symbolic structures. Just as psychologists have argued that disgust is a basic emotion from which nuanced shades of secondary emotions develop (see William Ian Miller's book *The Anatomy of Disgust* (1997) for a discussion of this), so 'good' and 'bad' become universal, binary linguistic operators for distinguishing people and things in our lives. From good and bad emerge a large variety of emotional shades, signified by varying linguistic operators, for example words such as 'uplifting', 'edifying' and 'satisfactory' for good; and 'worthless', 'poor', 'inadequate' or 'inappropriate' for bad. It is possible to see notions of good and bad situated as symbolic foundations around which an endless variety of judgements can be made. The deployment of the notions 'good' and 'bad' are thus not experienced as philosophical conundrums for actors – though they do engage in processes of 'weighing up' – as they become natural or taken for granted modes of interaction with the world. Judgements about people, their behaviours and material culture happen routinely, and are sometimes based on this binary opposition of good and bad, helpful or harmful, worthy or worthless. While some notion of 'good' and 'bad' becomes the basis or master scheme for a retrievable complex of resources or narratives used in everyday judgements, according to variables such as age, class, peer group and education level, we embellish these oppositions with a variety of words and concepts that give 'goodness' and 'badness' unique hues across different contexts. In this way, it is possible to see how the idea of distinguishing between good and bad types has particular relevance to the practice of consumption, for at its elementary stage, consumption is a process of selection or discernment of things that are perceived to satisfy. To fully consider this question of simultaneously classifying particular objects and one's 'world', we can look to the work of figurehead scholars from the *Année Sociologique*, a group centred around French sociologist Emile Durkheim in the early part of the twentieth century. Durkheim's work on religious sentiments and the sacred and profane within culture is valuable for understanding the symbolic dimensions of material culture, as is the work of his protégé, Marcel Mauss.

Durkheim, Mauss and cultural classification: the symbolic division of objects

We can begin by visiting the key points of Durkheim and Mauss' (1963[1903]) theory of classification, drawn from the book *Primitive Classification*. Their assertion is that the key problem for the human sciences, sociology in particular, is how cultural classifications are made. Psychologists have a particular approach to this question that is individual-centred. According to this view, classifications have salience because they allow the individual to make categorisations and demarcations which are an important element of individual psychology, yet such sortings tie individuals to the group: classifications entangle individuals within society. The task of the ethnographer, Durkheim and Mauss believed, is to discover the classifications people make. These classifications form the basis of daily life, and constitute fundamental cultural practices, for example assessments of things as good or bad, beautiful or ugly, rich or poor, self or other, and so on. Such processes allow things in the natural and social world to be classified within a system that is essentially symbolic. They help people make their way, so to speak, as individuals attempt to assemble facts about their world into a systematic and symbolic whole.

Human beings thus have a drive to classify – as we would understand a scientist to do – but they also cannot help but assign cultural value. Durkheim and Mauss' argument is that classification is a process of marking-off, of demarcating things that are related, but have distinct points of difference to another. These systems of ideas of relation and difference serve to connect and unify knowledge about the world. They build up a hierarchical system where ideas form chains of meanings, and where values can be assigned and competing discursive constructs weighed up. Importantly, the symbolic partnership of things is deeply, emotionally felt, so that violations of symbolic coupling are experienced and conceived as polluted and dangerous.

In primitive societies, classes of people and objects are grouped into classifications together, distinguished only by their relative location in a symbolic universe. As social complexity develops, so does the complexity of classifications, in accordance with a general model of evolutionary progress. Yet, despite this evolutionary understanding, Durkheim and Mauss maintain that the classifications primitive people make are not exceptional or singular and thus inferior in some way, rather that classification is a universal feature of human (social) thought that is scientific in nature. Here we can see affinities with Lévi-Strauss' structural anthropology developed over half a century later – classifications are about understanding one's place in the world relative to other people and other things, and developing a unified account of cultural symbols:

> The object is not to facilitate action, but to advance understanding, to make intelligible the relations which exist between things ... Such classifications are thus intended, above all, to connect ideas, to unify knowledge; as such, they may be said without inexactitude to be scientific. (Durkheim and Mauss, 1963[1903]: 81)

In *The Elementary Forms of the Religious Life* (1995[1912]), Durkheim extends this theory of classification in a couple of important areas. He maintains that the systems of representation people make of themselves, and the world generally, are of principal importance in understanding the distinctive nature of the social. Categories of understanding are the *modus operandi* of social beings, the 'solid frames that confine thought' (1995[1912]: 9). His principal interest is in religious sentiments, which he understands as eminently social and as the basis for the categorical divisions people make in society. Importantly, Durkheim points out that classifications are not merely dry, technical accomplishments but come to obtain their cultural authority by virtue of the moral quality they possess. Classifications of things have a moral force which animates them, and which contributes to their robustness and emotional depth. Thus, we can say that classifications of objects and commodities, and the aesthetic judgements implicit in them, are not merely representative of emptied-out, ersatz forms of individualism, but have an associated moral force that gives them durability and strength.

Do such processes hold up in consumer societies? Is it possible that difference and classification within consumer societies have a moral weight attached to them? We can answer this in the affirmative by looking to other research areas, for example, in Bourdieu's theory of taste, considered in the following chapter. We have also seen it as an implicit force in Hebdige's analysis of fashion and youth cultures: elements of material culture can be deployed to demonstrate challenges to conventional cultural codes, which in turn lend themselves to supporting particular moral stances. In a different tradition, Lamont's (1992) study of the manners and morals of middle- to upper-class citizens in France and the United States shows that people attach moral weight to what could be seen as rather mundane traits, objects and behaviours of others, including the things they consume, possess and display.

Durkheim's other significant insight in *Elementary Forms*, which is useful for our purposes, is that these systems of classification are inescapable evidence of the socialness of systems of representation. He says: 'as part of society, the individual naturally transcends himself, both when he thinks and when he acts' (Durkheim, 1995[1912]: 16). Hierarchies of classification develop as society develops – in fact, they are the basis of forms of sociality. Systems of classifying people, objects and things are thus linked to a collective consciousness – they obtain meaning by reference to other socially sanctioned classifications such that conceiving or classifying something is both learning its essential elements better, and also locating it in its place. In making such classifications, humans perform a commitment to the social, and bear out that 'society' is deep within them:

> Thus, in order to prevent dissidence, society weighs on its members with all its authority. Does a mind seek to free itself from these norms of all thought? Society no longer considers this a human mind in the full sense, and treats it accordingly. This is why it is that when we try, even deep down inside, to get away from these fundamental notions, we feel that we are not fully free; something resists us; more than that, because society is represented inside us well, it resists these revolutionary impulses from within. (Durkheim, 1995[1912]: 16)

Durkheim asserts that it is the nature of religious sentiment to divide the world into two distinct, polarised moral domains: the sacred and profane. Sacred things are not just gods or divine spirits, anything can be sacred. For example, an original artpiece by a famous artist, a first edition run of a book by a famous author, a highly valued consumer object like an iPod, or a pair of running spikes worn by a famous athlete. Any such thing has an aura, an iconic status, and comes to be highly regarded within certain communities. Sacred things are regarded as superior in dignity and power, profane things are set apart and forbidden. Each binary is held together – in symbolic opposition – by beliefs, rituals and practices which unite one single moral community (from a national society, to a subculture) through ritualistic practices of exclusion and commitment. These religious sentiments – the sacred and profane – allow people capacity to think about their worlds, others and the objects within them, and offer schemas for guiding social action. Its highest form is found in its social expression, enabled by a system of collective representations, whereby the individual participates in the world through navigating the universe of collective symbols. Durkheim imagined this extra-societal sentiment as a type of collective conscience, and the highest form of psychic life. Society is not possible without this collective conscience, and for this to exist individuals and things must be divided up into groups, and these groups must be symbolically classified in relation to one another:

> The individual realizes, at least dimly, that above his private representations there is a world of type-ideas according to which he has to regulate his own; he glimpses a whole intellectual world in which he participates but which is greater than he. (Durkheim, 1995[1912]: 438)

In contemporary research into everyday understandings of good and bad taste (Woodward and Emmison, 2001), investigators asked a sample of respondents how they would define 'good taste' and 'bad taste'. Though the survey question presented to respondents attunes them to ideas of 'good and bad taste', the sentiments respondents expressed were a perfect example of how things in the aesthetic and commercial domain have a particular moral weight. Thus, certain practices of taste and particular types or styles of contemporary material culture come to be evaluated as 'beautiful', 'timeless', 'elegant', 'vulgar', 'garish' or 'unsuitable', but in the end are classified as in the realm of good, or in the realm of bad. This is a simple, bipartite system of classification, and condensing the complexities of taste and aesthetic judgement to this binary scheme might be seen as somewhat reductionist. However, it has the advantage of illustrating how such judgements come to acquire an ethical force, and it allows actors the discursive space to make their own demarcations of the good and bad. These assessments are embellished with a variety of concepts and words by respondents, however in the end they are judged as satisfying or not, good or bad.

Marcel Mauss' study of gift exchange in primitive societies, *The Gift* (1967[1954]), also reinforces how activities within the domain of commerce and exchange can carry moral weight by allowing us to make relational classifications of people and things. What is the purpose of a gift, Mauss asks, when we understand that exchanging gifts does not enhance the absolute wealth of those involved in the exchange, and is not required for sustenance? Drawing on ethnographic studies from around the world, Mauss declares that gifts are supposedly voluntary, spontaneous and without self-interest, but in fact are obligatory, planned and self-interested. That gifts purport to be generously offered, free of self-consideration, is actually a form of social deception. For example, in Samoan culture to receive a gift is something which honours a person and brings them 'mana', or prestige. This in turn, brings with it the absolute obligation to return the gift. Gifts then are not inert but are alive and personified, and achieve a type of magical, spiritual hold over giver and receiver, such that receiving a gift is akin to receiving a part of a person's essence: 'to give something is to give part of oneself' (Mauss, 1967[1954]: 10). Gifts thus bring with them: (i) an obligation to repay, (ii) an obligation to give, and (iii) an obligation to receive.

Mauss extends his analysis of gift exchange on other cultures to note that even in western culture, where social and economic routines are apparently dominated by contracts and forms of instrumental rationality, economic activity incorporates more than a system of exchange, being one part of the enduring, wider social contract amongst citizens. Economic activity then brings with it a form of civility (1967[1954]: 81), so that trade and wealth generation brings with it general increases in living standards, social solidarity and peacefulness. Forms of exchange cannot be reduced to economy:

> It is our good fortune that all is not yet couched in terms of purchase and sale. Things have value which are emotional and material; indeed in some cases the values are entirely emotional. Our morality is not solely commercial. (Mauss, 1967[1954]: 63)

Developing a Durkheimian approach to objects: Alexander and Smith on sacred and profane discourses about technologies

As part of their development of a 'strong programme' in cultural sociology, Jeffrey Alexander and Philip Smith (see Alexander, 2003) have sought to integrate the structural analyses of Lévi-Strauss and Saussure, which as we have seen have focused on the codes, narrative and categories that inform culture. Alongside this structuralist tradition which emphasises the autonomy of cultural systems and codes, Alexander and Smith propose to enrich this model by applying a deeply interpretive, hermeneutic genre, inspired particularly by the anthropologist Clifford Geertz, and especially Durkheim's late work on religion. Their goal is to articulate a sociological paradigm that is both 'structural' in the Lévi-Straussian sense, and also 'hermeneutic' in Geertz's sense, allowing for the thick description of understandings, meanings and practices. Their work represents some of the most important recent work in the field of culture. First, we look at one of Alexander's empirical papers on discourses surrounding emergent computer technologies of the twentieth century. We can see it is a type of model paper allowing us to see how such a structural and hermeneutic analysis of material culture could unfold.

Alexander begins by laying out a key myth of modern life: the belief that science and rationality make the world a problem of purely technological means. That is, put another way, technological advancements will allow us to face and overcome any problems we encounter related to time, space and the natural elements. As a corollary, Alexander points out that the modern world is in an important way against culture – understood as things such as beauty, emotion, feeling, relationships and meaning – and is utterly materialistic. The modern world is inextricably directed by technologies which routinely allow us to accomplish tasks and goals that human bodies alone are unable to achieve. But the story of technology that is functional or utilitarian is not the only story to be told about technology:

Technology is rooted in the deepest resources and abysses of our imagination. It is religion and anti-religion, our god and our devil, the sublime and the accursed. (Alexander, 2003: 179)

Alexander asserts that understandings of technology have generally been identified as a materialist thing *par excellence*, 'the most routine of the routine' (2003: 180) that helps us to make a way and do business in the world. One might think of numerous examples of these routine yet highly powerful technological items on the basis of Alexander's suggestion: traffic lights, motor vehicles, electric lighting, writing implements, coats, socks and shoes, and so the list could go on. Simultaneously materialist and functional, and deeply constitutive of our way of thinking about doing things in the social world, such objects can signify a range of meanings. Technology, Alexander asserts, must be situated in a cultural order: a material thing, 'it is a sign, both a signifier and signified, in relation to which actors cannot entirely separate their subjective states of mind' (2003: 180). Alexander goes on to identify two broad traditions in the academic interpretation of technology. The first is indebted to Weber's ideas about bureaucracy, rationalisation, discipline and calculation, and is a pessimistic story of how technology gradually seeps into every bit of social life. The second is derived from critical theorists, notably Lukács and Marcuse, and emphasises technology as the means for subjugating labour as the growth of a technological culture begins to define modern capitalism.

Alexander's view goes beyond both of these inadequate or partial accounts. He urges us to see technology as a discourse – a sign system that is ordered by both semiotic structures or codes, and social and emotional demands. Technology is an object upon which people attach meaning, a 'good for thinking with' in the Lévi-Straussian sense:

Human beings continue to experience the need to invest the world with metaphysical meaning and to experience solidarity with objects outside the self. (Alexander, 2003: 184)

In terms of the specific meanings attributed to technology, Alexander uses the Durkheimian idea that humans divide the world into things and events that are sacred and profane. The sacred refers to images of the good that people strive to protect, while profane describes images of evil from which people need protection. For example, at the heart of our imaginings of the computer are a set of deeply felt oppositions, where machines have a capacity to embody both the hopes and fears generated by industrial society. Using a textual analysis of newspaper and magazine material from around the time of the computer's birth, Alexander shows how it is understood in sacred and profane terms. As a sacred object it is: a super-brain, superhuman, the closest thing to God, and can solve things that have baffled generations in a flash. As a profane object, the computer is: a colossal gadget, a Frankenstein monster, a mathematical dreadnought, a figure factory. The computer is thus understood as having the capacity to be both saviour and destroyer: as a sacred thing it 'is the vehicle for salvation' while its 'profane side threatens destruction' (2003: 191).

Working in the same tradition, Philip Smith (2003) develops some groundwork for a Durkheimian theory of punishment by exploring the meanings associated with a particular item of punishment technology: the guillotine. Following a similar logic to Alexander in his analysis of discourses about the computer, Smith makes the point that punishment technologies have moved in unison with the general tendencies of modernisation: toward rationality, reason and efficiency. This view of the relentless infiltration of modern imperatives into the pores of everyday life is consistent with Foucault's thesis in *Discipline and Punish*, who is perhaps the most important contributor to this tradition in criminology and social theory more broadly. Smith takes issue with this dominant thesis by looking at the guillotine case within the field of punishment, and assembles historical evidence from eighteenth-century newspapers, pamphlets and encyclopedias to show that a counter-discourse accompanies this 'rationality' discourse that is highly emotional, profoundly symbolic and founded upon grotesque and Gothic imagery. So, rather than the guillotine being a type of spectacular celebration of the punishment of deviance (for example, as was public torture or hanging), the guillotine was imagined to be an efficient, rational and passionless technology. As such, it eliminated the rich and possibly dangerous semiotic field that accompanied earlier modes of punishment, for example in Foucault's well-known contrast between the excruciating torture of Damiens and the prison timetable developed by Faucher which made the body docile, rather than destroy it. Smith summarises this 'passionless' view of the guillotine as another iteration of the story of the rationalisation of the world and the (Weberian) movement toward a bleak iron cage, where the guillotine would be identified as merely a dull and material expression of instrumental reason:

> Although intended as a material celebration of scientistic Enlightenment codes and dramatizing these in its efficient operation, the guillotine stimulated a febrile counter-discourse of heteroglossic, grotesque and Gothic symbolism. Totemistic collective representations, mythologies and vivid imaginative speculations became powerfully implicated in the evaluation of the penal technology by both advocates and critics. (Smith, 2003: 7)

Looking to give fruition to a Durkheimian theory of punishment, the resources for which remain latent in Durkheim's work, Smith shows that there were divergent cultural discourses surrounding the guillotine. He does not reject Foucault's emphasis on the guillotine as representing a rational instrument of science, but argues that such a thesis has displaced, even obliterated, a more culturally sensitive account of punishment. Smith argues his historical material shows that this object was an attractor for a range of cultural discourses, some rational and functional, some irrational and emotion-charged:

> The guillotine was a 'scientific' instrument; that its operations involved a rou-
> tinisation of bodily activity; and that an emergent professional gaze relent-
> lessly interrogated its embodied effects. Yet it will also become apparent that
> none of these came at the expense of more profound symbolic resonance. Far
> from eliminating or replacing vital symbolisms, the guillotine and its bodies
> became, in Lévi-Strauss's terms, *bonnes á penser* for a new set of mytholo-
> gies. (Smith, 2003: 30)

Mary Douglas: bringing Durkheim to consumption

One of the key proponents of the Durkheimian tradition in twentieth-century structural thought has been Mary Douglas. Her work with the economist Baron Isherwood, *The World of Goods* (1996[1979]), is an influential attempt to apply Durkheimian insights to problems of contemporary consumption. In this book Douglas and Isherwood seek to redress the poverty of economic theorising on consumption, which is identified to be overly narrow and obsessed with abstractions of consumer 'rationality' and utility, or alternately, taken with the Veblenesque notion that consumption is a crude game of conspicuous, 'competitive display'. In this latter tradition, consumption and consumerist tendencies are commonly castigated and scorned as 'greed, stupidity and insensitivity to want' (1996[1979]: vii). Douglas and Isherwood assert that neither moral indignation aroused by supposed excesses, nor micro-economic abstraction, is enough to understand the attractions of consumption.

In this work they provide what stands as probably the most systematic treatment of the nature of goods as cultural props. In the preface to this work, they assert a manifesto: 'goods are neutral, their uses are social; they can be used as fences or bridges'. The general goal is thus to contextualise consumption practice within the social and cultural process, broadly conceived, though uncovering its cultural codes, etiquettes and conventions. Along with this, it is necessary to understand the work they do to include, exclude and construct social identities and categories. This then, reads like a contemporary version of Lévi-Strauss' *bonnes á penser* (see previous chapter), but without the call-to-arms, strident structuralism that sometimes crept into Lévi-Strauss' work.

Douglas and Isherwood's core argument is that goods are resources for thinking, demarcating and classifying. They acknowledge that while goods, or consumer objects, originate in the system of capitalist production, at the same time 'all material possessions carry social meanings' and, as resources for thinking, commodity objects make 'visible and stable categories of culture' (2000[1966]: 38). Though goods 'come from' the economy, in order to understand their attractions and meanings we should conceptualise them autonomously from economic frameworks. As something for making sense of the world, consumer objects assist people in demarcating social categories, maintaining social relationships, and thus assigning worth and value to things and people (Douglas, 2000[1966]; Douglas and Isherwood, 1996[1979]). Consumption then has a moral component, in that choice and selection are not driven solely by utilitarian needs nor understood by consumers as 'simple choices', but, for the user, consuming objects acquires a deeper emotional significance. Certainly, we can hypothesise that this will be more likely for some goods more than others, and possibly for people of certain ages or social backgrounds more than others. Douglas and Isherwood recommend then, that to understand objects, analysts need to bracket out matters to do with markets and utility:

> ...we shall assume that the essential function of consumption is its capacity to make sense. Forget the idea of consumer irrationality. Forget that commodities are good for eating, clothing and shelter; forget their usefulness and try instead the idea that commodities are good for thinking; treat them as a non-verbal medium for the human creative faculty. (Douglas and Isherwood, 1996 [1979]: 40–1)

Consumption, then, is about meaning-making. The world of goods becomes a world of possible meanings for consumers. The attraction of consuming things, therefore, is only partly that it (temporarily) satiates needs. The more important attraction of consuming things is that it offers continuous opportunity to perform, affirm and manage the self. Social actors understand themselves in relation to others, and other things: they crave seeing themselves (or their potential, promised selves) reflected in other's talk and actions, and in the objects that surround them. So, one picks and chooses from the available array of goods within any particular class (e.g., canned tomatoes, bottled waters, motor vehicles, apples, strawberries and cherries) taking into accounts one's means and one's preferences, for example, for organic or environmentally sound produce, or for local rather than international goods, all the time keeping in mind the selections of others. So we must see that episodes of consumption are not merely shopping or provisioning expeditions, but opportunities to give meaning to or affirm one's social relationships and the wider social universe. A good example is within the world of sneakers where consumers have to navigate a variety of brands, styles and aesthetic preferences: Adidas, Nike, Reebok, Puma, K-Swiss, Converse, old or new school, retro or contemporary, global brand or no-name? Miles' (1996) ethnographic research into youth and their choice of sneakers shows this facet of choice and its weight with skill: youths need to think carefully about their choice of sneakers because what they wear positions themselves within a cultural universe that is played out on their neighbourhood streets, the high streets of their towns and cities, and their playgrounds. Another confirmation of this approach is found in Daniel Miller's (1987) ethnographic work on grocery shopping. Miller shows that routine shopping expeditions involving household provisioning are really opportunities for shoppers to think through aspects of their relationships with others. More on Miller's work later in this chapter.

Douglas and Isherwood pick up on Barthes' discussion of different ways to make coffee as an example of how routine, everyday acts of consuming things (coffee beans, liquid, cup, grinder) become opportunities to delineate crucial debates about self and non-self, the inauthentic and the truthful, the good and bad. Douglas and Isherwood dwell on the symbolic meanings of whether one chooses to grind coffee beans with a mechanical grinder, or pestle and mortar:

> The grinder works mechanically, the human hand only supplies force, and electric power can easily be substituted for it; its produce is kind of dust-fine, dry and impersonal. By contrast there is an art in wielding the pestle. Bodily skills are involved, and the stuff on which they are bestowed is not hard metal, but instead the noblest of materials, wood. And out of the mortar comes not a mere dust, but a gritty powder, pointing straight to the ancient lore of alchemy and its potent brews. The choice between pounding and grinding is thus a choice between two different views of the human condition and between metaphysical judgements lying just beneath the surface of the question. (Douglas and Isherwood, 1996[1979]: 50)

Goods and their consumption are more properly seen within systems of information. Utility is but one component of the nature of goods. Most importantly, they are social markers: not just of beauty and prestige, but all sorts of social categories which find expression in goods people are associated with, acting for the consumer's self, and for others who witness the consumption. Codes, messages and symbols circulate through commodities, as consumers attempt to be near the centre of message transmission in order to make sense of it and to participate.

Douglas and Isherwood extend their thesis by suggesting that consumption becomes the social system itself: the actual means for constituting self, society and culture. This notion has overtones of the recent Foucault-inspired governmentality literature, in that consumption becomes a means of expressing and managing self and populations. The significance of consumption, Douglas and Isherwood suggest, is that it actually constitutes the social system, with each episode or consumption event being merely one part of the process of building culture, through continuously expending, rebuilding and expending bits of it. In doing so, they suggest that consumption is more than just a way of social communication, but constitutive of it:

> But consumption goods are definitely not mere messages; they constitute the very system itself. Take them out of human intercourse and you have dismantled the whole thing. In being offered, accepted, or refused, they either reinforce or

undermine existing boundaries. The goods are both the hardware and the
software, so to speak, of an information system whose principal concern it to
monitor its own performance. (Douglas and Isherwood, 1996[1979]: 49)

Miller and studying material culture in societies of abundance

Daniel Miller's (1987) programme for material culture studies argues similarly for studies of consumption that acknowledge relations between
people and goods in industrial societies. Miller's work was very important in the articulation of the contemporary field of material culture studies. His key work *Material Culture and Mass Consumption* (1987) is a series
of mostly philosophical essays, drawing upon diverse theorists of modernity, to show how culture is dynamically constituted through meaningful
people–object interactions. In parts the work is dry and very abstract, and
in a critical mood one might decide that the conclusive bits of the work
really say little more than what Douglas and Isherwood said some years
earlier. Yet, in uniquely and impressively combining a variety of foundational theories of modernity, it is also a very powerful – and sometimes
elegant – statement about the purpose and scope of studying material culture that crystallised contemporary interest in the material basis of consumption. Miller cuts through academic discourses which (unhelpfully)
frame contemporary material culture as representing an inferior form
of primitive authenticity (classical anthropology), as objects of capitalist
oppression (Marxist and critical theory) or as the superficial excreta of an
era obsessed with surface (postmodernism). At its core is the belief that
anthropological insights can be readily applied to study contemporary,
'mass consumption'.

Miller makes the argument that even though we live in an era of material abundance where social life is increasingly experienced through a
vast array of objects, theoretical and conceptual knowledge of material
culture is rudimentary. One key reason for this is that academic study of
consumer culture – and the objects that comprise it – has presumed
objects to be either frivolous or oppressive. One of the reasons Miller
offers for this is spot-on, and amusing. Miller sees the cultural positions
of the scholars themselves as unreflexively reproducing such unsubtle
binaries. Though scholars are immersed in these fields of everyday material culture and often have the cultural and economic means to enthusiastically acquire an array of objects (for example, books, art, technology,
pleasantly furnished homes, tweed coats), scholars have generally
focused on the 'productive' sites of social life such as the workplace, preserving the myth that the objects one deals with have meanings which are
entirely personal or unworthy of academic reflection. The result has been
a double-standard whereby scholars analyse the thing called 'consumer
society' as if they did not participate in it, or were above it. Likewise, they
often assume – naïvely – that they somehow do not have aesthetic tastes.

Whatever else he did or cannot do, Bourdieu radically challenged such a proposition, and more importantly provided the conceptual means to do so. Miller's work has little in common with Bourdieu, but through different means allows us to focus the same questions regarding the cultural uses of things. Miller aims to take consumer societies seriously, without resorting to hackneyed discussions of authenticity, oppression or superficiality. The crux of his argument is neatly captured when he points out that we should not be so much concerned with what industrial, consumer culture forces upon us, but with what it allows us to be (or one might add what it allows us to think or feel). Scholars have rarely stopped to consider such questions:

> The argument that there is a thing called capitalist society which renders its population entirely pathological and dehumanised, with the exception of certain theorists who, although inevitably living their private lives in accordance with the tenets of this delusion, are able in their abstracted social theory to rise above, criticize and provide the only alternative model for society, is somewhat suspicious. (Miller, 1987: 167)

Miller switches the frame of analysis from the economic realm of objectification, to the process of consumer objectification. One of Miller's significant arguments centres on the important work consumers do in creating meaning from goods in industrial modernity, and in particular he emphasises the semiotic and cultural labour involved in, and after, the purchase of commodities (see also, Miller, 1998). It is in this period of time when a 'vast morass of possible goods is replaced by the specificity of the particular item' that it is chosen, and subsequently purchased (Miller, 1987: 190). The abstractions of production and exchange emphasised in structural accounts of consumption are replaced by the consumer's search for meaning. It is what happens as people come face-to-face with mass consumption objects which matters most for Miller. How can we understand them? How can we gather meaning from objects? How can we confer meaning on them? Miller thus understands the nature of consuming objects as fundamentally about the consumer engaging in transforming the nature and meaning of objects:

> consumption as work may be defined as that which translates the object from an alienable to an inalienable condition; that is, from being a symbol of estrangement and price value to being an artefact invested with particular inseparable connotations. (Miller, 1987: 190)

What Miller is referring to is the negation of exchange value – that is it's price – that must occur for people to invest meaning in an object. The meanings one gives are malleable – interpretations of objects will change according to social positions – age, gender, class and so on. Intuitively, as a consumer you might sometimes feel this hermeneutic process of transforming an object from exchange value to one invested with personal meanings. Think of a situation where you have paid quite a deal of money for something, perhaps a costly piece of technology, or an expensive item of clothing or footwear. Presumably, at some stage of the consumption process you were uncertain about purchasing this thing, or at least had to weigh up certain choices about brands, models, styles and of course, costs. At this stage, you may desire the object in question, but not possess it and certainly your relationship with it is mostly about rather abstract matters. Once you decide to purchase the object, you must then come to feel at one with the object – you must let it into your life and feel as if it is a natural 'part of you'. You probably remember that this takes some time, and perhaps personal rationalisation. Over time, the object comes to be valued, or not, and continually experienced through its (often changing) form. For example, a favourite tee shirt will fade and loosen up a little, as will a pair of canvas sneakers. Such changes in object form then require corresponding changes in the interpretation and use of the object, giving it a type of lifecourse. For example, the fading tee shirt may eventually be deemed unsuitable for wearing in public, becoming used for dirty or 'backstage' work like house cleaning or gardening.

Miller also outlines a series of contextual dimensions of material culture, which are summarised below.

- *The artefact as manufactured object*. Though most objects are functionally and symbolically flexible, some objects are intentionally produced for particular purposes, and, as such, are constrained by the very nature of their manufacture. One might note that art practices easily make such classifications irrelevant, as they transform things like machinery parts for artistic purposes such as sculpture. So, some artefacts do stand for particular types of production, but of course, this matters little for the users of an object.
- *Artefacts and function*. There are a variety of differentiations of objects based on their function, for example, in machinery or technology, or in types of soles worn on special use shoes. But, what is more important, Miller asserts, is symbolic and aesthetic variation, like the differences in shapes of bottles that contain different types of alcohol, or in the design of different types of shoes.
- *Artefacts and property*. Artefacts are tied up with the development of personal property rights, and also with our sense of self. For example, one owns the clothing they wear, but this clothing also represents an important boundary of self upon which others may not infringe.
- *Artefacts, space and time*. Social spaces acquire symbolic potency through the existence of particular objects and their location within space. Objects must also be contextualised in time. For example, a bus bench might be used for a variety of functions throughout a 24-hour period.
- *Artefacts and style*. Style refers to the capacity to arrange and order objects in an individual or unique way. The notion of style is easily observed in the domain of home furnishing, where objects are differentiated

along lines, and must be arranged in relation to one another in a coherent manner also as to convey a personal sense of 'style'. Home furnishers must take into account things such as colour, texture and scale, sometimes paying attention to tried and true schemes of good taste, and other times playing around with, even disturbing, such schemes to calculated effect.

Miller's contribution to material culture studies as the examination of contemporary consumption habits and processes can be more broadly situated in the context of consumption studies. Particularly, Miller's arguments are best understood in relation to the body of literatures, mostly sociological but also within cultural studies, human geography and business and marketing, that have sought to take consumption seriously as a domain of cultural importance in its own right. Miller (1995) asserts that instead of seeing consumption as something that alienates or oppresses people, there is a need to understand it as a social, cultural and moral project. Miller highlights a number of myths held by scholars about consumption, whom he claims operate with a number of ideological assumptions about the nature of consumption activity. These can be reduced to the idea that 'consumption is bad', and that 'consumption is good'. While the latter element of the binary has had far less circulation, it is sometimes associated with what might be called celebratory accounts of consumption which emphasise play, subversion and experimentation through domains of consumption. The former myth is dominant, and includes assumptions that consumption is associated with homogenisation, opposed to sociality and highly individualist, opposed to authenticity, and creates particular diminished forms of selfhood.

Miller's strong contribution has been to argue against either form of reductionism, urging scholars not to commit to simple theories of consumption. Rather, he wishes to change the focus in consumption studies to acknowledge the irreducible materiality of consumption processes – we cannot escape that most forms of consumption involve engagement with material things. Thus, consumption involves a generic process of engagement with goods through a process called 'objectification', whereby consumers use objects as a practice in the world (for example, to wear as shoes on their feet, or to hit a ball over a net with), and they also offer forms which afford modes of conduct and understandings to be enacted. Goods are thus simultaneously about practices and meaning construction. Under such a conceptualisation, the task of any modern individual is to locate themselves with schemes of object meaning, searching for desirable cultural expressions such as 'comfort', 'success', or 'skilful' through engagement with goods.

Two of Miller's empirical studies illustrate these general principles. In 'Appropriating the state on the Council Estate' (1988) Miller interviews a range of flat dwellers in lower-middle and working-class council-owned flats. He finds that even though these dwellers are not rich in economic capital, nor in the social group one would expect to enjoy the art of home renovation and decorating – they live in what some call 'valium estates' – his respondents enthusiastically use a range of techniques to re-decorate and personalise their kitchens. Feeling alienated by the regular kitchen fit-out, and the standard shape and size of their kitchens, householders follow a range of strategies. Some do nothing, another group try to aestheticise and essentially cover up their kitchen, using a variety of decorative objects to build a new kitchen façade and surface to essentially makeover the problematic appearance of the kitchen, while a final group went about completely or nearly completely replacing their kitchen. In doing so, they transform the once alienable kitchen space into something meaningful and personal, which overcomes the 'contradictions' inherent in broader industrial, mass society. On the basis of his interviews, Miller argues that the adoption of renovation strategies was significantly related to gender, and also identification (or lack of) and sense of belonging regarding living in the estate. In a later study – *A Theory of Shopping* (1998a) – Miller conducts an ethnographic inquiry into the shopping practices of a group of North Londoners. His theory of shopping is a study of the cultural practices and meanings of shopping behaviour which complicates the theory-heavy approach to consumerism by employing ethnographic techniques, and implicitly offers a strong critique of the postmodern account of shopping (1998a: 96). Miller shows the ritual aspects of shopping, whereby consumers use shopping expeditions to think about relationships and love, thrift and money-saving, and 'treats'. He shows that although shopping might sometimes be conducted alone, it is not necessarily an individualist pursuit, for it constantly involves the incorporation of imagined others into shopping practices. The material culture on the shopping aisles has functional uses, for sure, and this is why people purchase them as a form of provisioning, but more importantly goods and the shopping expedition is used as a way of imagining one's own goals, family life and relationships with members of the family.

The cultural life of commodities. Things have social lives

An important earlier essay which picks up on the theme of transformations of meaning in material culture through transformations in its status – evident as a central theme throughout Miller's work – is Igor Kopytoff's essay on the cultural biography of things (1986). Kopytoff maintains that commodities should not just be defined by their 'technical' commodity status – that is, in Marxian terms, as an item with use value that also has exchange value – but are immersed within cultural and cognitive processes. Commodities are therefore not inanimate, fixed and stable – they move in and out of various phases of being commodities and non-commodities. As we have seen, as Marcel Mauss argued in *The Gift*

(1967[1954]), the realm of the economy is shot through with cultural significance, so while we may talk of commodities in the sense that we purchase certain objects, such things are really always cultural markers of some sort, located within a moral economy where humans dedicate and assign value and *values* to things. Kopytoff points out the dichotomy that has existed in recent western thought where there is an analytic separation between people and things – at one end are inanimate commodities, and the other end are singularised individuals. The relationships between the two are thin, and instrumentally defined: people pick up things as they need them to accomplish various goals, but the relationships are limited to this. Kopytoff's principal goal is to suggest a 'processual' view of things (and by implication, persons also), whereby the status of objects undergoes transformations in category and associated meaning. Especially, Kopytoff is concerned with the process of commodification-decommodification-recommodification. Corrigan (1997) uses the example of a cat to illustrate this process. In western societies animals have been commodified – they can be purchased via market exchange in pet stores or breeding houses. Thus, sitting in the pet store awaiting purchase, the cat is a commodity. Once purchased, it is decommodified – incorporated into a caring family as a loved pet. Generally, it is unlikely the cat would be recommodified. A piece of art that has been purchased by an individual could, however be recommodified. Hanging on a gallery wall it is a commodity, once purchased it is decommodified as it hangs as art on someone's wall. Potentially, the piece could re-enter the market for resale sometime in the future. The general point is this: objects are never culturally fixed, but always in the process of being and becoming.

Kopytoff extends his argument to suggest that such transformations are akin to a type of biography. Thus, things, not just people, have social lives. Relevant questions to ask about such a biography are: Where does the thing come from and who made it? What has the thing been designed for? Who is likely to buy it, and what uses would they put this thing to? What has been the career of this thing so far, and what do cultural discourses tell us about the ideal career for this type of thing? Are there recognised stages in the life of this thing, and what will happen when/if it outlives its usefulness? (Kopytoff, 1986: 66–7). Kopytoff uses the example of a car. First, the car must be made by someone, or rather a team, who work for a large company. In this context, the car is part of the larger institutional and industrial contexts of that company related to things like profitability, marketing and product identity, the place of the car within the suite of cars produced by that company, and also similar cars produced by other companies. Another part of the car's biography relates to its record of performance, including reliability, repair and roadworthiness. A further aspect relates to its social biography: who owns and uses it, and to what purpose is it put? Is it a family or business car? What do its uses tell us about our culture more broadly? Finally, is there a time when the car will be re-sold, or traded on?

Kopytoff argues that the counterdrive to the commodity realm and the process of widespread commoditisation inherent in western economic culture is identified to be singularisation. Whereas commoditisation tends to reduce all things to exchange values (i.e. essentially monetary value), there is a strong cultural imperative to make some things singular, powerful and meaningful. In the Durkheimian sense, there is a drive to make certain objects sacred in order to render them culturally resonant within the larger cultural universe. Kopytoff argues this can happen at both a cultural level and an individual level. At a cultural level, sports fans may sacralise the bat, outfit or shoes of a legendary player; music fans may assign sacred status to the piano, violin or guitar of a composer or performer; a museum may recreate a furnished room designed by an esteemed person, such as the 'Living room from the Little House, Wayzata, Minnesota', 1912–14, originally designed by the architect Frank Lloyd Wright now in permanent display at the Metropolitan Museum, New York. This exhibit effectively sacralises the designs of Lloyd Wright, uniting a range of Wright's objects, styles and designs within a single setting, with some embellishments for the purpose of instructing and accommodating visitors. Along similar lines, much of the trick of marketing certain contemporary consumer objects is to link them to once singular objects of the past: sit in a faithfully reproduced chair originally designed by Macintosh, the Eames, or Panton; use a reproduction of the tea and coffee set originally designed by Saarinen for the SAS Hotel, Denmark. All of these objects are widely available in stores, or on the internet (as commodities), but their cultural value is constructed by a process of singularisation based on their scarcity, iconic status or other qualities.

At an individual level, in a world where commodities are abundant, people are constantly engaged in a private battle against homogeneity, which is frequently an impetus for a type of transformation involving customisation. The extensive range of accessories for the ubiquitous iPod digital music player is one simple illustration of this. One can buy different colour iPods, but frequently (one might say, classically?) they are plain white – suggesting to consumers an object that is cool, light and simple; but perhaps rather lacking in personality, especially from the standpoint of younger consumers. Thus, one can buy various 'skins' to personalize one's iPod, giving it colour and individual presence, as well as some protection. Or, a rock musician may attempt to singularise their 'Fender Stratocaster' style guitar through putting stickers on it, painting it or giving it other markings. Along the way, in all these examples, people go about constructing objects as they construct themselves.

In the introductory essay to the collection of papers that includes Kopytoff's piece, Appadurai (1986) talks about dual processes called 'paths' and 'diversions'. Paths are the customary, or taken-for-granted uses and trajectories of objects. Such uses are almost culturally prescribed, and seen to be embodied transparently in the design of goods. For example, one might perceive that there is one particular path for a mundane object like a safety pin, limited to particular uses and contexts related to clothing repair and construction. Diversions are where such 'cultural use paths' are interrupted and modified. One case is the existence of what Appadurai refers to as 'kingly things' – objects that come to represent the power, wealth or status of a monarch. In order to maintain the exclusiveness of such commodities, royalty 'enclaves' the object, maintaining exclusive use within royal contexts only. In more complex modern societies, the institutional domain of fashion is perhaps the greatest creator of such diversions from customary paths. In the safety pin example mentioned above, Dick Hebdige (1979) shows how safety pins were appropriated by punks in the 1970s and used in shocking ways, such as for nose piercing or as a type of perverse decorative broach. Along similar lines, they wore plastic bags as if they were clothing. We can also identify other examples within the domain of fashion. Major sneaker brands have looked back in time and place in order to find new ways of presenting the sneaker to contemporary youth. For example, wrestling boots and also basketball boots from the 1970s have been re-released by major footwear companies for the current youth fashion market, as part of a 'vintage' or 'classic' themed range. How is it that a boot worn by wrestlers in the 1970s could find a new life as a fashion sneaker of the current era? In a different realm altogether, the building material corrugated iron was long established in Australia as material used in light, working-class homes, and almost exclusively as a roofing material. Its undulating shape and light, tin appearance made it perfect for channelling rain from roofs. Yet, half a century later, it is used as a feature material within cutting edge architectural practice. The qualities which once strictly defined its functionality are now perceived as being desirable, aesthetic – and heritage – qualities which must very much go 'on show' in order to assert the individuality and cultural astuteness of the owner.

Art objects and the transformation of meaning

There are parallels to this type of cultural recirculation and recontextualisation within the art world. Marcel Duchamp is famous for his early twentieth-century series of 'readymade' or 'already made' sculptures, which included a snow shovel, a urinal, a bicycle wheel and a comb, amongst other things. Duchamp's interventions using material culture led to new ways of conceiving art, of negating art, and of understanding objects. For example: how does Duchamp make these objects art? Are they already art? How does changing context matter, in defining the nature of these objects? The trick Duchamp plays seems squarely about manipulating the symbolic meaning of objects by altering context: considered outside of typical context an object can seem absurd, for it is without the appropriate cultural props to provide a meaningful framework of interpretation. As Michel Leiris (2005) points out in his commentary on

Duchamp's arts and crafts practice, the core issue at stake is the legitimacy of representation, and its relation to recognition, repetition and their place within an aesthetic language. Along similar lines, the contemporary artist Jeff Koons has presented everyday objects like a basketball, or a porcelain puppy, as art. In the case of the basketball the object is presented in a glass case, though apparently unadorned by the artist's hand. In the case of Koon's porcelain sculptures, the skill is in actually affording the mundane object a sense of being too real, emphasising and indeed inflating its ordinariness and kitsch qualities.

In contrast to these unconventional (perhaps postmodern) artworks, in a piece on the career of August Rodin's sculpture 'The Burghers of Calais', Richard Swedberg (2005) illustrates the trajectory of a strongly modern, utopian artwork. Originally commissioned in 1884 by the City of Calais and first shown in 1895, the sculpture celebrates a local heroic act. The story represented by the monument goes like this: in 1347 during the Hundred Years' War between England and France, King Edward III held reign over the town of Calais, starving its citizens. He eventually threatened the citizenry they all would be killed unless six citizens presented themselves to him. Rodin's sculpture depicts the beginning of the six volunteers' journey to Edward III. The journey ended well, as the Queen persuaded Edward to spare the men, while Edward went about reconstructing the town according to his supposedly peaceful vision. The interesting question Swedberg deals with is: why has Rodin's sculpture been used as a monument throughout the world, including many nations in Europe, North America, Asia and Australia? First, Swedberg argues that the monument gained popularity in its local context because it helped to forge an identity for the city of Calais, and also functioned as a representation of a collective ideal of fraternity and solidarity for the nation of France, a way to understand and define painful histories and glorious futures. More generally, the sculpture appeals to honourable sentiments within modern individuals, related to a form of civil courage that helps to forge collective solidarity. The sculpture reminds ordinary citizens that to cultivate and maintain a civil society involves ordinary people making a variety of sacrifices for the good of others. Such sacrifices may be of the most mundane sort, but they may also be linked to heroism of ordinary citizens: the sculpture tells a very modern tale of social solidarity, suggesting to citizenry that 'the heroes of our time are not like the lonely and extraordinary individuals that you find on the top of pedestals in sculptures from earlier centuries' (Swedberg, 2005: 64). This explains how the sculpture became a highly mobile – perhaps iconic – representation, appealing to the heart of the modern spirit through the twentieth century.

Jeffrey Alexander (forthcoming) makes a similar point to Swedberg in his discussion of iconic experience and viewing Alberto Giacometti's sculpture 'Standing Woman'. Alexander's goal for his reading is more ambitious than Swedberg's, in that it relates to a general theoretical approach in sociology which gives priority to cultural experience, and in this case, the aesthetic component of such experience. Moreover, Alexander goes to more trouble to inquire into the aesthetic terrain of the sculpture and the experience of a viewer who stands before it, such as features of surface and depth, closeness and distance, and how these play out in the interpretation of the object. Alexander argues that it is through these aesthetic techniques that Giacometti draws the viewer into the object, affording access to the object's iconic meaning. The surface appearance of Giacometti's object is its expressive feature that is in turn 'felt' by the viewer. The object becomes a universal symbol, a 'collective representation' that draws us 'to the heart of the world' (Alexander, forthcoming: 10–11). In developing his argument, Alexander proposes an interesting model for understanding how such feelings of material attachment work. He proposes that what makes an object iconic is the way it affords movement from surface to depth – a form of 'immersion'. Immersion involves a dual process: one called 'subjectification' where people are able to seemingly draw an object into themselves, transforming it from object to subject, and allowing it to take on a life whereby one no longer sees the object itself, but 'oneself, one's projections, one's convictions and beliefs' (Alexander, forthcoming: 11). Simultaneously, through a process called 'materialisation', a person is drawn into an object, effectively becoming it, or what it is seen to stand for. What exists is not an object, nor a person, but a oneness of material and human, united by an emotional connection. Such connections – with material objects – are the basis for the performance and learning of cultural norms and discourses, becoming the basis for collective life and the negotiation of individuality within the collective.

Conclusion: evaluating cultural approaches to objects

Before proceeding to evaluate what I have called the cultural perspective in material culture studies, consider the following recap of its general features:

- First, remember that the cultural approach is almost the complete opposite of the Marxist and critical approaches, though it shares some important similarities with the structural and semiotic traditions. While the Marxist and critical approaches altogether obliterate the possibility of people finding meaning in objects (objects were instead the embodiments of exploitive capitalist relations and any perceived meaning would be evidence of a false consciousness), the cultural approach emphasises the *meaningfulness of objects*. While the structural and semiotic approach insists on the relationality of object-signs within a culturally embedded system of linguistic communication, the cultural approach takes a slightly more open approach to meaning making. In a sense, the idea that there are cultural codes, narratives and symbols that function like a cultural language is taken for granted – it is not considered necessary to trace over the ground covered by Saussure, and Lévi-Strauss particularly, in order to develop what are almost scientific models of symbolic communication. This was the task of an earlier era. The cultural approach instead emphasises the meaning-making capacities of objects, but does not do so using a strict semiotic model of communication.

- A key part of the conceptual platform of the cultural approach is the Durkheimian idea that cultural life operates principally through the formation, mediation and maintenance of classifications and categories. It is through making classifications about people, objects and events, that people come to define the boundaries of their community and their own values and beliefs. Durkheim proposed that the binary operators of sacred and profane form the basis of such classifications.
- These classifications are not merely technico-rational, mentalistic accomplishments. People make classifications in their everyday life and are thus akin to scientists, but the categories that are formed acquire a moral force: they have an emotional weight that begs the application of sanctions, penalties and general boundary maintenance work to ensure the integrity of these categories.
- Mary Douglas and Baron Isherwood provided the first direct application of Durkheimian thinking to the field of contemporary consumption. Douglas (an anthropologist) and Isherwood (an economist) argued that we must begin to move away from thinking about the functional or economistic aspects of consumer objects, and move toward the idea that such objects were really good for thinking. That is, recalling Lévi-Strauss's idea of *bonnes á penser*, objects allow people to understand themselves and their lives, others and culture at large.
- This approach insists, after the work of Daniel Miller, that contemporary consumption behaviours are not intrinsically individualist, ersatz or depthless, but are culturally meaningful behaviours worthy of academic attention.

To what extent does the cultural approach offer a viable set of theoretical resources for understanding material culture? The following arguments can be made in favour of such theoretical models.

- The major strength of this body of work is that it doesn't assume objects in general to be peripheral to the constitution of society and culture. What's more, it provides a much needed corrective to the modern assumption that objects enslave and empty-out via rationalisation, exploitation and technological determinism, and the postmodern assumption that consumer objects represent little but evidence of an individualist, accumulative and ironic culture. The cultural approach maintains that in order to understand the contours of culture even the most banal or trivial objects need attention.

- In assuming even the most mundane types of consumption and the most ordinary of individual consumers are agents of cultural construction, this approach strongly emphasises the agentic aspects of consumption, and constructive, agentic potential of consumers. In doing so, it turns on its head a century or more of critical and Marxist inspired theory and commentary that suggests the opposite: that consumers are cultural dupes, and that they are exploited.
- The cultural approach allows the introduction of questions of emotion and desire to come into play in the way sociologists understand people's relations to objects. Questions of rationality and instrumentality are not insisted upon, leaving theorists to more imaginative and potentially productive ways of understanding people–object relations, and the way they are constitutive of cultural forms.

The following argument is commonly used criticisms of the cultural approach.

- There is one major critique of the cultural approach. It is often maintained that the cultural approach lacks sufficient critical power, in the Marxist sense. That is, it pays too much attention to the operations of culture, and too little to questions of social–economic structure and inequality. For example, a more critical approach would require questions asked about who makes consumer objects, what type of pay and employment conditions they work under, and what are the global flows of such consumer objects?

SUGGESTED FURTHER READING

Model case studies of how to combine structuralist analysis with a Durkheimian sensitivity for generative cultural codes is found in Jeffrey Alexander's (2003) piece on the computer, and Philip Smith's (2003) evocative, visceral and fascinating paper on the guillotine. Along similar lines, Richard Swedberg's (2005) research on the Rodin sculpture from the journal *Theory, Culture and Society* is also a very interesting case study of how an object comes to represent universal cultural beliefs and myths across time and space. For fascinating research on the iconography and meaning of the guitar within various interest communities, see Bennett and Dawe's collection, *Guitar Cultures* (2001). Especially, consult the introduction and the chapter by Ryan and Peterson on the iconography of the guitar and types of guitar owners/players. Though I have briefly summarised the key ideas of Daniel Miller's book *A Theory of Shopping* (1998a) in this chapter, I'd recommend you have a further look at this to get a strong anthropological account of the meanings of contemporary shopping behaviours, which after all are expeditions dedicated to collecting consumable objects. For a work that links consumer brands to cultural mythologies, see Douglas B. Holt's *How Brands Become Icons* (2004).

PART III

OBJECTS IN ACTION

SIX

Objects and Distinction. The Aesthetic Field and Expressive Materiality

---

SUMMARY OF CHAPTER CONTENTS

This chapter looks at how objects come to acquire and represent status, aesthetic value and personal taste. It has four main sections which:

- give an historical introduction to how objects are linked to social status
- review the work of Immanuel Kant on how people judge beauty in objects
- summarise the work of Bourdieu on taste and the social implications of aesthetic judgement
- review the work of key modern theorists of fashion – Simmel, Veblen and Blumer – and their relevance to questions of social class, individualism, desire and collective belonging.

Introduction: Status and the taste for 'the beautiful thing' in consumer societies

Historical accounts of consumption practice (McCracken, 1988; McKendrick et al., 1992 [1982]; Mukerji, 1983; Williams, 1982) illustrate that consuming things is now – and has been for at least quite some time – as much a sphere for establishing social difference and position, and constructing self-identity, than it is a practice of sustenance. It is circumspect to remember that the use of novel objects for the explicit purpose of demonstrating cultivated distinction or personal style is not the only reason for, or mode of, consumption. Yet, contemporary consumer society is based upon the *materialisation of distinction*: the coding of cultural and status difference in objects themselves.

In an early paper Erving Goffman (1951) analyses the role of objects in managing status. For Goffman, co-operative, effective social activity was dependent on the harmonious differentiation and integration of different social statuses. Society requires this intersubjective communication of status, and status symbols are used by people to divide the world into categories of people. According to Goffman there are two principle roles for status symbols. First, status symbols have *categorical functions* in that they serve to distinguish and 'socially place' the person who uses the symbol. For example, in a consumer society we may read the brand or style of a watch as a symbol of status, or, we may also read particular occupational symbols which signal credentials like a lab coat, a stethoscope or a framed degree certificate. As well, Goffman says status symbols can serve *expressive functions*, relating to a person's own style, taste or cultural values, as either real or aspired to. In Goffman's vision, social life is underpinned by this type of symbolic circulation of objects and people in order to affirm, identify or express one's social status. This way, in advanced consumer society, finely tuned knowledges of the subtle differences in cultural meaning of objects that consumers interact with can become the means for social expression, social identity cultivation and social differentiation.

How is it that objects have come to embody desires and signify status, acting as proxies for a person's identity, dreams and social position? Drawing upon historical research, Grant McCracken (1988) has provided a careful analysis of three important historical eras to illustrate some of the ways and reasons consumer objects were increasingly desired as signs of status over the past few centuries.

(1) *Elizabethan England in the sixteenth century*. In the last quarter of the sixteenth century Elizabeth I used expenditure for the purpose of displaying, and establishing, the wealth and status of the monarch. In this era, the noblemen of England decorated their residences extravagantly, took new residences in London, and engaged in feverish rounds of hospitality to establish their own status, pre-eminence and social standing in order to gain the respect and attention of Queen Elizabeth. As McCracken puts it, describing the visit of the English nobleman to the court and London:

> When each nobleman was drawn to court to bid for the Queen's attention, he was drawn away from the locality in which he was the undisputed apex of a steeply hierarchical society ... this nobleman was suddenly one of a number of individuals with a claim to pre-eminence. His reaction to this new crowd of status-seekers was one of anxiety-stricken concern for his honour, his social standing, and his relationship to the monarch. It was almost inevitable that he should have been drawn into a riot of consumption. (1988: 12)

Rounds of status competition institutionalised these inflationary tournaments of consumption, and objects increasingly represented the monarch's legitimacy and status, aspirations of the kingdom, and the aura of its leaders. Increasingly complex regimes of value developed where differences in social status were signified by differences in the stylistic and aesthetic properties of objects. The preferences of the upper-classes dictated what was deemed fashionable, and their choices 'trickled-down' to everyone else.

(2) Consumption in eighteenth-century England. The world of consumer goods expanded dramatically during this period, in line with new production methods and new construction materials. Along with this, the opportunities for demonstrating social distinction enhanced the process – strongly stratified society, the opportunity to emulate the upper classes through cheaper goods, and increasing general wealth. Consumer objects became tokens of one's status. Consumption patterns also shifted – further from need and closer to fashion and wants, fashion cycles developed and sped up, networks of shops expanded, and shopping became as much a mode of sociality as an expedition for provisions. One of the well-known figures during this period was Josiah Wedgwood, whose ceramics are still widely produced, consumed and valued today. Wedgwood carefully marketed his goods to the upper classes, hoping those lower down would eventually follow. McCracken argues that Wedgwood was the first to fully understand and harness this trickle-down effect: the desire of those lower in the social hierarchy to emulate those above through the possession and display of *status tokens*. This type of emulatory dynamic was associated with the institutionalisation of fashion cycles, whereby aesthetic and stylistic features of objects were increasingly central to the circulation of objects. As McCracken (1988: 19) comments: 'That an object had not exhausted its usefulness was no longer sufficient grounds for its preservation. Whether it could satisfy the more important condition of fashionableness was now the deciding factor'. This shift precipitated broader social and cultural changes: goods were increasingly semiotically rich, selfhood was linked to possession and display of objects, city spaces transformed to cater for new interests in browsing, flaneurie, and public display of objects, people increasingly purchased for themselves not just their families, and increasingly consumers desired to be instructed about the 'right' ways, and things, to consume.

(3) Consumption in the nineteenth century. In this period there was not so much a new consumer boom – this had already happened – but a deepening and maturing of the consumer ethic established in the eighteenth century. The production of new consumer items increasingly became the motor of economic growth. Also, new modes for disseminating consumer objects developed, especially marketing in order to add 'desire value' to goods. Further, the department store was originated, which was associated not only with more elaborate and ornate modes of presenting consumer objects, but new modes of urban sociality which were increasingly democratic. Objects began to be encoded with more nuanced meanings, other than simply 'upper class emulation'. For example, department stores of the era developed interiors that signified different ethnic,

lifestyle and mythical themes. Objects and their modes of display were increasingly aestheticised. The consumer revolution of the period could not have found better housing, according to McCracken:

> This new institution helped change the nature of aesthetics by which goods were marketed, introducing powerfully persuasive techniques in film and décor that are still being refined. The department store also changed the very nature of the place in which people consumed, what they consumed, the information they needed to consume, and the styles of life to which this new consumption was devoted. (1988: 29)

This chapter considers how theorists have sought to explain the increasingly status-loaded nature of objects through the concepts of taste and fashion. The trends, that historical research has shown to exist in previous centuries, have deepened over the twentieth century. The rationale for a sociological study of taste becomes clear in this context: making choices is a fundamental skill, perhaps a 'duty' (Bauman, 1988), required for people who live in a consumer society. Taste is a core component of being a person in a consumer society. It is a basic capacity in consumer societies because 'taste is the basis of all that one has – people and things – and all that one is for others' (Bourdieu, 1984: 56). The rationale for a conventional sociological study of taste is that once these consumption choices are subjected to scrutiny, it is found that people do not possess the same objects or things – substantial variation does exist in regard to the choices people make and the visual-spatial ensemble they create on the basis of such choices (after Baudrillard, 1981: 34). Furthermore, the analysis of this difference will yield information that illuminates elemental information about contemporary society and the nature of people's lives within it. With this in mind, the broad aim of the current chapter is to review, analyse and assess theoretical perspectives on taste and aesthetics as they impact on our appreciation and use of objects. The basic question these theories address is: *what are the social processes by which people come to give value to objects, ascribe them status affirming capacity, and come to count them as important in defining the nature of selfhood and social identity?*

Four theoretical variations which address these questions are discussed and analysed in this chapter. The theoretical basis of each can be captured by keywords, which serve as a summary point for each position. The four models examined are characterised as: (i) the pure taste model, (ii) the class taste model, (iii) the emulation model, and (iv) the collective model.

Kant's philosophical aesthetics and sensing beauty in objects (the pure taste model)

The questions of what object is beautiful or possesses good taste, how to judge such beauty and taste in objects, and what criteria is to apply in its judgement, are central concerns of philosophical aesthetics. The heyday of such theories of taste was the eighteenth century – Kant, Voltaire, Hume, Cooper and Burke each wrote about the nature of taste, the experience of the sublime and beautiful, the weighing of value in judgements, and the experience of pleasure or displeasure in relation to things (Schaper, 1983). The philosophy of aesthetic choice, and its sub-concepts – taste, beauty, pleasure and the sublime – approach the question of taste in a different way to sociology. It is not the point of this chapter to distinguish itself through a unique philosophical reading of taste, but given much of the social writing on taste and aesthetics explicitly works from Kant's model – mostly as a point of departure – it is worthwhile considering the basic principles of his approach. Philosophical aesthetics tends to focus on how it is possible to judge something as beautiful or of good taste, the logical rules of such processes, and the variety of distinguishing types of pleasure and taste. In addressing such questions, philosophical inquiry is often characterised – after Kant – as the study of *pure taste*.

By contrast, the enduring tradition in the sociology of taste, to use Bourdieu's pointed expression at Kantian versions of aesthetics, is directed 'towards a vulgar critique of pure critiques' (1984: 485). What Bourdieu makes clear, in the broad tradition of diverse authors such as Veblen (1899[1934]), Lloyd Warner (Warner and Lunt, 1963; Warner et al., 1963,) and Goffman (1951), is that pure taste and the aesthetic theoretical system it is built upon, is in fact a bourgeois aesthetic which has at its base the refusal of facile cultural goods: things which are judged impure, shallow, cheap, frivolous or superficial (Bourdieu, 1984: 486). Given Bourdieu's vigorous engagement with the philosophical variety of aesthetics – the pointed subtitle of *Distinction* indicates his desire to generate a healthy sociological distance from Kant and the idea of a 'pure' aesthetic – it is worthwhile spending some time elaborating the philosophical account of aesthetics outlined in Kant.

In Kant's terms, judgements of taste are not based on logical, cognitive principles. That is, a person cannot objectively assess the beauty of an object through analytic, mental means. In order to judge what is beautiful, a purely 'esthetic' judgement must be made. The central component of this judgement is the feeling of pleasure or displeasure provoked in the viewer of an object. Moreover, this feeling of pleasure or displeasure must be 'wholly disinterested' (1952: 12), that is, a person must assess the thing in 'mere contemplation' (1952: 5), rather than be effected by a sense of the object's monetary value, or the value of its brand. Kant's notion of the roles of interest, and especially *disinterest*, in such judgements is a key sticking point for Bourdieu (1984: 41), who identifies a popular aesthetic or working-class aesthetic as contravening Kant's standard of taste because it is squarely based on the criteria of *interest* – gratification of pleasure through the senses, utility or moral position:

> Nothing is more alien to popular consciousness than the idea of an aesthetic pleasure that, to put it in Kantian terms, is independent of the charming of the senses. (Bourdieu, 1984: 42)

Thus in the Kantian aesthetic universe, where contemplation is emptied of notions of use, sensuous pleasures or pecuniary influences that might taint perception of beauty, people are freed to contemplate objects and judge their pure beauty based on the evocation of stirred feelings. Kant proceeds in his Second Moment of the Analytic of the Beautiful to contend that given the satisfaction of the criteria of disinterestedness, a person can reasonably assume that their assessment of something as beautiful (as opposed to merely pleasurable in sensual form) has a universal validity. It is here that Kant presents the tacit justification for a refined form of judgement that he labels 'reflective taste':

> Many a thing may be attractive and pleasurable to him; no one cares about that; but if he declares something to be beautiful, he expects the very same pleasure of others; he judges not solely for himself, but for everyone, and then speaks of beauty as if it were a property of things. Hence he says, the *thing* is beautiful, and he does not count on others agreeing with his judgement of pleasure because they did so occasionally in the past; rather he *demands* this agreement from them. He censures them if they judge differently and denies them taste, which he demands they should have. (Kant, 1952: 14–5)

The idea of universal validity has application to Kant's notion of a *sensus communis* of taste, presented in the Fourth Moment. From a sociological point of view, this suggestion of a common sense of taste is interesting, and seems related to later accounts of fashion and taste in the work of Blumer (1969), and also, though to a lesser degree, in Lyotard (1988). Both of these contributions are discussed in later parts of this chapter. Gronow (1997: 88) also draws out these theoretical threads clearly. What Kant argues is that tastes only seem to make sense, or acquire validity, in reference to others. This is so because given satisfaction of the criterion of disinterestedness, people should not fail to judge beauty in the same way – there is a harmony in social judgements which assumes an idea of 'common sense':

> In any judgement in which we declare something to be beautiful we allow no one to be of a different opinion. Yet we base our judgement not on concepts, but solely on our feeling. Hence, the feeling which we place at the foundation of the judgement of taste is not a private feeling, but a common feeling. Now this common sense, if it is to serve as this foundation, cannot be grounded on experience, for it is meant to justify judgements that contain an 'ought'. The common sense does not imply that everyone *will* agree with our judgements; it implies that everyone *ought*. I put forward my judgement of taste as an example of the judgement passed by the common sense and this is why I ascribe *exemplary* validity to my judgement. (Kant, 1952: 49)

Kant's notion of *sensus communis* acknowledges a collective basis for establishing standards of aesthetic judgement. It prefigures classical sociological work on the matter of taste communities, and has important implications for sociological research into the everyday schemes and narratives of taste. Yet, it is difficult to imagine how Kant's analysis of the judgement of beauty in objects works in a consumer society. Is it possible for people to make judgements of beauty independent of issues like marketing, brand, perceived status and cost? Such judgements seem reserved for special contexts where exchange value and symbolic value are effectively annulled, for example in institutional art galleries where questions of possession are irrelevant. The other main problem with Kant's proposal relates to the social implications, and possibility, of making disinterested judgements. In a society where important social divisions are based in consumption practices, is this possible? Given this question, it is pertinent to examine the high modern sociological critique of Kant's ideas in the work of Pierre Bourdieu.

Objects and class contexts. Bourdieu and the sociological psychoanalysis of objects (the class taste model)

Currently, any sociological discussion of taste must start by considering the foundational work of Pierre Bourdieu, directly through his principal work in the field, *Distinction*, and also via the theoretical foundation for sociological practice he has developed in other important works, for example, *Outline of a Theory of Practice*. Bourdieu's (1984) study of tastes and cultural consumption is based on surveys and interviews in 1960s' France, and one of its most important successes was to advance a strongly cultural and social perspective into the study of taste. In it Bourdieu argued that 'taste' was taken for granted as the natural domain of aesthetes who supposedly possessed a cultivated eye for assessing beauty. In Bourdieu's words, the fundamental dispositions that govern our choices can only be uncovered when '"culture", in the restricted, normative sense of ordinary usage, is reinserted into "culture", in the broad, anthropological sense and the elaborated taste for the most refined objects is brought back into relation with the elementary taste for the flavours of food' (Bourdieu, 1984: 99). The work of philosopher Immanuel Kant, to which Bourdieu's position is naturally contrasted has promoted a long-standing conception of taste that is thoroughly *anti*-social in the way it imagines taste to be a disinterested, pure appreciation of beauty; as though making aesthetic judgements were a gift of nature. However for Bourdieu, social science has empirically demonstrated this to be false and has exposed the aesthete's eye to be 'a product of history reproduced by education' (1984: 3).

Key principles in Bourdieu's account of aesthetic taste

The first point to note about Bourdieu's understanding of taste is that it is manifested in everything people do and possess: taste is 'the basis of all that one has – people and things – and all that one is for others' (1984: 56). That is, taste is not something reserved just for discussion of 'legitimate' painting, music or literature that is produced and consumed principally by what might be called the 'dominant' aesthetic classes. Rather, taste decisions are exercised in all social and personal domains across all social classes. This includes practical arts like fashion, hairstyles, home decoration and food preparation, along with leisure activities like reading, sport and cinema. As well as this, the bottom line of taste practice for Bourdieu is manifested in the way people present their bodies: 'the body is the most indisputable materialization of class taste' (1984: 190). The body is a fundamental site for the expression of taste through clothing and hair styles, objects of adornment, speech and manner. Additionally, the dimensions and shapes of the body as presented to others reveal the 'embodied' nature of taste, for example, dimensions like body volume and weight, shape and posture are clues to the social conditions which manifest them and the attitudes people hold toward their own body. In summary thus far then, for Bourdieu, taste is a universal practice because it applies for all classes of people across social groups, and it is also an inevitable practice because participation in the social world requires expressions and commitments of taste.

Two important principles follow as a result of Bourdieu's assertion that taste plays a role in determining all our interactions in the social and material world. The first is that the practice of taste takes on an appearance of being a 'natural' judgement. Judgements of taste are so routinely pervasive in everyday life, and are determined to such an extent by people's conditions of existence, that separating social relations from aesthetic judgements becomes difficult. In this way, taste judgements in Bourdieu's model come to serve as an aesthetic playing out of social relations. Since tastes are so thoroughly incorporated in to people's ways of being, acting and seeing in consumer society, they take on a 'natural' appearance and feel. It is this façade of naturalness that has fostered the ideology that some classes of people naturally possess good taste and others bad. Because inquiries into taste must attempt to uncover the basis of these highly routinised aesthetic judgements, Bourdieu comments in the opening to his first chapter of *Distinction* that 'sociology is rarely more akin to social psychoanalysis than when it confronts an object like taste' (1984: 11).

The second consequence of the chronic nature of taste judgements in consumer society is that there is an 'economy' of preference decisions available to be understood by the researcher. The economy of cultural goods is manifested in two ways for the researcher. First, it is identifiable in the particular combinations of cultural objects that classes of people consume. For example, Bourdieu's analysis of dominant tastes presented in a two dimensional plane diagram (1984: 262) show the particular distributions of preferences for musical works, composers, domestic interiors and cooking, plotted along with the degree of cultural and economic capital. Likewise, films seen in order of preference by Parisians are mapped to reveal the distribution of bundles of cinematic preferences held by secondary teachers, professions and industrial and commercial employers

(1984: 271). The outcome of this cultural preference mapping is the plotting of a cultural consumption economy, which for Bourdieu is a step along the way to understanding the space of lifestyles. The economy of preferred cultural goods, a product of people's tastes, is also manifested in the way people relate to culture. In Bourdieu's account, taste is not only something identifiable in *what* we consume, but also in the *way* we consume things. For example, he comments about the consumption strategies of the petit bourgeoisie that:

> The petit bourgeois do not know how to play the game of culture as a game. They take culture too seriously to go in for bluff or imposture or even for the distance and casualness which show true familiarity; too seriously to escape permanent fear or ignorance or blunders, or to side-step tests by responding with the indifference of those who are not competing or the serene detachment of those who feel entitled to confess or even flaunt their lacunae. Identifying culture with knowledge, they think that the cultivated man is one who possesses an immense fund of knowledge and refuse to believe him when he professes, in one of those impious jests allowed to a Cardinal, who can take liberties with the faith forbidden to the parish priest, that, brought down to its simplest and most sublime expression, it amounts to a *relation* to culture. (1984: 330–1)

In Bourdieu's analysis, other social classes relate to cultural objects in socially unique ways. The bourgeois class's mode of consumption attempts to emphasise authenticity and naturalness in their relation to culture, as though it was made especially for them. While bourgeois consumption may sometimes be permitted to be eccentric, it is held together by a confidence that goes with a flair for cultivating culture as nature. The bourgeois classes typically cultivate an art to living so that, for example, meal preparation becomes as much an artistic endeavour as a necessity. The point of such everyday activities that are based in modes of 'artistic consumption' is that they demand 'pure, pointless expenditure' provided by the 'rarest and most precious thing of all ... namely, time' (1984: 281). Alternately, the working class aesthetic is dominated by a rejection of aestheticisation and the cultivation of an art of living that is founded in modesty, pragmatism and simplicity generated by 'the taste for necessity':

> one sees examples in the behaviour of small craftsmen or businessmen who, as they themselves say, 'don't know how to spend the money they've earned', or of junior clerical workers, still attached to their peasant or working-class roots, who get as much satisfaction from calculating how much they have 'saved' by doing without a commodity or service (or 'doing it themselves') as they would have got from the thing itself, but who, equally, cannot ever purchase it without a painful sense of wasting money. Having a million does not in itself make one able to live like a millionaire. (Bourdieu, 1984: 374)

The final component of Bourdieu's account of taste that must be considered (briefly in this instance) is his notion of habitus, the mechanism by which tastes are cultivated and exercised. The habitus is the means by which people come to develop systems of likes and dislikes, and also the set of principles and procedures which people use in their relations with objects and people. In short, it is a set of dispositions, for use in practice, that orientates individuals in their relations with people and objects in the social world. The habitus is formed in individuals through historically and socially situated conditions of its production, it is the 'active present of past experiences' (Bourdieu, 1990: 54). While the habitus is a product of a determinate class of conditions, Bourdieu stresses that it retains some spontaneity and that while a person's habitus will typically direct them toward particular choices, it does not amount to obedience to rules. Bourdieu theorises the habitus as both *structured and structuring*. That is, it generates the principles by which people are able to classify and organise encounters in the social and material world, and it is also structured or generated by them in so far as these encounters are the product of regular associations and shared conditions of existence.

Bourdieu's account of tastes is the most ambitious and thorough yet to be published. The strengths of his approach in *Distinction* are multifaceted. Fundamentally, its forte rests on the range of quantitative data available to Bourdieu through his survey material and the techniques he employs in analysing the data. While Frow's (1987) deconstruction of Bourdieu's complicity in establishing a regime of cultural tastes and value is compelling in demonstrating the arbitrariness of his cultural categories, equally so Bourdieu's analysis of social and cultural correspondences along dimensions of cultural and economic capital is the best empirical treatment of the social patterns of taste that is available. But perhaps the most important reason for the work's substantial contribution to the study of taste is its application of an impressive theoretical basis that was developed by Bourdieu through a number of substantial prior works. Bourdieu's advance from a strong strand of structuralism (1963[1979]) to a more nuanced synthesis of objective and subjective principles (1977) – which came to rest on his theories about the role of different forms of capital, the habitus and dimensions of social space – is impressively operationalised in *Distinction*, despite any legitimate criticism which may be made of his approach.

To a less successful extent though, *Distinction* employs a range of interview data and case studies that are found through the text that seek, though in my opinion ultimately fail, to supplement the quantitative findings. The question of the stylistic efficacy of such an approach to his qualitative data has been noted, for example by Jenkins, who characterises *Distinction* as 'an intriguing pastiche of different blocks of text, photographs and diagrams' (Jenkins, 1992: 138). This is suggestive of a wider issue to do with how Bourdieu treats his qualitative data. Is it meant to stand alongside the quantitative material in terms of its value for the work, or is it of secondary importance? The principal way the concept of taste is operationalised in *Distinction* is through survey material and quantitative analysis – this is the most efficient way for Bourdieu to demonstrate his central thesis that what we think of as culture in a natural form, is in fact class culture. But such a methodological choice is not without its prejudices – it is not the 'natural' way to study tastes. A qualitative, open-ended approach to the problem would develop a unique theoretical treatment of taste that gives at least equal value to the meaning of actors who can be said to 'practise' taste through their relations with objects.

There are two principal critiques of Bourdieu's approach that are counterpoints to a more cultural, meaning-oriented account of people–object relations. The first is Bourdieu's methodological insistence that tastes be studied 'objectively'. The prevailing means Bourdieu uses to operationalise tastes in *Distinction* is through the idea of 'objectified' tastes. That is, survey measures are designed as indicators of the concept of taste, in order to map 'manifest preferences' for particular objects and things. These indicators are grounded in the principal domains of taste practice: music, art, literature, food, leisure and clothing. What this approach succeeds in doing is to map these domains of taste differentiation along lines of cultural and economic capital, and essentially, the point comes down to the matter of class. The value of such an approach should not be wholly discounted, but a different emphasis appreciated. Such a methodology affords the description of social patterns of the *indicators* chosen to represent 'tastes' – that is, of accounting for the things people possess and relate to – and in Bourdieu's case, provides evidence for his ideas about social reproduction and cultural domination. However, at worst, tastes become reified as cultural artefacts; and a creative, active process is reduced to 'knowing' or 'not knowing', 'having' or 'not having' particular cultural objects and knowledges. Such a methodological choice does not value interrogation of the subjective, hermeneutic aspects of tastes, ignores process, and is obliged to look over the tacit forms of knowledge involved in accomplishing and possessing 'tastes'. In addition, and perhaps as a corollary of the inability of survey methodology to come to grips with taste as a cultural practice, such an approach misses nearly altogether the *collective processes* associated with the everyday practice of taste. In summary then, Bourdieu's methodology emphasises tastes as a form of capital available for class differentiation. Such a focus supports his larger project of uncovering the social reproductive role involved in the assertion of a dominant taste, but in taking such a position it excludes the possibility of accounting for forces of integration through the social circulation of collective sentiments.

Being in fashion: social honour and the display of booty (the emulation model)

The legacy of Bourdieu's account is that one's tastes are principally seen as a product of social class: choices that are contingent on upbringing, education and social learning, rather than pure disinterested judgements.

This is the shattering power of *Distinction* – the sociological dissection of taken-for-granted claims of aesthetic infallibility. But to some degree, Bourdieu's *Distinction* has become too influential in the field of taste. *Distinction* remains a superior piece of critical sociological analysis of culture, but its dominance in the field has pushed earlier and other contributions to the margins. These have been either under-valued or forgotten, but their central sociological questions have never been dealt with in a satisfactory way.

The following section of this chapter moves away from the Kant–Bourdieu debate, and conceptualises some of the classical sociological writing on matters of taste, fashion and style. The critical power of Bourdieu's approach is missing from such earlier accounts, however, what is gained in these works are insights into the social dynamics of taste processes. Two key strands in classical studies of taste and fashion are identified. The first, best represented by Simmel and Veblen, has an interest in the public negotiation of taste and the social role of fashion. It is distinguished however, by the prominence of an elite-mass model of taste which relies heavily on notions of emulation, class distinction, imitation and conspicuousness. The second skein in this literature, marked by Blumer's (1969) article on collective tastes, emphasises the communal negotiation of style and taste, apart from the need for distinction and emulation. Admittedly, the model presented by Blumer is rather vague on specific mechanisms relating to the negotiation of such sentiments. However, he provides an updated, symbolic foundation for consideration of the collective dimension of taste. We turn first to consider the elite-mass *emulation* account of taste.

Like much of his work, Simmel's analysis of fashion and style is essentially an attempt to understand processes that propelled modernity, and in turn, their impact on the psycho-social development of the modern person. Fashion and style therefore, came to represent much more than merely clothes, home decoration or jewellery; they were fundamental processes of modern social life. Processes of conflict, compromise, elevation and adaption, all serve the basic Simmelian dialectic: generality/uniformity versus individuality/differentiation. Though fashion and taste represent unique conceptual components of a contemporary analysis of choice, for Simmel (like Kant and later Blumer), fashion and taste are central elements in one social-aesthetic process. Fashion was a kind of public playing out of taste mechanisms – it was a domain where levels of public taste were constantly established, then superseded (1997a: 194). Imitation was a fundamental component of this process, because it was the central practice or technique for individuals to orient themselves to the social. Because it involved reflection and mindless copying, Simmel characterised this central component of fashion as at once 'a child of thought and thoughtlessness' (1997a: 188). For the modern person, imitation wasn't only a negative thing, for it did free the individual from the responsibility of maintaining self and the work of generating an authentic individual style. However, in the process of copying, the modern imitator forfeited creativity and genuine self-purpose. The modern fashion imitator was merely a 'vessel of social contexts' (Simmel, 1997a: 188).

Given imitation was such a fundamental process in fashion, and hence a characteristic force of modernity as well, there must be a social group whose fashions served as models available to be imitated. It is because of this important demarcation between those who set the fashion agenda and those who followed, that Simmel's analysis of fashion is largely a class-based model of emulation, where the lower classes constantly sought to imitate upper class fashions. In fact, Fred Davis (1992: 111) suggests that Simmel's idea of fashion is a rather more subtle version of the classical trickle-down model. What Simmel goes on to argue is that fashion, in its most pure form (that is, its latest version), is the domain of the upper classes. Technically, the lower class can possess few genuine fashions of their own, and thus perpetually occupy the role of imitator most easily. Because fashion is the relentless striving for a social balance between differentiation and integration, fashions constantly change as the lower classes begin to effectively imitate the fashions of the upper classes. The ruthless striving for difference is frantic, though it is a one-way process only – always the lower classes look to the upper classes for the direction of fashion. Fashion is thus a supremely modern tool for differentiation that has a unique power to set in place a class-based dialectic of destruction and creative vitality that was ultimately based upon zero-sum principles.

> The very character of fashion demands that it should be exercised at one time only by a portion of the given group, the great majority being merely on the road to adopting it. As soon as an example has been universally adopted, that is, as soon as anything that was originally done by only a few has really come to be practiced by all – as is the case in certain portions of our apparel and in various forms of social conduct – we no longer speak of fashion. As fashion spreads, it gradually goes to its doom. (Simmel, 1957 [1904]: 547)

In his celebrated essay on fashion, Simmel suggests that there are a number of groups who more conspicuously engage in the search for fashionability. First are women, who are denied opportunities to express individuality in other civil and social spheres, and have to rely on fashion as a means of asserting a meaningful social personality. In addition, Simmel suggests that young people in particular are prone to display singular fashion behaviours (1997a: 201). But most of all, the middle classes are the real force behind the fashion dynamic. The lower 'masses' 'are difficult to set in motion and slow to develop' (1997a: 202), and on other hand, the highest social stratum are conservative, archaic and fear change (1997a: 202). The vitality rests with the middle classes, who have a psychological drive to scale social strata, and discretionary resources to achieve such an end.

The comparison of Simmel to contemporary work in postmodern consumer culture becomes clearer here, and is a feature worth commenting upon. Many of the ideas developed by Simmel have been emphasised as central components of the postmodern zeitgeist – the frantic hunt for novelty (1957[1904]: 545), the relentless striving for difference (1957[1904]: 546), the elaboration of fashion in multiple domains of social life (1957[1904]: 548), the playful nature of fashion (1997a: 194), and the intensified subjectivism and individuality of the times that Simmel emphasised in his work on style (1997b: 216). Such a list would clearly fit quite comfortably in contemporary characterisations of consumer culture found in the work of Featherstone (1987), Jameson (1991[1984]), or Lash and Urry (1994); though of course the central question in such a comparison would remain one of velocity and intensity, which is a more difficult proposition to empiricise.

Simmel provides a nuanced, important account of the sociological processes of fashion. His far-reaching project remained an examination of modern tensions of individuality and integration, and Simmel's analysis of fashion provides a classical psycho-social version of this 'adaption' problem. Simmel's model usefully emphasises the way that all excursions into fashion (including an anti-fashion stance) are techniques or resources for individuals to orient themselves to social forces. In this way, his model is classically *social*. The primary mechanism in Simmel's model of fashion is emulation. The fiscal power and psychological desire to engage with fashion is seen to lie with the middle classes. Those in the lower strata (presumably including the middle classes) seek status through imitation, or copying, of the upper classes, who are in a position to control the direction of fashion. This stance is problematic in a couple of ways. First, its assumption is that a motive for action is exclusion (by the upper strata) and emulation (by the middle and lower stratas). While Simmel shares some common ground with Bourdieu here, there have been serious recent challenges to such a position (for example, Halle, 1993 and Lamont, 1992), that assert mechanisms of aesthetics, judgement and taste are more complex than the distinction-emulation model suggests. Second, and this draws on central aspects of Blumer's (1969) critique, Simmel's analysis of fashion is in an important way staunchly modern – his construction of dichotomous social strata (principally upper, and then those in the lower strata), his assumption that lower classes have no genuine tastes or fashions (in contrast to Bourdieu and ideas about working-class tastes), and his lack of attention to the way particular taste (sub-)cultures could effect the implicit assumption of a direct hierarchy of desirable fashions and cultural values, mean that his model requires substantial reworking to fit contemporary trends, however useful his sociological insights may be.

In Thorstein Veblen's *The Theory of the Leisure Class* (1899[1934]) there is a more vulgar, witty and venomous expression of the elite-mass emulation model. While Simmel impresses with craftsmanship, subtlety and sociological force in the proposition of a class-based model of emulation, Veblen 'grinds away' (Davis, 1992: 111) relentlessly on the central idea of pecuniary honour. Both Veblen and Simmel however, tend to share a vision of public taste that is fundamentally charged by distinctions of class and the psychological attraction of aesthetic difference that only money can cultivate. The interesting theoretical component of Veblen's work arrives early in the form of an historical periodisation that provides the platform for an elaboration of the pecuniary zeitgeist of the times: in conjunction with the expanding trend of ownership in the contemporary phase of modern capitalism which drives people in a struggle for possession of various goods, a leisure class emerges whose primary skill is the accumulation and display of 'booty' which bestows a surplus of social reputability via pecuniary means.

In Veblen's model perpetual referencing or comparison to others is a crucial factor. People were chronically restless in their invidious comparison – once they reached the average standard of pecuniary reputability, ever higher targets were set. The person of status thus accrues social honour through being a connoisseur of tasteful objects. This person also had the responsibility of honing his own manner and carriage to reflect 'an air of leisurely opulence and mastery' (1899[1934]: 49). In Veblen's view, systems of pure aesthetic value became skewed in such a social arrangement. Cost was commonly substituted as a measure of aesthetic worth:

> ... any valuable object in order to appeal to our sense of beauty must conform to the requirements of beauty and expensiveness both. But this is not all. Beyond this the canon of expensiveness also effects our tastes in such a way as to inextricably blend the marks of expensiveness, in our appreciation, with the beautiful features of the object, and to subsume the resultant effect under the head of an appreciation of beauty simply. The marks of expensiveness come to be accepted as beautiful features of the expensive articles. (Veblen, 1899[1934]: 130)

This leads Veblen to a caustic dissection of pecuniary tastes in a variety of popular domains – flowers, lawns and pastures, animals and clothing are his main targets. Shots at fashion are rife:

> Among these everyday facts is the well-known liking which all men have for the styles that are in vogue at any given time. A new style comes into vogue and remains in favour for a season, and, at least so long as it is a novelty, people very generally find the new style attractive. The prevailing fashion is felt to be beautiful...
>
> It is extremely doubtful if any one could be induced to wear such a contrivance as the high hat of civilised society, except for some urgent reason based on other than aesthetic grounds. (Veblen, 1899[1934]: 177, 132)

The key idea in Veblen's account of consumption, fashion and taste is that people are strongly motivated to display pecuniary honour, and ultimately to forge a social difference to other classes. A principal point underlying his discussion is that the aesthetic tenets of simplicity and functionality are sacrificed for the sake of pecuniary canons of taste, and cycles of fashion were merely periodic phases where ugliness was heaped upon ugliness (Veblen, 1899[1934]: 177). No claims to an enduring or 'classical' pure aesthetic mattered as garnishing pecuniary honour and managing cultural distance through fashion was an inescapable motivation of the contemporary mode of capitalism.

The collective sentiment in aesthetic tastes: fashion objects and social solidarity (the collective model)

A strong interest in the sociological nature of fashion processes is a hallmark of Simmel's analysis. In fact, Simmel's analysis of fashion and style are key pieces in his attempt to understand the process of sociation and the central forces of social adaption and integration. More than any others, Simmel's writing on fashion emphasises this process most expertly. But there is a problematic element in Simmel's elaboration of the fashion process, and it centres on the way he conceives the social mechanisms and dynamics, which drive the direction of fashion and taste. Centrally, emulation and imitation were seen to direct a dual class system of fashion, where the lower classes copied the upper classes. Simmel thus focuses too heavily on the aspirational and emulationary elements of taste dynamic, at the expense of a more collective model where a diverse range of social and cultural factors could be seen to direct public tastes.

In part, Simmel's emphasis on incessant cycles of emulation and imitation as the *deus ex machina* of tastes is a product of his times: class systems were more starkly defined and more obvious than today, and there were relatively fewer opportunities for consumption, which meant that tastes were not as freely available to be 'purchased' as they are in the contemporary era. Nevertheless, while Simmel's writing on fashion mechanisms do not share the sometimes crudely simplistic characterisations of Veblen, they do concur in the way emulation and class difference generate fundamental modes of taste.

By way of contrast, Blumer's (1969) theory of fashion offers a more nuanced treatment of fashion and taste mechanisms than earlier theorists. While class differentiation was seen to drive fashion in conventional accounts, Blumer sought to elaborate a collective, almost market-driven dimension as the key element in the fashion and taste dynamic. In the first place, Blumer's analysis is an invitation to sociologists to take fashion seriously, and to grant it a significant place in any theorisation of modernity. While Simmel was (1957[1904]: 203) also cognisant of the way fashion was increasingly manifested in diverse social forms associated with the modern economy, Blumer's analysis – over half a century later – showed a more keen sense of how aesthetic work was becoming crucial to economic progress, and in some ways, is a prefiguring of contemporary notions of aestheticisation (see Featherstone, 1990; Lash and Urry, 1994). The core to Blumer's (1969) case is his critique of Simmel's essay on fashion, and the proposition of a different model of fashion, which essentially posited a unique conception of the *mechanisms* that shape fashions. The essence of Blumer's theory is that fashion and taste are formed collectively, rather than set by privileged elites as Simmel had earlier suggested.

On the basis of extensive observation of the women's fashion industry in Paris, Blumer identified a key feature of fashion to be 'an intensive process of selection' (1969: 278). Buyers in the industry developed a sharpened sense of discrimination 'which guided and sensitized their perceptions, and which channelled their judgements and choices' (1969: 279). What Blumer identified in the buyers was evidence of a common sense of the direction of public taste – a reading of codes, symbols and values inherent in new fashions which involved both an orientation to, and extension of, accepted fashions and tastes. In Simmel's earlier version of the mechanism of taste and fashion, the elite are centrally important as they determine the direction of public tastes. In contrast, Blumer characterised the elite as incorporated into the emergence of new forms as much as the lower classes. They have a desire to be acceptable to emergent forms of public taste; *to be in fashion* is the key motivation.

> The fashion mechanism appears not in response to a need of class differentiation and class emulation but in response to a wish to be in fashion, to be abreast of what has good standing, to express new tastes which are emerging in a changing world. These are the changes that seem to be called for in Simmel's formulation. They are fundamental changes. They shift fashion from the fields of class differentiation to the area of collective selection and center its mechanism in the process of such selection. This process of collective selection represents an effort to choose from among competing styles or models those which match developing tastes, those which 'click', or those which – to revert to my friends, the buyers – 'are stunning'. (Blumer, 1969: 282)

Blumer characterises the mechanism of fashion as one of 'collective selection'. Selection is the social process of arrival at a 'collective taste', and while Blumer posits a model of how this process might work, by his own admission it remains relatively vague and mysterious (1969: 282) and in need of further empirical treatment; however, this does not prohibit him claiming that this mystery 'does not contradict in any way that it takes place' (1969: 282). The social process of selecting tastes is described by Blumer almost like an auction of competing tastes in the social-aesthetic marketplace, where elite and mass groups pick and choose from emerging differentiations of forms and values according to their own needs:

> This common sensitivity and taste is analogous on the subjective side to a 'universe of discourse'. Like the latter, it provides a basis for a common approach to the world and for handling and digesting the experiences the

world yields. The value of a pliable and re-forming body of common taste to
meet a shifting and developing world is apparent. (Blumer, 1968: 344)

It is as if each acceptance or rejection of a new style or object constitutes
an economic vote for the public direction of taste:

The transformation of taste, of collective taste, results without question from
the diversity of experience that occurs in social interaction in a complex and
moving world. It leads, in turn, to an unwitting groping for suitable forms of
expression, in an effort to move in a direction which is consonant with the
movement of modern life in general. (Blumer, 1969: 282)

Blumer, then, provides the best developed account yet of how tastes are
framed and formed by a collective, seemingly marketised, process of
selection built on a common sensitivity to emergent styles and tastes.
Blumer's own sensitivity to the symbolic basis and interactionist qualities
of taste formation puts the study of tastes into a different domain than say,
the class model developed by Bourdieu. Blumer's theory suggests that
analysts need to better conceptualise the collective mechanisms and discourses which drive the emergence and formation of social ideas about
fashion and taste, and in addition, his theoretical foundation in symbolic
qualities of fashions suggests a better account of the semiotic element of
tastes needs to be developed.

What seems clear upon reading Blumer (1968, 1969), though it goes
unacknowledged in his work, is the legacy of Kant in Blumer's ideas. It is
as if Blumer provides the groundwork for a sociological treatment of a
key aspect in the Kantian theory of aesthetics. Whether Blumer intended
this to be is doubtful, but his notions of collective sensitivity, common sensi-
bility and collective selection are the sociological equivalent of Kant's idea of
the *sensus communis* of taste.

An earlier section of this chapter outlined Kant's theory of pure taste.
Without once again tracing through each logical step of Kant's philosophical investigation, it is enough to summarise by saying that Kant's notion
of disinterested contemplation develops by logic to his idea of universal
pleasure, where given the satisfaction of particular criteria, similar judgements of pleasure can be demanded of others. Under these conditions,
true judgements of taste can only be made when others have the same
feelings of pleasure provoked in contemplation – judgements of taste
cannot logically be made without consideration of this *sensus communis
aestheticus*. It seems obvious that Kant is not attempting to develop a
proto-sociological understanding of taste. However, his philosophical
logic does lead him to address the question of taste antinomies – the problem of a pure, universal judgement of taste in face of the tenet that judgements of taste are not based on communicable concepts (which denote a
particular type of interestedness), but feelings. In turn, the problem rests
on the issue of the universal communicability, a condition that must be

satisfied in Kant's aesthetic model. The idea that there is a 'common human understanding' (Kant, 1952: 151), whereby tastes are judged in reference to others is an important component of Kant's philosophical treatment. It is a logical condition of his idea that tastes are universally communicable – to judge tastes one must 'think from the standpoint of everyone else' (Kant, 1952: 152).

> However, by the name *sensus communis* is to be understood the idea of a *public* sense, i.e. a critical faculty which in its reflective act takes account (a priori) of the mode of representation of everyone else, in order, *as it were*, to weigh its judgement with the collective reason of mankind, and thereby avoid the illusion arising from subjective and personal conditions which could readily be taken for objective, an illusion that would exert a prejudicial influence upon its judgement. This is accomplished by weighing the judgement, not so much with actual, as rather with the merely possible, judgements of others, and by putting ourselves in the position of everyone else... (Kant, 1952: 151)

Conclusion

The quintessential social scientific way of researching 'taste' is associated with the work of Pierre Bourdieu. This chapter has been careful not to detract from the richness of theoretical, conceptual detail offered by his approach. Nonetheless, at a broader level his work is characterised by a relentless search for a *social map* of 'taste' indicators, where quotients of cultural capital are linked to specific cultural objects, and in turn are seen to play a role in reproducing broader social structures. This review has contended that such a tradition of analysis has excluded a parallel, marginal discourse on the social role of tastes.

Evident as early as Kant's idea of a *sensus communis aestheticus*, this alternative discourse on the role of taste has re-appeared in sociological literature in the work of Simmel, Veblen and later, Blumer. Though Simmel and Veblen's accounts are based substantially on emulation and status motivations, it has been suggested they contain an implicit acknowledgement of the way that tastes form community, binding individuals together through a collective orientation (see also Longhurst and Savage, 1996), even though their precise material choices may not be alike. In Blumer, we find clues as to the social exchange of symbolic meanings that assist in forming such a community, and a similar interest in the process of *negotiating* taste and aesthetic judgement. Looking to these classical accounts, and to some of the more recent speculations on the possibility of community in postmodernity (Bauman, 1991; Ferry, 1993; Gronow, 1997; Lyotard, 1988), encourages a research prospectus on taste and aesthetic value that inquires into the conceptual processes of making judgements, the types of subjective assessments involved, and the way that such decisions take account of collective norms.

SUGGESTED FURTHER READING

In addition to the historical works by Williams, Mukerji and McKendrick et al. discussed in the introduction to this chapter, Leora Auslander's study of how furniture styles are linked to power and authority in modern France, *Taste and Power* (1996), is instructive in associating aesthetic styles and forms with ruling-class values and institutional power. Despite the faults in his analysis, Veblen's *The Theory of the Leisure Class* (1899[1934]) is a witty and acerbic dissection of those who wish to be *in fashion*, that can still seem to have relevance today. I particularly enjoy Chapter 6 on pecuniary canons of taste. Two books on the social aspects of design are enjoyable and instructive: Peter Lloyd Jones' book *Taste Today* (1991), and Adrian Forty's *Objects of Desire* (1986).

SEVEN

Material Culture and Identity. Objects and the Self

SUMMARY OF CHAPTER CONTENTS

This chapter surveys a range of material that looks at how objects are used at an individual level, principally in the identity-related task of understanding oneself. The chapter has five main sections which:

- define identity and its major dimensions, and establish how objects assist in the formation and performance of self and social identities
- introduce object-relations and psychoanalytic theory to illustrate some of the important psychodynamic relations between people and objects, with special reference to D.W. Winnicott's idea of transitional objects
- review explanatory theories of consumption which have underlying psychological components centred around Baudrillard's notion of 'lack'
- use the example of youth sub-cultures to show how collective identities are established through the working out of norms and values through particular objects
- review research material on objects as self-extensions.

Objects and identity

How and why do people use objects as aids to developing, presenting and managing their identity – the psycho-social activity of understanding who they are, and letting others know who they are? We are defined as people not only by what we think and say, but by what material things we possess, surround ourselves with, and interact with: our clothes, shoes, motor vehicle or other forms of transportation, pens, computer and other personal technologies like mobile telephones or PDAs, and so on. All of these material things help to establish, mediate and assist us in the performance of our personal and social identities.

You will recall that a fundamental principle of material culture studies is that objects have the ability *to stand for other things* – or establish social meanings – on behalf of, or more precisely *along with* people. The theoretical principles upon which this claim is based have already been touched upon, but are worth briefly revisiting. In the previous chapter, we saw how Goffman distinguished between objects that allow for social confirmation of *categorical status* (such as a uniform), and objects that afford *expressiveness*, which he saw as reflecting a person's style of life, preferences, or personal tastes – in effect what we could understand as their identity. Along similar lines, Harré (2002) distinguishes between the *functional* and *expressive* orders of objects. While the former order relates to the functional purpose to which an object can be put, the latter capacity relates to social hierarchies of status and honour, which individuals negotiate. Harré (2002: 32) comments: 'Material things can be understood in their full human significance only if their roles in both these orders are identified. A Maserati Biturbo Quattroporte is a useful device for bringing the weekly groceries home from the supermarket. It is also a visible expression of wealth, style and so on'. This chapter will look more closely at the links between objects and identity, but before progressing with this task, the first thing that needs to be agreed upon is exactly what identity is, its definition and major components.

Defining identity

Identity is a modern conceptual construct used in the social and behavioural sciences to refer to people's sense of themselves as distinct individuals in the context of community. At a basic level, we could say that identity refers to people's socially determined sense of who they are – like a social statement of *who one is*. Referring to the distinct features and attributes of self, such as personality traits or values, identity is what distinguishes oneself from another person. It includes the personal sense someone has of themselves as an individual, with particular corporeal and emotional qualities. It also includes a person's location within society, especially the multiple types of social roles they can occupy and perform at different times and places, for example, as student, partner, father, boyfriend and so on.

Sociologists and social-psychologists typically think about three aspects of identity: (i) *social or objective* identity, referring to a person's belonging to various social groups, and the distinguishing socially relevant features of such belongings, for example like gender, social class or ethnicity; (ii) *self or subjective* identity, referring to the unique combination of one's personal features, traits and preferences; and (iii) *ego* identity, referring to the feeling one has of knowing who they are and how they 'fit in', giving the person a sense of stability and continuity that helps to sustain their outlooks and actions. In reality, separating out these elements as discrete aspects of identity is difficult. Contemporary understandings of identity emphasise that having an identity means belonging to multiple groups, performing a variety of roles, drawing various resources from each of these networks, and from society broadly (e.g. media discourses) to forge a sense of self.

Essentially, it is this *expressive capacity* of objects that affords individuals the opportunity to articulate aspects of self through material engagements, in an attempt to communicate something *about* – and indeed *to* – themselves. Objects have the capacity to do 'social work'. Objects might signify sub-cultural affinity, occupation, wealth, participation in a leisure activity, or an aspect of one's social status – all aspects of *social identity*. On the other hand, objects also carry personal, cultural and emotional meanings, related to *subjective identity* – they can facilitate interpersonal interaction, and help a person to act upon him or herself. For example, wearing certain clothing may make a person feel empowered by changing their self-perception. Objects, then, can assist in forming or negating interpersonal and group attachments, mediating the formation of self-identity and esteem, and integrating and differentiating social groups, classes or tribes. The actual qualities of these objects do not always matter greatly for sociality, and may be secondary to its possession. At some level it is the mere *possession* of the thing that matters for people's attachment to material objects (Dittmar, 1992: 9). The fact that one has exclusive control and ownership of an object is the crucial aspect mediating the boundaries between self (who controls the object) and the other (who doesn't). In this way, *possession* of the object *affords* cultivation of *identity*, sometimes irrespective of an object's aesthetic or functional qualities.

Identity and late-modern society: the emergence of identity as 'capital'

The postmodern perspective on consumption, which dominated the intellectual landscapes of the 1980s and 1990s, took the ability of consumption to signify identity to an extreme. In radically turning Marxist and critical perspectives on their heads, postmodern accounts emphasised consumption freedoms, largely unfettered personal choice, and consumption as a form of play. The gist of the postmodern claim is that consumption exists within a culture of hyper-commodification, where newness, beauty and status are god-like in the minds of consumers, and are the keys to forming one's identity. The contrast made commonplace in commentary on consumption processes is that if consumption could ever be characterised in historical perspective as strictly utilitarian or functional, then by contrast it is now characteristically self-constructive: identity-forming, reflexive, expressive and even playful.

The postmodern mode of expressive, identity-forming consumption has been enabled by a number of large-scale social changes. First, the widespread, frenetic commodification of all spheres of human life has encouraged people to purchase the most fundamental human needs of self-worth, love, sex and happiness, through commodities. Associated with this – the argument goes – we live in an era where our self-identity is created or discovered, and constantly monitored, relatively free from the constraints of social class, family and work life. Being responsible for our own identities, people use the abundant resources of consumer markets to construct a viable identity, based around the skilful assemblage of certain commodities which assist in building a sort of commodified self. Third, commodities are not desired purely, or even mostly, for their function, but have become aestheticised. That is – consistent with Baudrillard's thesis about sign value being paramount – objects must look good, as well as work. All sorts of consumer goods come to mind to illustrate this dictum: watches, shoes, mobile telephones, domestic lighting and so on, are all resolutely functional consumer objects that have been thoroughly *aestheticised*. Finally, there is evidence of a fragmentation of old hierarchies of cultural tastes, meaning pop-culture objects and even 'kitsch' objects can have as much aesthetic cachet as objects valued by the upper-classes, depending on social context. This has meant that products easily available to everyday consumers can be seen as 'art', and contribute to a credible personal style. For example, think of many of the cheap, cheeky and clever goods made by the French designer Philippe Starck. In part, social status involves the masterly manipulation of symbols in order to establish one's good taste, discernment or superior cultural style. Clever consumers, especially youth within particular sub-cultures, have usurped the link between high levels of personal style or taste and wealth. In our consumer culture, a person doesn't need a Rolls-Royce and a country-estate to establish their personal style and good taste. Establishing superior style can now be done through a cool pair of old sneakers, some faux rich jewellery purchased from a flea market, a retro pair of sunglasses and a cheap 1980s styled, electronic watch. Or, at least that's what the new rules of our consumer culture tell us.

Picking up on the dimensions of these new social formations and patterns that de-emphasise structure, regulation and universal life paths, James Côté (1996: 424) proposes that late-modern society requires individuals to cultivate and apply forms of 'identity capital', which he takes to refer to the 'wherewithal individuals use when … they attempt to negotiate the tricky passages created by the obstacles of late-modern society'. Côté's (1996) 'identity capital' thesis suggests that in late-modern culture individuals have the potential to develop situated, contextual modes of self-presentation that are reflexive and self-monitoring, allowing ease of forms of 'cultural mobility' through time and space. Identity capital constitutes investments people build in themselves, which assist them in making their way in a variety of personal and professional arenas they aspire belonging to. This variant of capital includes things like: development of social and technical skills, enhanced behavioural repertoires, and associations within networks. One could add that the possession of particular object tokens that afford desired identities could be included as part of the 'tangible resources' for identity capital Côté refers to (1996: 426). Such material tokens – the right 'look', clothes, jewellery, motor vehicle, and so on – all become passports into desired social, cultural and institutional spheres.

What can objects do for our social and personal identity?

All of the previous discussion suggests that in contemporary society objects can play a very important role in establishing our social and personal identities. In terms of social identity, objects can *stand for* particular features of a person, in the absence of interpersonal contact. Thus, visually identifying an object within someone's possession can tell us much about a person, without us having to speak to him or her to confirm such a status. In terms of personal identity, objects *assist the credible, effective performance* of an identity – they are integral parts of an effective social performance whereby objects (seem to) fuse with their possessors in order to offer a convincing social performance. It should be noted that there are some important cautions against easily accepting this view, however, which really suggests the need for a better specified model of the communicative aspects of objects. For example, Colin Campbell (1996) cautions against the idea that goods necessarily or simply communicate some aspect of a person's identity. For many consumers, it may be the case that buying new clothes is strongly associated with an item of clothing meeting functional requirements (for example, such as comfort, being right for a particular task like gardening or jogging, able to be worn to work). Also, it is difficult for us to assume the reasons why a person is wearing what they are, even the person themselves may not be aware of the reasons as they may wear things habitually, or 'automatically'. Then, even when clothing-conscious people do choose particular outfits, with particular features, colours, cuts and shapes, and so on, it is unclear how such ensembles are 'read' by others. All in all, while it is plausible to assume objects like clothing relate to a person's social identity and are actively chosen, it is more difficult to describe and explain such a process in precise detail, especially when it is complicated across multiple time–space contexts. The next sections of this chapter survey the literatures which in some way show that material culture is crucial to identity, along the way helping to specify some of the processes at play. We turn first to look at how objects assist important dimensions of human psychological development.

Object-relations and psychoanalytic theory: the role of objects in human psychological development

The social and human sciences tend to focus on the socially and culturally communicative properties of material culture. Indeed, this has been the predominant theme of the current work, which seeks to review and represent these traditions. This focus within the human sciences has been at the expense of meaning-centred analyses of objects, and more so at the expense of individual-centred approaches which investigate the motivations, drives and attachments between individuals and objects.

The associated pros and cons are, briefly, thus. It is correct that the selling machinery of advanced capitalism makes consumer objects more and more available, marketing them vigorously and ingeniously in order to sway consumer preferences. But then, such objects clearly have great emotional and cultural power for users, who project their own meanings onto any given object and in turn they incorporate things into their self. The advantage of psycho-cultural approaches is they investigate some of the emotional or personal reasons for attachments. Making use of a psychodynamic approach could be especially useful in consumption studies, where a range of pivotal theories of *why* people consume make suggestive, tentative use of psychological and psychodynamic approaches. A more rigorous application may yield useful insights.

The following section outlines some key tenets of the 'object-relations' school of psychoanalytic theory that are useful for studying material culture. Before doing so, one area of potential misunderstanding needs to be cleared up: the 'objects' in object-relations theory are not always or necessarily hard, material things, though they can be. An object within this theoretical tradition can be a person, a part of another person, or indeed an item of material culture. In suggesting the application of this tradition of psychoanalytic theory to the study of material culture we can make general use of the theoretical endeavours recently charted by sociologically oriented psychoanalytic theorist Nancy Chodorow (1999, 2004) who argues the efficacy of paying attention to the internal worlds of fantasy and affect to explain individual experience and action, and also cultural complexity. She suggests that all social and cultural experiences are transformed through people's psychic lens: people are historically located, but psychodynamically create a sense of meaning and selfhood. Chodorow's elegant summary of the psychodynamic perspective is instructive:

> People create and experience social processes and cultural meanings psychodynamically – in unconscious, affect-laden, non-linguistic, immediately felt images and fantasies that everyone creates from birth, about self, self and other, body, and the world – as well as linguistically, discursively, in terms of a cultural lexicon. Social processes are given, and they may lead to some patterns of experiencing in common, but this experiencing will be as much affective and non-linguistic as cognitive. (Chodorow, 2004: 26)

Important work originating from psychoanalytic theory, coming under the rubric of object-relations theory, is a potentially fruitful area for new research innovations within material culture studies. Object-relations theory can be considered a sort of modern adaptation of the Freudian psychoanalytic approach. Sigmund Freud originally used the term 'object' to refer to anything (not necessarily a material object) that a person used in order to satisfy drives. So, in Freud's sense, objects are targets towards which people directed their desire for instinctual satiation. For Freud, these were of two main types: libidinal and aggressive. Object-relations theory moves away from the somewhat reductionist approach of Freud's libidinal theory, to an emphasis on the use of objects in establishing relationships for certain types of emotional sustenance, psychological development, or need. The emphasis in object-relations theory is therefore on fixing upon objects that satisfy key relationship needs. People choose certain objects from within their environment to develop, manage and mediate their sense of self, others and the external environment.

The psychoanalyst Melanie Klein distinguished between part-objects and whole-objects. For example, a parent would be a whole-object, while the particular bodily part of the mother's breast would be a part-object. Klein's point is that all human drives become directed or centred around such objects. Once again, the object which affords psychological sustenance and growth need not be a particular material object, though it could be. Thus, within object-relations theory, objects can be people (such as one's mother, or partner) or material things (such as so-called 'transitional objects' with which we form attachments). These objects and a person's relationship with them are incorporated into a sense of self, becoming integral parts of maturing personhood. For example, children form relationships with toys, which act as transitional objects in the formation of the child's sense of self. As adults, some people form strong relationships with food and alcohol, which are objects used to service or overcome their anxieties or grief. Adults also have a range of special objects, to which they feel attached: a favourite mug, a photograph, a special item of clothing, a pen, item of jewelry, and so on. So the term 'object' is more inclusive for understanding how humans form and preserve a sense of self, as well as relationships with others, through forming relationships with a variety of object things. Within psychoanalytic theory this tendency to invest objects with power and energy – meaning – is called *cathexis*.

Transitional objects and human development: a life-long search for meaningful objects?

D.W. Winnicott's (1971[1953]: 1) elucidation of the idea of the 'transitional object' is an important early statement in object-relations theory that still has relevance. Winnicott noted that around the second half of their first year infants become fond of holding and playing with objects. He specifically suggested many infants become attached to dolls, but the repertoire of objects probably extends further than this, to whatever is within their reach. These objects become special objects for the infant, perhaps even objects to which the infant appears 'addicted'. Winnicott argues that it is not just that the infant seeks oral excitement and pleasure from fondling objects, or that fondling diminishes an infant's anxiety, but *the object they attach to offers deeper psychological gratification* around the psychic satisfaction of learning about self, and others. Winnicott says that engagements with objects occur within 'potential spaces', which are a type of intermediate space some-where between subject and object – not the individual subject, nor the exter-nal object environment, but the spaces of creativity and play that are created when both meet. Winnicott says that potential space is at 'the interplay between there being nothing but me and there being objects and phenom-ena outside omnipotent control' (1971[1953]: 100). Within this space, objects are 'imaginatively elaborated', or invested with meaning through cathexis (1971[1953]: 101).

According to Winnicott's theory, such playing with objects assists in the development of a 'personal pattern' through the infant's capacity to recognise the object as *'not-me'*. This is an important realisation, for it permits the infant to recognise the boundaries or borders or their self through handling/sucking/throwing the object. It also confirms to the infant that they can manipulate their environment (for pleasure, comfort and satisfaction), and that they are indebted to others by forging bonds of reciprocity and learned manners (for example, through the way parents frequently encourage an infant to say 'ta' after accepting an object). The object therefore assists in teaching the child important lessons.

A couple of fundamental psychoanalytic processes are at play in all types of human relations with objects (Chodorow, 1999: 15). The first is *projection*. When we project, we put our own feelings, beliefs, or parts of self into another person or object. The second is *introjection*, where elements of an object are taken into the self. There is thus a *dialectic of transference* of energies at play in people–object relations. On the one hand people *project onto* objects particular meanings, fantasies, desires and emotions, and on the other, objects are being *taken into* the self, used, elab-orated, played with and eventually exhausted. We can see how such theoretical resources can be of use for inquiries into the nature of con-sumer societies, especially people's desires for consumer objects. It sug-gests that people seek objects in order to cultivate/satiate desires and needs, and that particular objects are sought out because they are invested with particular meanings that tap into these desires, needs and fantasies. In suggesting this, such approaches take us away from emphases on the social and cultural dynamics of social communication, honour and status, fashionability and cultural capital. Yet, they allow us to get to the core of questions of human desire for objects of consumer culture, potentially complementing the focus on traditional sociological questions of con-sumption and social difference. Some of the sociological material which gestures in this direction is discussed in the next section.

Psychological lack and consumption: objects and desire

Given the sociological tendency to explain consumption through the logic of class and group membership analysis, it is not surprising that even though studies of emotion and embodiment have gained greater currency within social theory generally, this has not yet had a significant effect on the consumption studies literature (see Boden and Williams, 2002). In part, this has to do with the intellectual trajectory of consumption studies. As Miller (1995) has pointed out, and has been discussed earlier in the current work, there has been a reliance on a reductionist paradigm which posits consumerism as either a social and personal 'bad', the lineage of which can be traced from Marx through twentieth-century varieties of critical thought such as Marcuse, and Horkheimer and Adorno (as reviewed in the first section of the current work); or as a potentially liberating 'good', interpreted through the lens of theorists such as de Certeau, Benjamin and Shields. While theoretically enabling, neither position has encouraged a complex view of consumption practice.

This relative paucity of investigation into the interaction between emotion, self and consumption in social research is surprising given the fact that a small number of persuasive and influential attempts to actually explain the sustained existence of the cultural ethic of consumerism have employed strong social-psychological, emotional orientations in their explanations. Prominent in this field are Baudrillard's (1996[1968]) theory of a psychological 'lack' at the core of consumerist psychology, Campbell's (1987) account of the self-sustaining, autonomous ethic of consumerist desire, and McCracken's (1988) theory of consumption as an act of 'displaced meaning'. An important caveat is apt at this point. Reading these works one picks up strongly on such psychodynamic and psycho-social aspects – it should be noted such theoretical influences are not developed as an explicit part of the authors' theoretical model. It is important to note therefore that these authors are not necessarily psycho-analytic in their approach. What is correct, however, is that in a crucial part of their explanation and analysis of consumption they do encourage a focus upon deep psychological/ideational meanings driving consumption that could assist in the development of such an approach.

It is the rather psychically chilling idea of 'lack' that is at the core of Baudrillard's writings on the nature of consumption practice in a consumer society (1996[1968]). We require some brief revision of Baudrillard's ideas from his work *The System of Objects* before moving to the main point. At the base of Baudrillard's analysis of consumerism is the theory that while we may consume physical objects, in fact we are really consuming *the idea of an object*. These ideas are tied to inner motivations and drives, rather than utility. Baudrillard's point is that objects eventually, inevitably, perpetually disappoint – they never really satisfy the deep psychological needs that direct us toward them in the first instance. Consumption and consumer capitalism is thus founded upon a *psychological lack* that it perpetually stimulates, but cannot satiate. The possession of objects is not just about *having*, but *being*. Thus, to talk about 'my car', 'my shoes', 'my i-Pod', 'my earrings', and so on is to bring objects into our own possession and domination, projecting our own feelings onto a particular object that we use *in order to be who we are* (Baudrillard, 1996[1968]: 101). Baudrillard's (1996[1968]: 204) pessimism about this type of unquenchable need for objects is cavernous, and his indebtedness to psychoanalytic variants of critical theory and Marxism is apparent when he says that consumption has a dynamic derived from the 'ever-disappointed project now implicit in objects'. Furthermore, the motivation to consume comes from a deep, 'disappointed demand for totality that underlies the project of life' – a cavernous, irrepressible, 'lack' (1996[1968]: 205). With such gloom and barrenness, the reason for Baudrillard's postmodern turn may well be clear.

McCracken's (1988) theory of displaced meanings is similar to Baudrillard's notion of lack, though better specified. McCracken also postulates a psychological motivation for consumption. In his theory, a chronic aspect of the psycho-social aspect of everyday life is the gap that exists between the real and ideal in people's everyday lives; in consumer societies the pursuit of desirable objects is an important resource for making bridges between the real and ideal. Dreaming and fantasising – and drawing upon advertising discourses and the real or imagined lives of others – are important, for it is in this imagined domain that people come to define and build up their notion of an ideal. In consumer societies, objects come to represent a bridge from the real to the ideal. Objects are resources that attract meaning for people. It is on particular objects that people tag their hopes, dreams and desires. The psychological pang comes when people acquire elements of their dream, as represented in objects, and invariably discover that their lives soon settle back to a mundane reality. After a short high, the theory postulates that people realise their 'dream consumer object' does not satiate a deep, inner dissatisfaction. At this point, the cycle of dreaming for newness begins again.

Campbell's (1987) theory is even more elaborate and ambitious, primarily because of the historical argument it is predicated upon. Campbell's thesis is that, alongside the bourgeois, rationalist and technical ethic which characterised Weber's theory of capitalist development, there is a romantic, pleasure-seeking, hedonistic spirit which drives modern consumerism. Central to the cultural complex of consumerism is daydreaming, fantasising and self-delusion. A major part of consumption is imagination – consumers desire objects because they believe them to offer something novel, empowering or edifying. People do not thus have an actual desire for acquisition of objects *per se*, but the acquisition of 'dreams and the pleasurable dramas which they have already enjoyed in imagination' (Campbell, 1987: 90). As in McCracken's theory, so too for Campbell, purchase simply eventually leads to further disappointment, and the cycle of longing and desire begins again. This is the sublime power of the consumer society – to offer objects that promise meaning and satisfaction, but ultimately fail to satiate at the deepest level, over a long time period. As beings that crave continual confirmation of identity and honouring of the self, it is only reasonable that humans search for, and find some, satisfaction in using objects for the purpose of managing such demands of their psyche.

Youth culture and objects

Within the British cultural studies tradition there have been a range of important ethnographic studies into the lives of various marginal groups, especially young people. These have taken as one of their main goals to show how members of such sub-cultural communities construct meanings to differentiate themselves from mainstream groups. Rather than being a sign of selling-out, or submission to dominant ideologies, such studies take youth sub-cultural forms like fashion or music to represent types of resistance and political action. For example, in Chapter 4, we considered Dick Hebdige's analysis of youth sub-cultural styles, which illustrated how the semiotic 'command' of objects like safety pins, ripped shirts, leather belts and so on, enabled youth to symbolically challenge conventional stereotypes and mores. Within punk sub-culture, for example, the emphasis was on having objects 'out of place' – consequently disturbing semiotic coherence and the 'natural order' of things – in order to give an object a threatening type of cultural power. Another scholar in the same tradition is Paul Willis, whose ethnographic studies of 'profane' or 'common' culture showed how what were apparently the most mundane elements of everyday life were open to subversive symbolic usage via creative acts of appropriation. Such acts of appropriation were most effective when they deployed the symbols of the dominant classes. Consumer objects can be taken out of context, developed and repossessed to express something very different to that which they were originally intended. In his book *Profane Culture*, Willis (1978: 7) writes:

> ...these cultures teach us that revolutionary cultural change will only come from reinterpretations, reformations of consciousness, and fermentation from below around the most trivial, everyday and commonplace items .... It concerns thinking and feeling and how things are seen: new eyes on old objects.

In his ethnography of 'the motor-bike boys' Willis found the 'motor-bike object' as the central stylistic focus of bike culture. Much of the culture of the group he studied was taken up discussing aspects of motor-bikes: their style, capacity, features, handling and ride, and so on. Within the group, an individual's status was accorded in part by the type of bike they rode, and their levels of competence around riding and mechanical knowledge. And more than this, *the type of experiences* one has with a bike accorded status within the group: the breadth, depth and associated understanding one had which was akin to a type of citizenship within the biking community. The motor-bike was the perfect material accompaniment – or equivalent – to the broader cultural universe of the motor-bike boys.

While the boys were masculinist, direct, physical and respectful
of status, 'the solidity, responsiveness, inevitableness, the strength of the
motor-bike matched the concrete, secure nature of the bikeboys' world'
(Willis, 1978: 53). Willis continues, making the links between the object
and the identity of the bikeboys explicit:

> It underwrote in a dramatic and important way their belief in the common-
> sense world of tangible things, and the secureness of personal identity. The
> roughness and intimidation of the motor-bike, the surprise of its fierce accel-
> eration, the aggressive thumping of the unbaffled exhaust, matches and sym-
> bolizes the masculine assertiveness, the rough camaraderie, the muscularity
> of language, of the style of social interaction. (Willis, 1978: 53)

Willis saw the motor-cycle impacting on the full range of the cultural reg-
ister. Its mechanical qualities were recognised and to be understood, and
an important part of attaining status within the group. Its mechanical
qualities were also incorporated into a mode of understanding one's
experiences on the bike: how it rode, handled and responded was important. In the end however, it is not a cybernetic relationship: 'bike' and
'boy' do not merge. Rather, the drive was to practically and symbolically
'control' the bike, to make it a distinctive and meaningful cultural construction. In the end, this anthropomorphised (to give something human
qualities) the cycle: effectively honouring it equal communicative status
within the bikeboy's cultural universe.

Within the field of youth and risky behaviours, Cynthia Lightfoot (1997)
links risk-taking to the development of youth identity. Risks are not plain
stupid, meaningless or nihilistic, but serve much the same function as
Winnicott's 'transitional objects' discussed earlier in this chapter: they offer
young people an opportunity to apprehend their own identities, feelings,
desires and fears, within the context of their peers: 'worn like badges –
of autonomy, or defiance, or group membership – risks are declarations of
the self' (Lightfoot, 1997: 9). Lightfoot talks about how within their peer
group, adolescents go about constructing new *talismans*: objects of status
marked with culturally approved magic signs, which are seen to confer on
its bearer supernatural powers. While engagements with such 'talisman'
objects come about within the context of play and fantasy, they are powerful forms of expressing youth identities: 'adolescents are makers of new
talismans. The clothes they wear; their music and media choices, their
language and slang, their hangouts: all of these are forms expressing who
they are, and who they would like to be' (Lightfoot, 1997: 9).

Objects as extensions of self

Russell Belk's (1988) extensive, interdisciplinary essay on possessions and
how they 'extend self' is the key work in this field. Belk makes the point

that human beings are more than their physiology – their bodies and their minds. People value very highly and extremely personally objects in their external environment, especially those they deem to 'possess'. At one level, these things are purely technological and functional – they assist people to undertake social action with greater efficacy, and across time and space (for example, a mobile telephone, motor vehicle, or an electronic diary assistant). More than this, external objects take on deeper meanings – they can afford a variety of projections. The psychologist William James asserts that the self – who 'I' am – is understood not just to be 'Me', as in my body and my thoughts, but also what is 'mine'. So, effectively, James understands that we cannot separate selfhood from things external to it, which a person believes and acts *as if* a thing is equivalent to their self. Hence, a human being's world of meaning extends well beyond their empirical self, to objects, things and other people in their environment. On the way external objects become associated with selfhood, James says: 'we feel and act about certain things that are ours very much as we feel and act about ourselves' (William James, in Belk, 1988: 140).

Psychological research backs up James' theories about where people believe their 'self' begins and ends. It suggests objects and things are very much a part of people's sense of self. Belk (1988) reports Prelinger's research on limits to selfhood that shows people tend to understand themselves first and foremost as embodied, though objects also rank highly in significance. In order of ranked importance, people imagine their self as: specific body parts (eyes, face, legs), psychological processes of their mind (like a person's beliefs, values or their conscience), their personal identifying attributes (age, occupation), their possessions (watch, computer, CDs), abstract ideas (one's moral viewpoints), other people (partner, parents), objects within one's close physical environment (pens, lamps, books), followed finally by objects within distant environments (where one has travelled, one's workplace). Interestingly, note how the possessions category ranks more highly than 'other people' in imagining the self, suggesting the strong importance of objects. A potential factor at work in this ranking is the degree of personal control people perceive they have over things, which influences their perceptions of the relative closeness of these components of self. People can personally control objects more than they can other people, and hence feel a closer attachment to them. Thus, the more we believe we possess, or are possessed by an object, the closer we feel it to be part of our selves (Belk, 1988: 141). Summarising, Belk (1988) concludes on the basis of his review that the following are perceived by people as important components of self, in ranked order of importance: body; internal processes; ideas and experiences; persons, places and things we feel attached to. The following sections review research which looks into various dimensions which structure the relationships between the self and objects.

Favourite objects, treasured possessions and meaning creation

Csikszentmihalyi and Rochberg-Halton (1981) interviewed over 300 people from 82 different families within the Chicago City area for their influential study that set out to empirically account for the transactions between people and objects within homes. Their research approach is underpinned by a belief that objects are symbols that can tell researchers who people are, who they have been, and who they wish to become. When asked what things in their homes were most important to them, and why, respondents reported the following categories most frequently. This list is followed with a brief summary of the major reasons why they nominated this object:

1   furniture (chairs, sofas and tables that fill the home, providing com- fort, structuring routine and sometimes embodying memories)
2   visual art (paintings and posters that have aesthetic and stylistic value but equally importantly refer to memories, familial attach- ments and values of the self)
3   photographs (of family and loved ones, preserving memory, per- sonal ties and suggesting perpetual presence of departed kin)
4   books (these refer to one's past achievements, current interests and are tokens that represent one's ideals and values)
5   stereo (music is an important mood moderator for many people and an important referent for people's identity)
6   musical instruments (an important symbol of a person's creative expression and a referent for their enjoyment of music, sometimes refers to a past interest one has had to give up)
7   TV (like music, TV helps to moderate moods and provide enjoy- ment, it also provides an artificial form of sociality for those who live alone)
8   sculpture (three-dimensional artefacts, standing for family relation- ships, cherished experiences, and sometimes aesthetic qualities)
9   plants (provide an opportunity for people to care for something, grow- ing healthy plants represent a personal accomplishment and refer to people's sense of connection with the environment)
10 plates (includes heirlooms, gifts, exotic objects and curios which tie one to others and refer to significant events in one's life).

Csikszentmihalyi and Rochberg-Halton (1981) also found important differences in how objects were cherished across the life-course. On the basis of their generational sampling approach, they suggest a master binary scheme for interpreting age-related differences between: (i) objects that are cherished for affording of *action* (for example, a ball, or a bike, or a kite), and (ii) objects that are cherished for affording *contem- plation* (for example, a photograph, an old plate, a sculpture). The objects young people and children tend to nominate as their most cherished are things that cultivate or encourage action – they are instruments for *doing*, and require physical manipulation and engagement, such as musical instruments, sports equipment, bikes and skateboards. On the other hand older people, the grandparents within the study sample, tend to cherish objects that require mostly mental and emotional engagement, such as photographs. The middle generation tended to nominate objects toward the contemplative end of the spectrum, resembling the older generation within the sample. The general trend the authors identify is for meanings of objects to shift over time, from what one can do with an object to what one has done in the past. Thus, as one gets older objects serve to connect one with the past, affording continuity of self into the future presumably as one's life changes, becoming more challenging and more complex in various ways. Csikszentmihalyi and Rochberg-Halton are careful to point out that such a binary distinction between action and contemplation can be misleading. For example, both older and younger generations ranked the stereo highly as a cherished object. In such a case, the object can clearly afford a range of meanings, and can be used flexibly by people to suit their needs. For the young person the stereo thus plays the latest pop songs, loudly, energetically and urgently; while for the older person it can induce sentimental moods or be a source of relaxation. The authors suggest more broadly that this 'decentring' of cherished objects – from objects that directly and physically engage self to objects that link self to others – corresponds to Piaget's stage model of cognitive development.

Laura Kamptner (1995) researched the treasured possessions of adolescents. Kamptner was interested not only in the range of treasured objects, but the reasons why people nominated such possessions. Kamptner found that adolescent males listed the following categories of objects, in order, as their most treasured: music (CD player, musical instruments), sports equipment (from surfboards to baseball bats), motor vehicles, small appliances (mostly TVs but also computers, cameras and videogames), and clothing (including shoes). Females listed the following objects, in order: jewellery, stuffed animals, music, clothing and small appliances. Csikszentmihalyi and Rochberg-Halton (1981: 107) report a similar type of finding from their study. Males tend to report *instrumental* objects more frequently, such as furniture, TVs, stereos and musical instruments, while women tend to rank highly *expressive* categories such as photographs, visual art, sculpture, books and plants. In terms of the meanings derived from their most treasured objects, according to Kamptner's data males were most likely to refer to enjoyment (mood enhancement such as 'feeling good' or 'escape'), utilitarian reasons (such as it 'gets a job done', or fulfils a role), and self (the object represents a part of one's identity); while females were most likely to list the social meanings of objects (objects that have some type of link or tie to another person) as the most important meaning, followed by self and enjoyment. In this sense, there are important gender differences: men tend to focus on objects that get things done, fulfil perceived important roles or tasks and which give direct enjoyment, entertainment or pleasure; while women tend to focus on objects that afford kin and friendship ties (for example, of memory, or direct current association).

In terms of age and object attachment, Kamptner finds that, compared to when they were young, older respondents suggested they treasure objects now for their utilitarian roles, rather than comfort or entertainment reasons. So, the kinds of objects treasured did change with age, generally from 'emotional comfort' to 'utilitarian' and 'enjoyment' roles. Kamptner suggests this change mirrors the developmental stage of adolescents, who use objects to generate autonomy and independence, generate a sense of self-identity, and engage with peers, and find excitement and stimulation. In summary, objects afford identity-related developmental opportunities for adolescents.

In her research into object meanings, Marsha L. Richins (1994a) distinguishes between the public and private meanings of possessions, while noting the interpenetration of such categories. Public meanings relate to meanings assigned by members of society at large. While there will be some variation and misinterpretation, by and large, members of a community can agree on the meaning of many objects as they are shaped by meanings around fashion, style, status and stigma. Private meanings are what a possession means for an individual. This might include some aspects of the owner's personal history, especially related to significant kin relationships. In terms of the types of possessions valued by respondents in her study, Richins found the following categories of objects, in ranked order: sentimental objects (gifts, photo albums), assets (house, property, money), transportation (car), practical objects (tools, kitchen appliances), recreational objects (sports equipment, musical instruments), personal appearance related things (hair dryer, hair straighteners, jewelry), extensions of self representing personal accomplishments (trophies, degree certificates), and aesthetic objects (paintings, sculptures). Richins' multi-stage study shows a good degree of consensus amongst her respondents regarding the intended private and public meanings of objects. To some degree this is expected: the public meanings of an object result from shared socialisation experiences, and participation in social activities. Private meanings tended to be nuanced and idiosyncratic. Thus, respondents could tell the researchers more about the private meanings they attach to objects, because an individual's direct experience with objects is shaped by the very personal nature of their life history and associations. As Richins (1994a: 517) observes: 'the range of uses and experiences provided by a vacuum cleaner, for example, is much more limited than those provided by an automobile or hiking boots'.

Some interesting research has extended the process of valuing possessions to more general personal traits, especially how materialistic a person is. Materialism refers to how strongly a person desires and values possessions as part of their identity. A materialistic person is one who highly regards the capacity of possessions in their life, and who considers possessions important ingredients for a variety of facets of their life, such as happiness, success or self-worth. Do materialistic persons value different objects, and do they ascribe them different meanings to less materialistic people? For example, while two people may equally value a car to get them from A to B (as the saying goes), a materialistic person would demand the car have various attributes which they perceived as meeting their sense of self. Likewise, a 'universal' type of clothing such as jeans could be worn by both a materialistic and less materialistic person, though the type of jeans preferred would be vastly different in price, brand and possibly design. Richins (1994b) finds that less materialistic people value objects likely to be used privately, or visible within the home only, whereas more materialistic people value objects that are worn, or used, in public spaces. Further, the more materialistic a person, the more expensive the items they highly valued. High materialism respondents were more likely to refer to financial value when describing objects, and less likely to mention interpersonal ties. Those who were low in materialism were more likely to value objects for their interpersonal meanings, rather than instrumental values. Appearance related meanings – or aesthetic values – were more highly scored by high materialists when determining their satisfaction with objects. In a unique and interesting study into the psychic world of materialistic individuals, Kasser and Kasser (2001) applied a psychoanalytic-inspired approach to survey people about the content of their dreams. By classifying people according to a materialism scale, they found that highly materialistic people were more likely to have dreams around insecurity themes (for example, like falling, or dying), conflictual interpersonal relationships with significant others, and concerns about their self-esteem. By comparison, less materialistic individuals reported dreams suggesting they strove toward greater intimacy, and felt empowered to overcome danger. Despite noted methodological limitations in their otherwise careful approach, Kasser and Kasser suggest that highly materialistic people may suffer more readily from self-doubt and threats to their identity-security, have poor interpersonal relationships, and have a self-esteem that is either low or contingent on a range of external factors.

Conclusion

Within consumption studies, a recent shift has been toward accounts which have emphasised, even privileged, the idea of identity as central in explaining the motives and social purposes of consumption. Typically, this trend toward identity-centred approaches has been most strongly displayed within cultural studies, and more meaning-centred sociological analyses. Such moves have largely been in response to the longer history of marginalising consumption within more structural and materialist analyses. The popularity of such 'identity' approaches has been such that moves back the other way toward structural, (materially) contextualised accounts of consumption have been called for in the general tradition of Pierre Bourdieu.

The move away from identity, before adequate empirical treatment can be afforded to account for its role, is premature. This chapter has reviewed work which shows that at the very centre of people–object relations are questions of identity. This is not necessarily the 'identity' of the more colourful cultural studies and sociological accounts that suggest identity is merely something to be played or flirted with. Rather, this chapter has tried to review work that shows the centrality of people–object relations to the 'hard' identity questions of self-cultivation, psychological meaning and personality development. Objects have crucial roles to play in this psychodynamic activity of constituting and understanding self, from birth and the cradle, throughout the lifecourse.

SUGGESTED FURTHER READING

On the big questions of identity, possessions and objects the first place to look is any work by Russell W. Belk. Belk is a Professor in the field of business studies who writes with analytic clarity, and an interest in cultural explanations of consumption. On self-image, consumption and attachment also see papers by Schultz et al. (1989); Dittmar and Drury (2000) and Ahuvia (2005). More generally, *The Journal of Consumer Research* has a range of consistently good qualitative and quantitative pieces on all facets of consumption. On theories of identity generally, also consult Anthony Elliott's work *Concepts of the Self* (2001) but if you like the material on object-relations discussed in this chapter also consult Elliott's useful overview of psychoanalytic theory *Psychoanalytic Theory: An Introduction* (1994). For more on object-relations specifically, see Lavinia Gomez's *An Introduction to Object Relations* (1997), while advanced readers should browse D.W. Winnicott's important *Playing and Reality* (1971[1953]). For work on identity and sub-culture, see Paul Willis' *Profane Culture* (1978). For an updated version of British sub-culture research, see Paul Hodkinson's *Goth: Identity, Style & Subculture* (2002). Though both these works are not about material culture *per se*, look for references to how objects help to define the sub-culture's norms, experiences and values. For a design perspective that tackles questions of consumption, attachment and psychic 'lack' and stacks them up against very serious questions of waste, the biosphere and environmental degradation see Jonathan Chapman's book *Emotionally Durable Design* (2005).

EIGHT

Material Culture, Narratives and Social Performance. Objects in Contexts

SUMMARY OF CHAPTER CONTENTS

This chapter looks at how objects come to life through narrativisation and social performance. It has four main sections which:

- define and discuss the concepts of narrative and social performance, outlining their value for studying objects
- discuss the example of the home as a special context for studying material culture
- outline a range of environmental and social-psychological, and sociological, approaches to studying domestic objects
- use case studies to investigate the polysemic nature of people–object relations in the home.

Objects in contexts

Along with a discussion of the application of the concepts 'narrative' and 'performance' in studies of material culture, this chapter uses interview and case study material from a study the author conducted on practices of home decoration. Its aim is to examine two important perspectives on how objects acquire cultural meaning and efficacy within social contexts. These perspectives amount to ways of investigating or accounting for objects, and can be summarised by the terms 'performance' and 'narrative'. The rationale for this chapter is that objects cannot have cultural efficacy without these two important ingredients: *narratives* and *performances*. Before moving to the body of this chapter, the basis of this rationale is briefly considered.

First, without narrative storylines, be they accounts spoken by individuals or accounts that hold more general sway within a population such as a discourse, an object is rendered virtually invisible within a culture. An object may perform a crucial role (like the many thousands of individual rivets in an aeroplane) but it is taken for granted, and effectively ignored. One might observe that sociologically this practice of ignoring is important, for it is partly in ignoring an object that we learn its place. Much of the material within the growing field of actor-network theory (ANT) starts from this premise to some degree. However, this chapter is more interested in the *narrativisation* of objects, meaning the way people talk about objects as a way of talking about their lives, values and experiences. So, the way consumer objects acquire their cultural meaning is within local settings, where participants confer objects a social life through offering active, creative accounts, or narratives. It is stories and narratives that hold an object together, giving it cultural meaning. Rom Harré's (2002) paper is helpful in illuminating this point. He proposes a number of principles for theorising objects. Two of these are:

> An object is transformed from a piece of stuff definable independently of any story-line into a social object by its embedment in a narrative.
>
> Material things have magic powers only in the contexts of the narratives in which they are embedded. (Harré, 2002: 25)

Second, because objects are material things that humans interact with in an environment, they are part and parcel of all types of human activity. We can say that objects are part of any social performance, whereby people go about actively constructing and communicating meanings. For example, try to picture Jimmy Hendrix without his guitar, Satchmo without a trumpet, Groucho Marx without a cigar, Charlie Chaplin without his cane, a bus conductor without his portable ticket machine, a B-Boy without his 'kicks' (sneakers), Flavor Flav (the rapper from the group Public Enemy) without the clock around his neck, a business person without their PDA or mobile phone. Of course it is possible to picture the person without the object, but in thinking about each of these people, the *person and the object go together*. There is mutuality and complementarity between person and object (Gibson, 1986). The effective performance of any identity thus relies on particular engagements with, and presentations of, objects. In this sense, we can say that *objects have a performative capacity*, being a result of social context and reflexive presentations of self in relation to objects. Extending this view more broadly to questions of consumption, we can conceive consumption as a performative accomplishment, where social actors draw upon narratives, codes and symbols to continuously enact their identity and give meaning to material possessions. There is a dual quality to this relationship between social action, things and words which Pels et al. sum up in their excellent introduction to a special issue of the journal *Theory, Culture and Society*:

Objects need symbolic framings, storylines and human spokespersons in order to acquire social lives; social relationships and practices in turn need to be materially grounded in order to gain temporal and spatial endurance. (2002: 11)

Objects and narrative: things and words

The previous section has examined how, in conjunction with humans, objects are routinely part of any social performance – they act and are acted upon to achieve social goals. Along with this performative capacity, objects also require accounting for, and narrativisation. They are part of the stories we tell about our experiences and values. Narratives refer generally to stories or accounts that are told individually and at the macro, societal level. At an individual level, narratives consist of the accounts or stories people tell themselves, and others, in order to both *make sense of –and make through practical means* – their lives. Narratives are thus reflective, accounting for events that have already taken place. But they are also active as a site for articulating an individual's values and beliefs – they provide the resources and frames for constructing a person's future. Individuals tell their lives through stories, though these stories are not simply there waiting to be told – they are actively constructed for particular audiences, plots and contexts (Riessman, 1993). This process of narrativisation tells us about the meanings people apply to their lives.

There is a second type of narrative that is relevant to our concerns. Narratives are not only mentalistic or idealistic aspects of selfhood, but important components of culture. That is, narratives are not just told by individuals to others or to oneself. They circulate within culture, telling members of a group about their own culture, and therefore about objects. Thus, the reader will remember Smith's historical study of the guillotine (see Chapter 5), and the way it was understood – 'framed' – through particular cultural narratives about science, medicine, the human body and spirit. Likewise, Alexander's study of the computer (in the same chapter) showed the cultural narratives that existed over time about this new object, and how it was narrativised through public discourse alternately as a saviour, or a threat.

Objects and social performance

Social life is not just made up of performances, but of accounts of these performances which provide the meaning and context for social action. Taking the example of consumption, we can see it as driven by the need to establish cultural identities and affiliations, then, conceptualising it as a type of 'consumption performance' where actors harness symbolic codes, narratives and objects to achieve certain ends, can offer new paths for conceptualising consumption. Recent developments in performance theory have emerged from a range of theoretical traditions. Goffman (1959) used the concept of performance to explain the enactment of social roles according to the logic of status management. More recent developments in performance theory (Alexander, 2004a, 2004b; Butler, 1997[1988]; Geertz, 1973; Schechner, 1993; Turner, 1982) seek to understand the performative character of identity by drawing upon theoretical resources of symbolic action, ritual and social drama to show how social action is contingent upon history and collective sentiments, but must be brought into existence by continuous performative acts which actualise and reproduce the identities of social actors (Butler, 1997[1988]: 409). In his exposition of the elements of performance Alexander (2004b: 529) defines cultural performance as:

> the social process by which actors, individually or in concert, display for others the meaning of the social situation. This meaning may or may not be one to which they themselves consciously adhere; it is the meaning that they, as social actors, consciously or unconsciously wish to have others believe. In order for their display to be effective, actors must offer a plausible performance, one that leads those to whom their actions and gestures are directed to accept their motives and explanations as a reasonable account.

Alexander (2004b) goes on to develop a model of the elements of cultural performance. These include a variety of things that compose a social performance, such as: a body of collective representations to which social actors orient their actions (goals, morals, beliefs); actors and audiences; *mise-en-scène* (the elements of the scene within which people act); social power (some performances are understood as natural and appropriate, others as inherently challenging and iconoclastic). A final element of Alexander's model of social performance is especially relevant for discussions of material culture: the means of symbolic production. By this, Alexander is referring to the range of 'mundane material things' (2004b: 532) that allow and empower people to act socially. This consists of objects that serve to represent things to others, frequently through iconic means. These material things are a crucial part of any social performance because they assist social actors to 'dramatize and make vivid the invisible motives and moral they are trying to represent' (2004b: 532). Erving Goffman referred to such things as 'expressive equipment'.

A few relevant examples of material things that have a performative capacity come to mind. The first relates to mobile phone use. Imagine you are talking to a friend when their mobile phone rings. What does this signal to you? One of the things it is likely to suggest is that this person is busy, perhaps having many things on their plate, and has a range of other commitments to meet. In fact, your friend answering their mobile phone whilst in conversation with you may be a signal for your conversation to end. Another example relates to formal wear, such as a tie. Imagine you see a male friend who is usually dressed very casually wearing long trousers with a coat and tie. What is this likely to signal to you? Two things come to my mind: either they are about to attend a job interview, or a funeral. There may be other possibilities, but the tie sends a strong signal that a person is dressing formally for a special occasion requiring 'proper' dress. There are a whole range of other possible examples which illustrate how particular materials or objects signal to others a person's understanding of the social situation and their own part in it. Alexander makes the point that an individual's social performance can be received as 'fused' (successful), 'de-fused' (failed and incomplete) and 're-fused' (re-made as successful), depending on a range of factors such as an individual's command of the situation and its requirements. Ultimately, the goal of any social actor is to harness the symbolic things and objects at hand in order to successfully convey their meaning to others. Material things become part of most social performance.

The home: objects in a special context

In the next section of this chapter we consider the home as a special context for people–object relations. There are a number of reasons why the home is a good case study: it is a focal point of most people's lives – both physically and emotionally, where they interact with the most important others in their lives; it is the most substantial monetary investment the majority of people will make and an important signifier of achievement and success, as well as personal values; and finally, it embodies elements of being both highly personal and strongly social such that it encompasses private and public meanings. In the following review the research relating to psychological, cultural-anthropological and sociological elements of dwellings is critically discussed.

The psychological components of dwellings: maintaining self and individuality in a social context

Social psychological research into the house and home constitutes a large body of total research into dwellings. Researchers in this tradition have recognised the environmental and psychic importance of the home space and objects inside the home, given their centrality to modern life broadly and everyday existence. Gaston Bachelard's (1958[1994]) *The Poetics of Space* explores the phenomenological and psychoanalytic aspects of space, and in doing so emphasises the philosophical implications of the psychological perspective. Bachelard is a rather idiosyncratic place to start an analysis of the psycho-social aspects of the home – his ideas have an imperial tone, yet are nearly entirely speculative; however, he does manage to convey some essential aspects of the phenomenology of dwellings and the objects inside them. For Bachelard the house is a place of memory and dreams that is the centre of the human universe – 'For our house is our corner of the world. As has often been said, it is our first universe, a real cosmos in every sense of the word' (Bachelard, 1958 [1994]: 4). A sub-text that runs through Bachelard's discussion is that modern life (presumably through work, technology, gadgetry) dispossesses people of the benefits of truly knowing their dwelling; modern processes slacken people's 'anthropocosmic ties' (1958[1994]: 4). What the house should offer people is 'psychological elasticity' (1958[1994]: 6) – the chance to recall and hone memories, and a secure space in which to foster imagination. Here the psychoanalytic basis of Bachelard's approach becomes clear. He proposes that people are by nature closer to poets than historians, who live fixations of happiness through memories and their images. Those memories which have the most salience are ones generated in the protective cradle of the home. For Bachelard, daydreaming – essentially an important psychological process of reflection – is crucial to phenomenological well-being. Bachelard even suggests 'topoanalysis' as an auxiliary of psychoanalysis (1958[1994]: 8) to encourage, for therapeutic purposes, people to reflect on important intimate sites in their lives, and the relations of these spaces to self, security and happiness.

There are a number of important psycho-social themes in Bachelard's work that recur in more recent work of psychologists. Based on the psychological idea of the self and non-self, Bachelard proposed that divisions of geographic space are fundamentally divided between house and non-house, enclosing interior space, and excluding outside. In addition, the house has a façade (or 'mask' in Jungian terms), the public face that we choose to present to others. The materiality of the house thus facilitates, or provides, the physical means for people to think through issues of privacy that define the public and private self. Two examples are interesting on this matter: the verandah on Australian colonial style houses is a type of liminal space, necessitated by the temperate-subtropical climate, which allows for elasticity in the public/private dichotomy. The verandah places people in public view, but at the same time offers them a fence as a symbol of privacy – on the verandah a person straddles both public and private setting. In a similar vein, Vera (1989) shows how large windows which are found in many Dutch homes allow people's private spaces to become part of the public domain, and in turn, afford a surveillance point for monitoring of public activity.

In their cross-cultural analysis of house forms Altman and Gauvain (1981) also argue that the individual/society dialectic is the principal theme for analysis of domestic space. This basic thesis is elaborated by the identification of two associated processes. The first is the 'identity/ community' distinction, which highlights the way displays of status, distinction, decoration and individuality are tempered by community norms, which sanction the possibility of being 'too unique'. The second dialectic is 'accessibility/inaccessibility', where zones of the house acquire a security status that varies with the nature of interpersonal relationships within the house and cultural norms associated with certain parts of the house. For example, if the main bedroom has an ensuite, which members of the family are allowed to use it? Is the living room an appropriate place to eat breakfast? Does a family member knock before entering another's bedroom? Lawrence (1987) uses the phrase 'privacy gradients' to describe the role of these spatial, cultural boundaries which define appropriate manifestations of the interior/exterior dialectic throughout the house.

Just as space is culturally inscribed, Werner (1987; Werner et al., 1985) demonstrates the importance of time in structuring divisions of household space. Not only does the house and its spatial/cultural demarcations change over time in a linear fashion (Csikszentmihalyi and Rochberg-Halton 1981: 138) depending on group needs (for example, a family having more or less children to house), but the material culture of the house plays an important cyclical role in the habits of everyday lives: bedrooms, kitchens, bathrooms, sunrooms and verandahs are typically used throughout the day at particular times.

Broadly consistent with Werner et al.'s (1985) transactional approach to people–environment relations, Csikszentmihalyi and Rochberg-Halton (1981) present findings from a significant empirical study of material culture in North American homes that was discussed in the preceding chapter. One of the key areas Csikszentmihalyi and Rochberg-Halton's (1981) study addresses is the relations between people, their psychic development and well-being, and the material objects in their homes. Their research demonstrates that people use objects to signify information about themselves, their relationships with others, significant past experiences and personal aspirations – 'the fact remains that the transactions between people and the things they create constitutes a central aspect of the human condition' (Csikszentmihalyi and Rochberg-Halton, 1981: ix). Objects within the home can possibly perform a range of diverse functions including the mediation of conflicts within the self (à la Freudian psychology); expression of desired qualities of the self; the representation of status, fashionability or authenticity; and the expression of the goal of personal and familial integration. In the most broad terms then, it can be said that material objects in the home are crucially linked to human psychological development. In psychological terms, this idea is associated with the process of affordance (Gibson, 1986; Werner et al., 1985), where rather than just focusing on the physical capacity of objects, they are perceived according to human-generated meanings through processes of appropriation, attachment and identity investment. In an empirical cross-cultural study of living room spatial systems in Italy and France that applies this idea of affordance, Bonnes et al. (1987) suggest that the arrangement of objects in the home is related to the psychological need for optimisation of the environment according to what is most valued by householders. Thus, privacy, self-expression, identity formation and aesthetic principles may all play a role depending on the socio-cultural backgrounds of the householders.

Considered critically, Csikszentmihalyi and Rochberg-Halton (1981) characterise people's relationships with their homes as driven by the psychological goal of the search for meaning: 'Meaning, not material possessions, is the ultimate goal in their lives' (1981: 145). Although their study is insightful and empirically interesting, it is in their key word – meaning – that we have the opportunity to see a basic sociological point. Csikszentmihalyi and Rochberg-Halton do not focus on social meaning, but psychological meaning. As the following section outlines, a sociological treatment of their data would pay more attention to questions of social group formation, class and taste, symbols and signifiers.

The home: taste and its signifiers

A principal tenet in any sociological account of the home is that objects and their placement in the home signify things. By this, it is meant not only that objects have cultural or psychological weight, they reference sociological factors like class, status and taste. Quite apart from sociological knowledge of patterns of tastes, or the analysis of lifestyles and the expression of good taste, is the idea that underpins notions of a collective account of tastes – one person's tastes are meaningful only in relation to another's tastes. This force of taste to be at once integrating and differentiating is what gives it potency as a key resource for social differentiation. But in order for specific tastes in clothing, music, or home decoration to acquire a cultural power, they must be able to be decoded by people, in everyday practice, as embodying elements of a particular style, aesthetic mode or taste. This is an assumption which underpins both psychological and sociological analyses of tastes, though it is not an unproblematic one.

In Bourdieu's study of tastes, the home is one part of the larger system of taste. It is a domain which is incorporated into his notion of a 'space of lifestyles', where different practices of home decoration, presentation and use are distributed across the space of social positions. As part of his survey instrument Bourdieu asked respondents what words they would associate with their ideal notion of home. He finds that aesthetic categories ('studied', 'imaginative', 'harmonious') are used more frequently by those in higher levels of the social hierarchy (measured by occupation). Alternately, the proportion of functionalist choices ('clean and tidy', 'practical', 'easy to maintain') is more important for the middle and lower classes (1984: 247–8). This refusal of particular categories does not just occur between classes however, as fractions within each class are able to mobilise nuanced logics which defend the particular basis of their choices. In this way the broad rules which govern the aesthetic management of the home are merely different applications of universal systems of taste interpretation. Thus, Bourdieu finds similar 'modes of living' in other taste domains like food and clothing. In all, the aesthetics of organising and presenting domestic space are an important domain for the positive display of difference and the refusal of other choices.

Bennett et al.'s (1999) reproduction of Bourdieu's survey work in the Australian context asks respondents an identical question about their notion of the ideal home. Their findings suggest gender is an important factor in social constructions of the desirable home. The distribution of responses by gender in their data shows that men tend to place emphasis on more abstract ideas like 'modern', 'well-designed' and, importantly, 'distinctive'. Women seem more concerned with practical, everyday notions like 'uncluttered', 'clean and tidy' and 'lived-in'. What is important for women, Bennett et al. (1999) suggest, are inward oriented understandings of home, while for men expression, distinctiveness and style are more commonly emphasised.

Bennett et al.'s (1999) finding on gender is interesting, though there are few sources of data to compare it with. Bourdieu has stated that women tend to occupy an aesthetic position close to the working-classes, a disposition which oscillates toward the practical and real (1984: 40). In this sense, Bennett et al.'s (1999) Australian finding seems broadly consistent with Bourdieu's, even though Bourdieu does not present his specific findings on gender notions of the ideal home, preferring to frame his discussion in that section with a stratification by occupation only. However, it would seem reasonable to hypothesise that women would favour aesthetic notions more than men, who would be more likely to remain grounded in the practical aspects of the home like spaciousness, simplicity and organisation. Bennett et al.'s (1999) qualitative data is helpful here. Their case studies of middle-class women emphasise the importance of aesthetic expertise in the home, particularly the successful coordination of aesthetic signifiers. In contrast, they propose working-class homes are managed to ensure order and cleanliness, and to foster the principle of family happiness – in sum, the privileging of non-aesthetic categories. This finding suggests that women are at least principal managers of domestic space, but probably more than that, they are often taste experts. Daniel Miller's (1988) study of kitchen renovation on a London council estate offers an interesting counterpoint to the finding that working class residents perceive the home using un-aesthetic frameworks. Miller found two basic types of kitchen were installed when the estate was built, and accordingly, his goal was to account for the aesthetic changes made to the kitchen over the 15 or so years since they were built. Miller found that a small group of males had made no changes at all to the layout and decoration of the original kitchen, supporting the finding that the aesthetic domain of the home is female centred. Men did engage in expressive activities, but these generally occurred in other rooms of the house. Overall, Miller established that a significant degree of aesthetic work had been done to the kitchens, and that the kitchen was valued as a site constructive of social and kinship relations. Miller describes the process in terms of 'dealienation', where consumption is a process of transformation through giving meaning to alienated elements of material culture (see also Miller 1987; 1998a for similar themes).

David Halle's (1993) research on the consumption of artistic styles in a sample of North American homes constitutes an original and valuable empirical interpretation of this broader theoretical debate about the relative weight of themes concerning cultural dominance and class, and a diverse range of other cultural and social-psychological factors. At the centre of Halle's research is the rationale that public tastes for art are best understood within the material culture of the house and neighbourhood, and its related myths, values and ideologies associated with family, modernity and sub-urbanisation. As Halle points out, art history is commonly thought about as the history of 'great artists' (1993: 3), and a lack of a decent theory to explain the consumption of art has meant that one-dimensional, caricatured accounts have taken hold. Halle characterises these theories as 'art as status', 'art as ideology' and 'art as cultural capital'. Halle's primary finding is that the meanings consumers give to art in their home are not totally individualistic and unhinged from structural processes, but that idiosyncratic meanings and interpretations arise out of people's interactions within broader social contexts such as suburbanisation, modernisation and family life. For example, Halle postulates that the general preference for de-populated landscapes is linked to a modern leisure sentiment that favours the position of the private spectator.

Madigan and Munro's (1996) study looked at the home as a site for consumption, specifically considering the theoretical tension between the home as an expressive space and the familial and class patterns which are overlain onto individual aspirations. In relation to the question of gender and the home, Madigan and Munro (1996) did find that women bore more responsibility for aesthetic choices in the working- and lower-middle-class homes that made up their sample; furthermore they expect an even greater level of aesthetic responsibility for women in middle-class and lower-middle-class homes. Madigan and Munro's findings on class and home aesthetics generally support findings from elsewhere. They identify the most important factor in choice to be the social and interpersonal relations embodied in such aesthetic choices. Thus, making people feel 'welcome, comfortable and relaxed' (1996: 53) is more important than individualist notions of style and expression. This is a strategy that presents the self as decent, respectable and reliable, and requires a domestic space that is suitably tidy, sober and modest. Accordingly, Madigan and Munro (1996: 46) found that firm notions of aesthetic style were relatively under-developed in their sample, though younger people were found to be more aspirational and have a need to be perceived as distinctive and individual in their choices (1996: 52).

Madigan and Munro (1996) suggest that there is a lack of freedom to manipulate the symbols and images of home decoration which is associated with lower-income households that simply serves to re-emphasise their lack of resources. Notions of self-expression are seen as the privileged domain of the upper-middle classes. The attraction of this viewpoint is clear. Nevertheless, it must be questioned on two matters. First, are 'non-aesthetic' modes of living in homes *truly* non-aesthetic, or merely a different type of aestheticism which is relatively undervalued in conventional standards of good taste? Second, there is some research which indicates that even the most socially disadvantaged and deprived groups engage in forms of living space decoration, (Hill, 1991; Miller, 1988), suggesting that the distinction between modes of home presentation based on social class are likely to de-emphasise or leave out a range of other cultural and social-psychological factors.

Domestic objects: their narrativisation and role in social performance – some cases

The final section of this chapter seeks to apply these ideas to research conducted on how people decorate their homes. The key ideas of this chapter – material culture and narrativisation, and material culture and social performance – should be evident in the cases discussed but I do not want to reduce the discussion to these factors as a range of other matters are evident that nicely illustrate many of the themes of this book. The cases discussed show how these ideas work in practice, within particular research and social settings, and allow the reader to identify a number of important elements of how objects 'do cultural work'. These include the following:

- How objects are polysemic, meaning they contain a variety of messages and (within limits) can be interpreted flexibly by their users.
- How objects within the home are not merely functional, but tied to broader narratives about oneself, one's life and one's personal tastes.
- How objects are related to a person's life history and their current life context.
- How objects, through the activity of home decoration, allow people to grapple with larger questions about their personal values, outlooks and desires.

(1)   Helen: domestic technology, design and aesthetics. First, to a consideration of the case of Helen who was also discussed in an example used in Chapter 1: the 'New England' style chair. A little more information about Helen's life helps to contextualise what follows. Helen, her husband, and two young girls live in a large house in one of the most prestigious suburbs in the city. Helen is articulate, informative and speaks with a tone of clear-headed precision about her home, how she has come to decorate it, and the objects she has filled it with. Throughout the interview Helen portrays a high level of aesthetic competence – she has transformed her material tastes into a coherent and accountable whole to the extent that they are manifest as harmonious ambience.

The home is important for Helen; although she has a busy professional life she is someone who places a high value on appropriate styles and choices, to the extent that she works with an interior designer through important phases of home renovation. In the accompanying survey, Helen chooses 'clean and tidy', 'uncluttered' and 'comfortable' to describe her ideal home. On the one hand such choices are surprisingly 'unaesthetic', though they may in part be explained by Helen's busy professional life. Nevertheless, these choices fit her preferred mode of presentation of an 'understated' style. Toward the end of our conversation I ask if she has a favourite object:

> I love my B&O stereo. I love that, I love that – I'm very happy with that. I often wonder, again ultimately if we did that back room modern and kept the navy theme, I might actually have it mounted on the wall and make it a feature itself.

Helen's 'B&O' (an abbreviation of the renowned brand 'Bang & Olufsen') encapsulates the principles of technologised, abstract, modernist design. Apart from the suggestion of a silver disc shape, it presents as a dark, rectangular object in a design style that could be considered avant-garde, given contemporary designs for stereo systems. Because of its minimalist intention the 'B&O' does not look like a conventional stereo system. Bearing in mind she already has an impressive range of original art in her home, how could Helen contemplate making the stereo a feature by mounting it on a wall? More to the point, why does Helen choose it as one of her favourite things?

(2) Marie: kinship ties and memory. Helen's choices can be partly understood by studying a dissimilar example. For the purpose of contrast, take the case of Marie, who lives nearby Helen in a mid-century house she is currently renovating. Marie lists her occupation as 'home duties', her husband is in the insurance business, and, like Helen, she has been living in her current house for two years. When I asked Marie about her choice of favourite things she replies by listing two items:

> Honestly, my favourite things would be my photos, those photos. I can honestly say the favourite piece that I have is the plate that I told you about...

During our tour of the house a little earlier in our interview, Marie had pointed out the plate and commented to me:

> That one we bought on the Left Bank in Paris about 20 years ago and we bought it for about $5, and we were just so proud of this piece because we were over there with no money and to spend $5 on a cup of coffee or a bread roll was a big deal. So yes ... but we absolutely love that and actually we were talking, one of my daughters was over on Friday night and she said 'mum, do you remember the day I cracked that?' and anyway we had it mended and she said 'mum, you were upset and you got some boot polish and fixed it up so that dad wouldn't see it' because that's what mothers do.

A couple of important points of difference emerge upon a comparison of how Marie and Helen have decorated their homes. The first hinges on the dichotomy of warmth and coolness as *flavours* of decoration (Riggins, 1994). Helen is very much committed to decorating her home in soft, neutral, unobtrusive colours. The patterns she chose in consultation with her interior designer were invariably pale green and blues. Helen's favourite chair – discussed in Chapter 1 – is an exemplar to her and connotes this cool style. She comments during our interview: 'To me that chair, that sums up my idea. That's me. I love that. That sort of cream, neutral, New England look'. Helen's choice of the 'B&O' as a favourite object is a manifestation of this desire for simplicity and neutrality in the technological domain. We can see how Helen uses the chair and stereo to stand for her values: part of herself is represented in the chair, and having the chair or stereo in view reminds herself of 'who she is'. In comparison, one is struck by the busier, audacious use of colour in Marie's home. The rich, deep shade of pink used in her dining room suggests warmth and drama, rather than the coolness and simplicity of Helen's home. In Marie's home, the furniture is stained darker, the floors are polished in a dark oil that Marie describes as 'old fashioned', and gold is frequently used in various accessories including curtain rings, picture and photograph frames. When I ask about her use of colour, Marie says: 'Well, I think colours are not so sterile, are they? Therefore it gives more of a softness to it rather than the harsh, plain colour'.

The other obvious difference is in the nature of the objects Marie and Helen choose. Marie selects her family photographs and her sentimental plate as most important; these are objects that signify family achievements, kin relations and love. On this matter, David Halle (1993) provides evidence that informal family photographs are very common in middle- and working-class homes, that there is a trend toward informality in photographs, and that clustering on tables or dressers is a common mode of presentation. In contrast to Marie, Helen selects her 'B&O' stereo, an object of design value and quality no doubt, but also a significant status object. Much like the cachet of a prestige motor vehicle, possessing the 'B&O' attests to Helen's taste and appreciation of good design, but also her ability to *afford* the good design. Having the 'B&O' also demonstrates her competence across a range of aesthetic fields including art and technology, which is reminiscent of the pattern of the omnivorous consumer (see Peterson, 1992; Peterson and Kern, 1996). This comparison is not meant to suggest that Helen is a status-seeking snob, and that Marie is simply caring, good-hearted, and family oriented – the analysis cannot be reduced to this. My interest is more in the different ways that people use ideas about taste and material culture as resources, to continually find and define themselves, and their place, in the world. The object thus affords people to perform self. What seems more important than the actual *physical* properties of what these interviewees choose to talk about – the specific colour, or texture, or style, or object – are the *means and resources* they have for expressing these preferences and the relation of these schemes to the process of narrative construction. The physical tastes and preferences are thus merely the material elements of more interesting cultural and social discourses, which can be imagined as embedded 'beneath' the talk of principles of taste and material culture. A final, striking example – the case of Anna – illustrates this point.

(3)   Anna: the dilemmas of high-end kitchen goods. Anna's oven is a contentious, problematic object. Its polysemic nature – a combination of matters which seem to relate to style, context, price and role – necessitates much work by Anna to convert the oven to something which can sit naturally and comfortably in her home. Anna's talk about the oven demonstrates the way aesthetic choices can relate to political values as well as to the functional nature of objects; and how objects can offer frames through which the nature of household relations is clarified. In renovating her kitchen the task of balancing new, glossy surfaces with the traditional structures and materials inherited with the historic home has been a chief goal. Consequently, Anna's notion of what is aesthetically acceptable hinges on generating this 'balance':

> ... we struggled over the style because we wanted it to fit In with the house, which is 120 years old, um ... so we wanted the benefits of modern technology with a sympathy with the house, we ended up with the wooden cupboards and um ... mimicking the old safe doors, to break that total timber look with the stainless steel benches which are pretty utilitarian, but still I think actually blend in ... I think it goes really well with the timber as well as being utilitarian, so it's not just utilitarian it's the look that it creates which is a blend of sort of modern practicality with traditional style.

The object in question here, the oven, is modern in appearance; though its straight, solid styling also allows it to signify a sense of classicism and authenticity above and beyond its stainless steel shine. It is a large European-brand oven, priced at many thousands, made in stainless steel and glass. The style of the oven is currently fashionable, though not yet widely popular because of its cost and size, and the industrial connotations some consumers may assign to it. Its shape and lack of decorative parts suggest an economy of design: an elegant sturdiness; but, its make and materials denote European standards (at least as seen from the perspective of the Australian consumer). This is an oven for those who are aware of the aesthetics of food preparation and the role of cooking equipment in preparing good food. But rather than focus on its aesthetic qualities and status signifying capacities, in the following exchange Anna represents her new oven through a range of frames, many of which are non-aesthetic. What is apparent through this exchange is the psychic work invested in the incorporation of the commodity object into a system of meaning that is subjectively experienced, but built upon relationships at a range of social levels:

Anna (A):	It's almost kind of like an art piece because visually you see it coming through that open space, and it fits in with the house, and I guess it says something fairly traditional, not necessarily that I espouse completely to those ideals.
Interviewer (I):	What message does it send?
A:	Well, I guess something about the relationship of food and household, and that's involved in nurturing ... there's a lot of debate about that actually ...
I:	What about?
A:	Well my partner's very ... has a high input into domestic decisions which is fairly unusual I gather after talking to the people who sell commodities, they've had to take a negotiating role ...
I:	So what is the debate about?
A:	My partner liked it, he wanted it more than I did, I said, 'I don't cook enough to justify this kind of oven, does this mean that you're going to cook'?
I:	So did he see it as an art piece?
A:	No, I see it as an art piece because I don't use it enough to justify it.
I:	How do you feel about an oven being commodified as an art piece?
A:	To me, it's just a pragmatic resolution of 'ok, I'm not going to hang on to this one', and it's really nice looking and we do use it enough.
I:	What sort of oven would you have gone for?
A:	Something out of sight ... something smaller ... but considering the pragmatics that this is a fairly large space, I mean if we're going to use it, then it does balance the space and something smaller would look ridiculous ... so against that I've got my sense of balance and space ... those sorts of things are pretty important as well as whether something is utilitarian or useful, beautiful or ...
I:	So you like the styling and the look?
A:	Yeah yeah, it's just really if I spend that there's a pressure to ... you know, and I don't see myself as someone traditional who spends a lot of time cooking every night, but on the other hand I do have a bit more time now and we're spending more time um ... creating meals that are attractive and more of an art form than something just to eat.

Through the course of this exchange we see both Anna, and the interviewer, seeking an understanding of how the oven is interpreted by Anna. There is no straightforward answer, because the oven is pivotal in Anna's account of the aesthetic, spatial and economic issues involved in renovating the kitchen. In her first statement on the oven, Anna confirms that the aesthetic qualities of the object are critical by suggesting the oven is 'kind of like an art piece'. However, this sparks a range of other issues to be addressed, before Anna returns to her perception of the aesthetic qualities of the oven at the end of the extract through ideas about spatial balance, scale and beauty. Through the middle of the extract, and thinking through her ideas about the object, we can see where Anna problematises the purely aesthetic nature of the oven. She identifies how the oven is placed within political issues related to gender roles in the family associated with nurturing and domesticity, and how choosing the oven involves aspects of compromise and power that need to be reconciled within her own relationship with her partner. The crucial point to emphasise here is the way Anna thinks through the object in the course of the conversation – within a narrative framework it is deployed by her to explain and account for a range of important issues. By weighing-up alternative accounts and meanings for the researcher, Anna provides a narrative context for the object, and accomplishes her personal account of taste within the setting of the research interview. The object – elsewhere I have called these things 'epiphany objects' (Woodward, 2001) – allows Anna control of her narrative through the deployment of a concrete example, and in turn, emerges from the interview as a key resource for the researcher to offer a synopsis of her narrative.

Conclusion: a note on reflexive methodologies and material culture

The data gathering process for the research cases reported above are not without methodological dilemmas: management of the domestic setting prior to the interview, and respondents saying what they perceive the researcher wants to hear are issues that need to be considered. However, there are two strong counterpoints that circumscribe the weight of these matters. The first is that this impression management itself constitutes a significant source of data (see also Lamont, 1992: 21). The aspirations people have for their home, and their ideal ways of presenting and talking about their home and the objects inside it, are just as important as how they might actually live in their home. The second point relates to the astute use of other verifiable forms of data available to the researcher in the domestic setting. For example, is the interviewee generally consistent in their aesthetic and moral relations with the home? Is what the interviewee says about an object realistic given other cues in the home and the interview? This need to fit object-relations into a larger picture of household and interpersonal relations may explain why the case-study approach is often used as an aid to the development of theory in socio-cultural accounts of consumption and lifestyle (Bennett et al., 1999; Bourdieu, 1984; Lamont, 1992; Riggins, 1994).

Perhaps more critically in terms of developing procedures for proposing an interpretive account of taste, consumerism and material culture, researchers should bear in mind how such an interpretive account deals with methodological issues of truth and fiction, reality and representation. Thus, should the interview data presented here be seen as the literal, authentic truth of their relations with objects? To what degree have the normative process of interviewing and the presence of a researcher in their private, domestic space influenced people's responses? Even more fundamentally – and problematically – as Denzin (1997) asks, to what extent can researchers assume that subjects have unproblematic access to their own lived experience? In the study of domestic material culture through face-to-face interviews, we might even expect such potential problems to be heightened. Justifying their taste using an explicit aesthetic rationale is difficult for many people to accomplish.

The answer to each of the questions may well highlight a multitude of epistemological quandaries that have the potential to challenge core assumptions about the nature and purpose of social research. However, this is not necessarily a problem but a strength that can be turned to the theorists' advantage. In fact, it illuminates a crucial theoretical position about taste, aesthetics and domestic material culture which is assisted by the insights of reflexive ethnography and theories of social accountability (Shotter, 1984). What these data demonstrate is how having taste is an ongoing narrative accomplishment and part of a social performance, as much as it is an objective, fixed form of cultural capital. In identifying and narrativising their tastes for the researcher, the respondents account for themselves, their home, and implicitly a universe of others through the construction of a taste narrative. Talking about taste and aesthetic choice with people in their homes offers opportunities for exploration of cultural, emotional and aesthetic meanings that can be manifested in domestic objects. The material culture discussed in the research interviews thus affords an important role for the respondent: they allow abstract ideas about style, taste and aesthetic preference to be concretised, affording respondents opportunity to elaborate their narrative using material culture. In turn, the strategy of focusing on household objects is also profitable for the researcher, as the objects respondents chose to talk about signify some element of a person's aesthetic ideal.

The implications for research into aesthetic taste and material culture is that ethnographic studies, conversation analysis and narrative analysis can yield profitable insights. Judgements of taste and forms of aesthetic expertise are reflexive accomplishments, based in talk and narrative construction, and are presented to visitors, guests and researchers alike, as they are required. Even the most emptied-out, banal objects of modern domestic material culture have a role to play.

SUGGESTED FURTHER READING

For introductory books which give thorough reviews of work on narratives see C.K. Riessman's book *Narrative Analysis* (1993). For a discursive approach to narrative see John Shotter's *Social Accountability and Selfhood* (1984), Shotter and Kenneth J. Gergen's *Texts of Identity* (1989), and Jonathan Potter's *Representing Reality* (1996). Social performance is an emerging area in cultural sociology, but has been around for longer in other disciplines. See any books by Richard Schechner on the topic of performance – I found *Performance Studies, An Introduction* (2002) especially useful to get a handle on core ideas and diverse approaches within performance studies. Also see essays by Jeffery C. Alexander from the journal *Sociological Theory* in 2004, and the book by Alexander et al. called *Social Performance* (2006) for a cultural sociological development of the idea of performance. If you are interested in reading more about the home and objects see Daniel Miller's collection *Home Possessions* (2001), Amos Rapoport's *House Form and Culture* (1969), and Madigan and Munro (1996). For a completely anachronistic, pop-sociology account of home, manners and self-presentation see Russell Lynes' book *The Tastemakers* (1954). For more advanced readers Gaston Bachelard's *The Poetics of Space* (1994[1958]) isn't only about homes, but is a stimulating philosophical piece on the phenomenology of space that should kindle new thinking about the meaning of domestic spaces and the objects we fill them with.

PART IV
CONCLUSION

NINE

Conclusion: Objects and Meaning in Consumer Culture

Writing on adornment, Georg Simmel (1950) gets at the crux of psycho-cultural processes related to people's use and display of a special class of objects. Objects of adornment, Simmel observes, are generally of considerable value, or at least made to appear as though they are; for example, a string of pearls, a diamond ring, a chunky gold wristwatch, a pretty pair of shoes, or a pair of flashy sunglasses. The dynamic at play in the act of adornment, Simmel finds, is the strangest of sociological processes. Simmel had an uncanny knack of observing and unearthing such kernels of sociological truth in the smallest and most trivial kinds of things. Admittedly, the dynamics of fashion and stylisation have changed substantially since Simmel's time, though his observations are always worth considering for their poetic form of social explanation. He writes that adornment is at once about 'being-for-oneself' and 'being-for-the-other'. On the one hand to adorn oneself is an entirely selfish, competitive act of trying to 'enlarge' one's ego by bringing attention and envy from others. At the same time, it is an act which 'enlarges', or cultivates, social solidarity. It is a 'gift' to others, even though it works at the other's expense, by elevating the wearer of the adorning object. Viewers also offer back a type of social gift – they observe and give attention to the person who has adorned themselves. Though they may feel inferior, they have the gratification of playing a part in the synthesis of the great convergent and divergent forces: society and the individual. Such is the capacity of objects of consumption.

The main thrust of this work has been to examine, compare and evaluate the major ways of approaching objects within social and cultural theory, and within various domains of everyday practice. A substantial portion of it is based in interpreting and representing modern social and cultural theory and research. Formal, sometimes conventional, sociological assumptions bleed through repeatedly, though hopefully not excessively. Despite this disciplinary basis, the work is an endeavour to progress a general, cultural understanding of objects which is both drawn from, and useful across, disciplines including sociology, cultural anthropology, consumer behaviour studies and environmental psychology. To date, the nomenclature of 'material culture studies' has tended to encourage sympathetic research on the meaningful and constructive aspects of people–object relations within cultural anthropology, cultural studies and sociology. However, this work has presented exciting and provocative work from a range of other fields, including consumer behaviour research and a range of psychological sub-disciplines (like object-relations psychoanalytic theory) and cultural theory more generally. This conclusion revises key concepts, summarises major conceptual frames in new ways, and points to areas of future interest in studying people–object relations. For the introductory reader this conclusion serves the purpose of revising core material, but through a new synthesis. For the advanced reader, the conclusion articulates and discusses a modest agenda for research into material culture.

It should be clear to the reader – not only through the weight given to certain matters, but the verve and energy devoted to them – that there are a number of biases that reveal my own intellectual preferences for studying objects in culture. These predispositions can be summarised by three abstract concepts: *cultural, interpretive* and *pragmatic*. It is hoped the way these concepts are developed and applied will be clear to any reader who has progressed to this point, though the section below points directly to the meaning of each. First, the term 'cultural' refers to what might be called the meaning-making affordances of objects – the symbolic capacities objects offer to *think through and about* diverse aspects of social life in such a way as to cultivate solidaristic as well as differentiating effects; practical action in addition to reflection. Second, the term 'interpretive' refers to a dual process of interpretation. In the first instance it refers to a particular interest in the way individuals deal with, frame, negotiate and understand objects, as well as the approach taken by social and cultural researchers to 'discover' and report such relations. The nature of this hermeneutical dialectic encourages researchers to think reflexively about the social world, and the methods needed to adequately describe it. Finally, 'pragmatic' refers to the fact that objects do things to people, and people do things with objects. There is a type of intersubjectivity – yet to be fully understood or investigated by researchers – between persons and objects that makes *materiality* a fundamental platform, and media, of sociality. Alexander's (2004b) model of cultural pragmatics is instructive here on the broader meaning of the term 'pragmatic', highlighting its integration of processes of cultural extension and psychological identification in the continuous performance of the social.

A major component of this book has examined core traditions in social theory that are useful for the study of objects as culture. Using the overarching idea of meaning-making, it is worth looking back at each tradition in order to generalise about their points of difference, strong suits and weak points. The hegemonic position of Marxist and critical theory for understanding objects and consumption has been noted within consumption studies and material culture studies. The materialist analyses of the Marxist approach emphasised the genuine lack of possibility of finding meaning in objects. What's more, they suggested if individuals professed to finding meaning, it was merely evidence of false consciousness and a deficiency of critical awareness. Through the twentieth century, Marxist accounts were refined, and more likely to take into account psychological and psychoanalytic factors in their exploration of culture as an ideological construct continually reproduced by under-developed individuals who were essentially cultural dopes. Such a view of objects amounted to a warning that 'objects are not as they seem', that people's relationships with them were self-deceptive and alienating, and constitutive evidence of an 'insane society', to play with Erich Fromm's expression. Essentially, this is a culturally reductive account, with a deterministic, anthropologically naïve and inflexible view of the human capacity for agency, imagination and cultural creativity. Seeing objects as defined principally through technical, economic concepts – such as a 'commodity' – means this view cannot elaborate a useful account of the material as culture.

Structural and semiotic accounts of objects offer a more sophisticated theoretical ensemble for capturing meaning-making processes with objects. Developed principally through the writings of Saussure and Lévi-Strauss, this oeuvre highlighted how cultural objects are relationally ordered, symbolic, and how they can be understood within larger language-like systems of cultural meaning which have communicative capacity akin to language. This body of work affords an opportunity to develop an autonomous model of cultural communication which doesn't rely on forces such as the 'means of production' to explain how objects embody meanings. It offers therefore, a much more robust and nuanced model of how material things circulate within systems of cultural meaning. In the later writings of Barthes and Baudrillard this account of how objects embody and represent meanings, affording a range of cultural communications, was applied to the study of advanced consumer societies. What we have in this skein of literature is an important body of theoretical material on the autonomous communicative capacities of objects – a recommendation for its enduring relevance for material culture studies. What is not so evident in this body of theoretical tools, however, are ways for studying objects as they move away from systems of communication, to frames of meaning, individual interpretation and human intersubjectivity. The final major body of theoretical resources this book has considered deals with this capacity of objects. Combined with the structural and semiotic tradition which focuses on the internal, relational ordering of objects, this more deeply cultural view offers a powerful account of the moral signatures and imperatives of cultural classifications of objects, the processes of singularisation and subjectification that social actors use to make objects meaningful, and the ways in which objects are 'de-commodified' through a range of psycho-cultural strategies. To summarise, such accounts are: (i) *processual* in that they emphasise the trajectories of objects through diverse spaces and times of human activity, (ii) *transformative* in that they show how objects are able to be continuously shaped and re-shaped by their human users through the interplay of physical and symbolic manipulation, and (iii) *contextual* in that they show how objects are situated within broader discourses, narratives, myths and frames that assist in the construction of cultural meaning and its interpretation.

The latter section of the book demonstrates how objects become crucial parts of social and psycho-social patterns and relations, within a range of important fields, including status, honour and distinction; the formation and maintenance of self, social and ego identity; and the narrativisation and performance of self. Above all, what these sections show is that there can never really be one account or interpretation of an object. To take an example used in the previous chapter, an object like a new oven can be about one's aesthetic taste and status, or about the family and sharing meals, or about spending a lot of money on a kitchen renovation, or about dealing with one's partner's needs, or about the personal anxiety or guilt sometimes associated with spending large sums of money on consumer goods. Any one account – an interpretation – will always be different to another, by virtue that is comes from someone who has a different history and biography, or is articulated by the same person on a different day, in unique contexts. A material thing thus has a range of different potential roles or 'affordances' (Gibson, 1986), each dependent upon a different embedding narrative – its uses are not limited by its physical features, or design. As Harré (2002: 30) notes: 'if material things become social objects in so far as they are embedded in narratives then the question of whether this is the same or a different social object depends on whether and how this is the same or different story'.

While much of this book dwells on domains and examples from within consumption studies, it is important to remember that materiality can be approached through frames other than consumption, and that consumption is about more than relations with objects and materiality. In addition, consumption is about more than identity construction and expression, and social distinction. Many of the examples used need to be considered with this point in mind: they are partial accounts of social relations that seek to understand people–object relations within the broad field of consumption, frequently through logics embedded in a consumption studies paradigm. Despite this specificity, what is inescapable is the capacity of an object to do cultural work. It may sometimes appear as if people have selective, fleeting relationships with objects that are made on their own terms: people routinely look at them, pick them up, become entangled with them, use them, dispose of them and move on. In fact, a more accurate and telling observation may be the contrary: in ways that many people never know *objects have a type of hold on them*. In the end, objects cease to be external to the individual: objects are their constitution, their subjectivity. Far from being a sign of human weakness, self-deception or oppression by the dead hand of a malevolent social system, the patterns of relationships between people and objects suggest people actively seek out – and require – these bonds with objects. Explaining the nature of these attachments and affiliations is why material culture studies is valuable for understanding the crux of the social: the balancing of individuals with society; of emotion, embodiment, meaning and action, with collective values, cultural discourses and solidarities.

References

Adorno, Theodor W. (1991) The Culture Industry: Selected Essays on Mass Culture, (ed. J.M. Bernstein). London: Routledge.

Ahuvia, Aaron C. (2005) 'Beyond the extended self: loved objects and consumers' identity narratives', *Journal of Consumer Research*, 32(1): 171–84.

Alexander, Jeffrey C. (2003) *The Meanings of Social Life: A Cultural Sociology*. New York: Oxford University Press.

Alexander, Jeffrey C. (2004a) 'From the depths of despair: performance, counterperformance, and "September 11"', *Sociological Theory*, 22(1): 88–105.

Alexander, Jeffrey C. (2004b) 'Cultural pragmatics: social performance between ritual and strategy', *Sociological Theory*, 22(4): 527–73.

Alexander, Jeffrey C., (forthcoming), 'Iconic Experience in Art and Life: Standing Before Giacometti's "Standing Woman"'.

Alexander, Jeffrey C., Giesen, Bernhard and Mast, Jason (eds.) (2006) *Social Performance: Symbolic Action, Cultural Pragmatics and Ritual*. Cambridge: Cambridge University Press.

Altman, Irwin and Gauvain, Mary (1981) 'A cross-cultural and dialectic analysis of homes' in Lynn S. Liben, Arthur H. Patterson and Nora Newcombe, *Spatial Representation and Behaviour Across the Life Span*. New York: Academic Press. pp. 283–320.

Appadurai, Arjun (1986) 'Introduction: commodities and the politics of value', in Arjun Appadurai (ed.), *The Social Life of Things: Commodities in Cultural Perspective*. Melbourne: Cambridge University Press. pp. 3–63.

Attfield, Judy (2000) *Wild Things. The Material Culture of Everyday Life*. Oxford: Berg.

Auslander, Leora (1996) *Taste and Power. Furnishing Modern France*. Berkeley: University of California Press.

Bachelard, Gaston (1994[1958]) *The Poetics of Space*, trans. Maria Jolas. Boston: Beacon Press.

Barthes, Roland (1967) *The Fashion System*, trans. M. Ward and R. Howard. New York: Hill and Wang.

Barthes, Roland (1979) *The Eiffel Tower and Other Mythologies*, trans. R. Howard. New York: Hill and Wang.

Barthes, Roland (1993[1957]) *Mythologies*, trans. A. Lavers. London: Vintage.

Bataille, Georges (1985) *Visions of Excess: Selected Writings, 1927–1939*, ed. Allan Stoekl, trans. A. Stoekl. Minneapolis: University of Minnesota Press.

Baudrillard, Jean (1981) *For a Critique of the Political Economy of the Sign*, trans. C. Levin. USA: Telos Press.

Baudrillard, Jean (1996[1968]) *The System of Objects*, trans. J. Benedict. London: Verso.

Baudrillard, Jean (1998) *America*, trans. C. Turner. London: Verso.

Baudrillard, Jean (1998 [1970]) *The Consumer Society: Myths and Structures*. London: Sage Publications.

Bauman, Zygmunt (1988) *Freedom*. Milton Keynes: Open University Press.

Bauman, Zygmunt (1991) *Modernity and Ambivalence*. New York: Cornell University Press.

Beck, Ulrich (1992) *Risk Society. Towards a New Modernity*. London: Sage.
Belk, Russell W. (1985) 'Materialism: trait aspects of living in the material world', *Journal of Consumer Research*, 13: 265–80.
Belk, Russell W. (1988) 'Possessions and the extended self', *The Journal of Consumer Research*, 15: 139–65.
Belk, Russell W. (1995) *Collecting in a Consumer Society*. New York: Routledge.
Belk, Russell W., Wallendorf, Melanie and Sherry, John F. Jr. (1989) 'The sacred and profane in consumer behaviour: theodicy on the odyssey', *The Journal of Consumer Research*, 16(1): 1–38.
Bennett, Andy and Dawe, Kevin (2001) *Guitar Cultures*. Oxford: Berg.
Bennett, Tony, Emmison, Michael and Frow, John (1999) *Accounting for Tastes. Australian Everyday Cultures*. Cambridge: Cambridge University Press.
Blumer, Herbert (1968) 'Fashion', in David L. Sills (ed.), *International Encyclopedia of the Social Sciences*. New York: The Macmillan Company and The Free Press.
Blumer, Herbert (1969) 'Fashion: from class differentiation to collective selection', *The Sociological Quarterly*, 10: 275–91.
Boden, S. and Williams, S.J. (2002) 'Consumption and emotion: the romantic ethic revisited', *Sociology*, 36(3): 493–513.
Bonnes, Mirilia, Giuliana, Maria Vittoria, Amoni, Flora and Bernard, Yvonne (1987) 'Cross-cultural rules for the optimization of the living room', *Environment and Behaviour*, 19(2): 204–27.
Bourdieu, Pierre (1979[1963]) *Algeria 1960*. Cambridge: Cambridge University Press.
Bourdieu, Pierre (1977) *Outline of a Theory of Practice*. Cambridge: Cambridge University Press.
Bourdieu, Pierre (1984) *Distinction. A Social Critique of the Judgement of Taste*. London: Routledge.
Bourdieu, Pierre (1990) *The Logic of Practice*. Cambridge: Polity Press.
Butler, Judith (1997[1988]) 'Performative acts and gender constitution. An essay in phenomenology and feminist theory', in K. Conboy, N. Medina and S. Stanbury (1997) *Writing on the Body. Female Embodiment and Feminist Theory*. New York: Columbia University Press.
Butler, Rex (1999) *Jean Baudrillard: The Defence of the Real*. London: Sage.
Campbell, Colin (1987) *The Romantic Ethic and the Spirit of Modern Consumerism*. Oxford: Basil Blackwell.
Campbell, Colin (1995a) 'Conspicuous confusion – A critique of Veblen's theory of conspicuous consumption', *Sociological Theory*, 13(1): 37–47.
Campbell, Colin (1995b) 'The sociology of consumption', in D. Miller (ed.), *Acknowledging Consumption. A Review of New Studies*. London: Routledge.
Campbell, Colin (1996) 'The meaning of objects and the meaning of actions: a critical note on the sociology of consumption and theories of clothing', *Journal of Material Culture*, 1(1): 95–105.
Carson, Rachel (1962) *Silent Spring*. Boston: Houghton Mifflin.
Chapman, Jonathan (2005) *Emotionally Durable Design. Objects, Experiences, Empathy*. London: Earthscan.
Chapman, William Ryan (1985) 'Arranging ethnology: A.H.L. F. Pitt Rivers and the typological tradition', in G.W. Stocking Jr. (ed.), *Objects and Others. Essays on Museums and Material Culture*. Wisconsin: University of Wisconsin Press.
Chodorow, Nancy J. (1999) *The Power of Feelings: Personal Meaning in Psychoanalysis, Gender, and Culture*. London: Yale University Press.
Chodorow, Nancy J. (2004) 'The sociological eye and the psychoanalytic ear' in Jeffrey C. Alexander, Gary T. Marx and Christine L. Williams. *Self, Social*

Structure, and Beliefs: Explorations in Sociology. Berkeley: University of California Press.

Cohen, Stanley (1972) *Folk Devils and Moral Panics*. London: MacGibbon and Kee.

Corrigan, Peter (1997) *The Sociology of Consumption*. London: Sage.

Côté, James E. (1996) 'Sociological perspectives on identity formation: the culture-identity link and identity capital', *Journal of Adolescence*, 19: 417–28.

Csikszentmihalyi, Mihaly and Rochberg-Halton, Eugene (1981) *The Meaning of Things. Domestic Symbols and the Self*. New York: Cambridge University Press.

Culler, Jonathan (1983) *Barthes*. London: Fontana Paperbacks.

Davis, Fred (1992) *Fashion, Culture and Identity*. Chicago: University of Chicago Press.

Denzin, Norman (1997) *Interpretive Ethnography: Ethnographic Practices for the 21st Century*. California: Sage.

Dittmar, Helga (1992) *The Social Psychology of Material Possessions: To Have is to Be*. New York: St Martin's Press.

Dittmar, Helga and Drury, John (2000) 'Self-image – is it in the bag? A qualitative comparison between "ordinary" and "excessive" consumers', *Journal of Economic Psychology*, 21(2): 109–42.

Douglas, Mary (2000[1966]) *Purity and Danger. An Analysis of the Concepts of Pollution and Taboo*. New York: Routledge.

Douglas, M. and Isherwood, B. (1996[1979]) *The World of Goods. Towards an Anthropology of Consumption*. New York: Basic Books.

Durkheim, Emile (1995[1912]) *The Elementary Forms of the Religious Life*, trans. Joseph Ward Swain. London: Allen and Unwin.

Durkheim, Emile and Mauss, Marcel (1963[1903]) *Primitive Classification*, trans. Rodney Needham. London: Cohen and West.

Eco, Umberto (1976) *A Theory of Semiotics*. Bloomington: Indiana University Press.

Elliot, Anthony (1994) *Psychoanalytic Theory: An Introduction*. Oxford: Cambridge.

Elliot, Anthony (2001) *Concepts of the Self*. Malden: Blackwell Publishers.

Emmison, Michael and Smith, Philip (2000) *Researching the Visual. Images, Objects, Contexts and Interactions in Social and Cultural Inquiry*. London: Sage.

Featherstone, Mike (1987) 'Lifestyle and consumer culture', *Theory, Culture and Society*, 4: 55–70.

Featherstone, Mike (1990) 'Perspectives on consumer culture', *Sociology*, 24(1): 5–22.

Featherstone, Mike (1991) *Consumer Culture and Postmodernism*. London: Sage.

Featherstone, Mike (1992) 'Postmodernism and the aestheticisation of everyday life', in S. Lash and J. Friedman (eds.), *Modernity and Identity*. Oxford: Blackwell.

Ferry, Luc (1993) *Homo Aestheticus. The Invention of Taste in the Democratic Age*, trans. Robert De Loaiza. Chicago: The University of Chicago Press.

Forty, Adrian (1986) *Objects of Desire: Design and Society 1750–1980*. UK: Thames and Hudson.

Foucault, Michel (1977) *Discipline and Punish: the Birth of the Prison*, trans. A. Sheridan. New York: Pantheon Books.

Frisby, David (1986) *Fragments of Modernity: Theories of Modernity in the Work of Simmel, Kracauer, and Benjamin*. Cambridge: MIT Press.

Frisby, David (1992) *Simmel and Since: Essays on Georg Simmel's Social Theory*. London: Routledge.

Fromm, Eric (1955) *The Sane Society*. New York: Rinehart.

Fromm, Eric (1976) *To Have or To Be*. New York: Harper & Row.

Frow, John (1987) 'Accounting for tastes: some problems in Bourdieu's sociology of culture', *Cultural Studies*, 1(1): 59–73.

Galbraith, John Kenneth (1987[1958]) *The Affluent Society*. Harmondsworth: Penguin.

Geertz, Clifford (1973) *The Interpretation of Cultures*. New York: Basic Books.

Gibson, James J. (1986) *The Ecological Approach to Visual Perception*. New Jersey: Lawrence Erlbaum Associates.

Goffman, Erving (1951) 'Symbols of class status', *British Journal of Sociology*, 2(4): 294–304.

Goffman, Erving (1959) *The Presentation of Self in Everyday Life*. New York: Doubleday.

Gomez, Lavinia (1997) *An Introduction to Object Relations*. London: Free Association Books.

Gronow, Jukka (1997) *The Sociology of Taste*. London: Routledge.

Halle, David (1993) *Inside Culture. Art and Class in the American Home*. Chicago: University of Chicago Press.

Harré, Rom (2002) 'Material objects in social worlds', *Theory, Culture and Society*, 19(5/6): 23–33.

Harvey, David (1989) *The Condition of Postmodernity*. Oxford: Blackwell.

Hebdige, Dick (1979) *Subculture: The Meaning of Style*. London: Methuen & Co.

Hebdige, Dick (1988) *Hiding in the Light: On Images and Things*. New York: Routledge.

Held, David (1980) *Introduction to Critical Theory: Horkheimer to Habermas*. Berkeley: University of California Press.

Heskett, John (2002) *Toothpicks and Logos: Design in Everyday Life*. Oxford: Oxford University Press.

Hill, Roland P., 'Homeless Women, Special Possessions, and the Meaning of "Home": An Ethnographic Case Study', *Journal of Consumer Research*, 18 (December): 299–310.

Hodkinson, Paul (2002) *Goth: Identity, Style & Subculture*. New York: Berg.

Holt, Douglas B. (2004) *How Brands Become Icons. The Principles of Cultural Branding*. Boston: Harvard Business School Press.

Horkheimer, Max (1982) *Critical Theory: Selected Essays*, Trans. M.J. O'Connell and others. New York: Continuum Publishing Corporation.

Horkheimer, Max and Adorno, Theodor W. (1987[1944]) *Dialectic of Enlightenment*, trans J. Cumming. NY: Continuum.

Jacknis, Ira (1985) 'Franz Boas and exhibits: on the limitations of the museum method of anthropology', in G.W. Stocking Jr. (ed.), *Objects and Others. Essays on Museums and Material Culture*. Wisconsin: University of Wisconsin Press.

Jameson, Fredric (1991[1984]) *Postmodernism, Or, The Cultural Logic of Late Capitalism*. London: Verso.

Jenkins, Richard (1992) *Pierre Bourdieu*. New York: Routledge.

Jones, Peter Lloyd (1991) *Taste Today. The Role of Appreciation in Consumerism and Design*. New York: Pergamon Press.

Kamptner, N. Laura (1995) 'Treasured possessions and their meanings in adolescent males and females', *Adolescence*, 30(118): 301–18.

Kant, Immanuel (1952) *The Critique of Judgement*, trans. J.C. Meredith. Oxford: Clarendon Press.

Kasser, Tim and Kasser, Virginia G. (2001) 'The dreams of people high and low in materialism', *Journal of Economic Psychology*, 22: 693–719.

Kellner, Douglas (1989a) *Critical Theory, Marxism and Modernity*. Cambridge: Polity Press.

Kellner, Douglas (1989b) *Jean Baudrillard: From Marxism to post-Modernism and beyond*. Cambridge: Polity Press.

Kleine III, Robert E. and Kernan, Jerome B. (1991) 'Contextual influences on the meanings ascribed to ordinary consumption objects', *Journal of Consumer Research*, 18: 311–24.

Kleine, Susan Schultz, Kleine III, Robert E. and Allen, Chris T. (1995) 'How is a possession "me" or "not me"? Characterizing types and an antecedent of material possession attachment', *Journal of Consumer Research*, 22: 327–43.

Kopytoff, Igor (1986) 'The cultural biography of things: commoditization as process', in Arjun Appadurai, *The Social Life of Things. Commodities in Cultural Perspective*. Cambridge: Cambridge University Press.

Lamont, Michele (1992) *Money, Morals, and Manners. The Culture of the French and American Upper-middle Class*. Chicago: The University of Chicago Press.

Lash, Scott and Urry, John (1987) *The End of Organised Capitalism*. Cambridge: Polity.

Lash, Scott and Urry, John (1994) *Economies of Signs and Space*. London: Sage.

Law, John (2002) *Aircraft Stories: Decentering the Object in Technoscience*. Durham: Duke University Press.

Lawrence, Roderick J. (1987) 'What makes a home a house?', *Environment and Behaviour*, 19(2): 154–68.

Leiris, Michel (2005) 'On Duchamp', *October*, 112 (Spring): 45–50.

Lévi-Strauss, Claude (1962) *Totemism*, trans. R. Needham. England: Penguin Books.

Lévi-Strauss, Claude (1966[1962]) *The Savage Mind*. London: The University of Chicago Press.

Lévi-Strauss (1968[1963]) *Structural Anthropology*, trans. C. Jacobson. England: Penguin Books.

Lévi-Strauss, Claude (1979) *Myth and Meaning. Cracking the Code of Culture*. New York: Schocken Books.

Lightfoot, Cynthia (1997) *The Culture of Adolescent Risk-Taking*. New York: Guilford Press.

Longhurst, Brian and Savage, Mike (1996) 'Social class, consumption and the influence of Bourdieu: some critical issues', in S. Edgell, K. Hetherington and A. Warde (eds), *Consumption Matters: The Production and Experience of Consumption*. Oxford: Blackwell Publishers.

Lukács, Georg (1971) *History and Class Consciousness: Studies in Marxist Dialectics*, trans. R. Livingstone. Cambridge: MIT Press.

Lunt, Peter K. and Livingstone, Sonia M. (1992) *Mass Consumption and Personal Identity: Everyday Economic Experience*. Philadelphia: Open University Press.

Lupton, D. and Noble, G. (2002) 'Mine/not mine: appropriating personal computers in the academic workplace', *Journal of Sociology*, 38(1): 5–23.

Lury, Celia (1996) *Consumer Culture*. Cambridge: Polity.

Lynes, Russell (1954) *The Tastemakers*. New York: Grossett & Dunlap.

Lyotard, Jean-Francois (1988) *Peregrinations. Law, Form, Event*. New York: Columbia University Press.

MacKenzie, Donald and Wajcman, Judy (1999) *The Social Shaping of Technology*. Philadelphia: Open University Press.

Madigan, Ruth and Munro, Moira (1996) 'House beautiful: style and consumption in the home', *Sociology*, 30(1): 41–57.

Maffesoli, Michel (1996) *The Time of the Tribes. The Decline of Individualism in Mass Society*, trans. Don Smith. London: Sage.

Marcuse, Herbert (1976[1964]) *One Dimensional Man*. London: Abacus.

Marx, Karl (1954[1867]) *Capital. A Critical Analysis of Capitalist Production*. Moscow: Progress Publishers.

Marx, Karl (1975) *Economic and Philosophical Manuscripts of 1844*, trans. M. Milligan. New York: International Publishers.

Mauss, Marcel (1967[1954]) *The Gift: Forms and Functions of Exchange in Archaic Societies*, trans. I. Cunnison. London: Cohen and West.

McCracken, Grant (1988) *Culture and Consumption: New Approaches to the Symbolic Character of Consumer Goods and Activities*. Bloomington: Indiana University Press.

McKendrick, Neil, Brewer, John and Plumb, John H. (1992 [1982]) *The Birth of a Consumer Society. The Commercialisation of Eighteenth-Century England*. London: Europa Publications.

Michael, Mike (2000) *Reconnecting Culture, Technology and Nature: From Society to Heterogeneity*. London: Routledge.

Miles, Steven (1996) 'The cultural capital of consumption: understanding postmodern identities in a cultural context', *Culture and Psychology*, 2: 139–58.

Miles, Steven (1997) *Consumerism. As a Way of Life*. London: Sage.

Miller, Daniel (1987) *Material Culture and Mass Consumption*. Oxford: Blackwell.

Miller, Daniel (1988) 'Appropriating the state on the Council estate', *Man*, 23(2): 353–72.

Miller, Daniel (1994) 'Artefacts and the Meaning of Things' in Tim Ingold, (ed.) *Companion Encyclopedia of Anthropoly: Humanity, Culture and Social Life*. London: Routledge, pp. 396–419.

Miller, Daniel (1995) 'Consumption as the vanguard of history', in Daniel Miller, (ed.), *Acknowledging Consumption: A Review of New Studies*. London: Routledge.

Miller, Daniel (1998a) *A Theory of Shopping*. Cambridge: Polity Press.

Miller, Daniel (ed.) (1998b) *Material Cultures. Why Some Things Matter*. Chicago: University of Chicago Press.

Miller, Daniel (ed.) (2001) *Home Possessions: Material Culture Behind Closed Doors*. Oxford: Berg.

Miller, Daniel and Tilley, Christopher (1996) 'Editorial', *Journal of Material Culture*, 1(1): 5–14.

Miller, Peter and Rose, Nikolas (1997) 'Mobilizing the consumer: assembling the subject of consumption', *Theory, Culture and Society*, 14(1): 1–36.

Miller, William Ian (1997) *The Anatomy of Disgust*. Cambridge: Harvard University Press.

Mukerji, Chandra (1983) *From Graven Images: Patterns of Modern Materialism*. New York: Columbia University Press.

Packard, Vance (1957) *The Hidden Persuaders*. Harmondsworth: Penguin Books.

Packard, Vance (1959) *The Status Seekers: An Exploration of Class Behaviour in America*. Harmondsworth: Penguin Books.

Pels, Dick, Hetherington, Kevin and Vandenberghe, Frédéric (2002) 'The status of the object. Performances, mediations, and techniques', *Theory, Culture and Society*, 19(5/6): 1–21.

Peterson, Richard A. (1992) 'Understanding audience segmentation: from elite to mass to omnivore and univore', *Poetics*, 21: 243–58.

Peterson, Richard A. and Kern, Robert M. (1996) 'Changing highbrow taste: from snob to omnivore', *American Sociological Review*, 61 (October): 900–7.

Pettit, Philip (1975) *The Concept of Structuralism. A Critical Analysis*. Berkeley: University of California Press.

Potter, Jonathan (1996) *Representing Reality: Discourse, Rhetoric and Social Construction*. London: Sage.

Rapoport, Amos (1969) *House Form and Culture*. New Jersey: Prentice-Hall.

Richins, Marsha L. (1994a) 'Valuing things: the public and private meanings of possessions', *Journal of Consumer Research*, 21(3): 504–21.

Richins, Marsha L. (1994b) 'Special possessions and the expression of material values', *Journal of Consumer Research*, 21(3): 522–33.

References

Riessman, Catherine Kohler (1993) *Narrative Analysis*. California: Sage.

Riggins, Stephen Harold (1994) 'Fieldwork in the living room: an autoethnographic essay', in Stephen Harold Riggins (ed.), *The Socialness of Things. Essays on the Socio-Semiotics of Objects*. Berlin: Mouton de Gruyter. pp. 101–47.

Rose, Nikolas (1992) 'Governing the enterprising self', in P. Heelas and P. Morris (eds), *The Values of the Enterprise Culture: The Moral Debate*. New York: Routledge.

de Saussure, Ferdinand (1966[1916]) *Course in General Linguistics*. London: Peter Owen.

Schaper, Eva (ed.) (1983) *Pleasure, Preference, and Value: Studies in Philosophical Aesthetics*. Cambridge: Melbourne.

Schechner, Richard (1993) *The Future of Ritual. Writings on Culture and Performance*. London: Routledge.

Schechner, Richard (2002) *Performance Studies, An Introduction*. New York: Routledge.

Schor, Juliet B. (2000) *Do Americans Shop Too Much? Boston*: Beacon Press.

Schor, Juliet B. and Holt, Douglas B. (2000) *The Consumer Society Reader*. New York: New Press.

Schultz, Susan E., Kleine III, Robert E. and Kernan, Jerome B. (1989) 'These are a Few of My Favourite Things. Toward an explication of attachment as a consumer behavior construct', *Advances in Consumer Research*, 16: 359–66.

Schumacher, E.F. (1973) *Small is Beautiful. A Study of Economics as if People Mattered*. Great Britain: Abacus.

Shotter, John (1984) *Social Accountability and Selfhood*. New York: Basil Blackwell.

Shotter, John and Gergen, Kenneth J. (eds.) (1989) *Texts of Identity*. London: Sage.

Simmel, Georg (1950) 'Adornment', in Kurt H. Wolff, *The Sociology of Georg Simmel*. New York: Free Press.

Simmel, Georg (1957[1904]) 'Fashion', *The American Journal of Sociology*, LXII(6): 541–8.

Simmel, Georg (1997a) 'The philosophy of fashion', in David Frisby and Mike Featherstone, *Simmel on Culture*. London: Sage.

Simmel, Georg (1997b) 'The problem of style', in David Frisby and Mike Featherstone, *Simmel on Culture*. London: Sage.

Slater, Don (1997) *Consumer Culture and Modernity*. UK: Polity Press.

Smith, Adam (1969[1759]) *The Theory of Moral Sentiments*. New Rochelle, New York: Arlington House.

Smith, Philip (2001) *Cultural Theory. An Introduction*. Massachusetts: Blackwell.

Smith, Philip (2003) 'Narrating the guillotine. Punishment technology as myth and symbol', *Theory, Culture & Society*, 20(5): 27–51.

Sombart Werner (1967[1913]) *Luxury and Capitalism*, trans. W.R. Dittmar. Ann Arbor: University of Michigan Press.

Sparshott, Francis Edward (1958) *An Enquiry into Goodness, and Related Concepts: With Some Remarks on the Nature and Scope of Such Enquiries*. Chicago: University of Chicago Press.

Swedberg, Richard (2005) 'August Rodin's The Burghers of Calais. The career of a sculpture and its appeal to civic heroism', *Theory, Culture and Society*, 22(2): 45–67.

Sweet, Fay (1999) *Philippe Starck. Subverchic Design*. London: Thames and Hudson.

Taylor, Betsy and Tilford, Dave 'Why Consumption Matters', in Juliet Schor and Douglas Holt, (2000) *The Consumer Society Reader*. New York: New Press. pp. 463–477.

Turner, Bryan (1993) 'Baudrillard for sociologists', in Chris Rojek and Bryan S. Turner (eds.), *Forget Baudrillard*? London: Routledge.

Turner, Victor (1982) *From Ritual to Theatre. The Human Seriousness of Play*. New York: Performing Arts Journal Publications.

Veblen, Thorstein (1899[1934]) *The Theory of the Leisure Class: An Economic Study of Institutions*. London: Unwin Books.

Vera, Hernan (1989) 'On dutch windows', *Qualitative Sociology*, 12(2): 215–34.

Wallendorf, Melanie and Arnould, Eric (1988) '"My favourite things": a cross-cultural inquiry into object attachment', *The Journal of Consumer Research*, 16(1): 1–38.

Warner, Lloyd W., Low, J.O., Lunt, P.S., and Srole, L. (1963) *Yankee City*. New Haven: Yale University Press.

Warner, Lloyd W. and Lunt, P.S. (1963) *Status System of a Modern American Community*. New Haven: Yale University Press.

Werner, Carol M. (1987) 'Home interiors. a time and place for interpersonal relationships', *Environment and Behaviour*, 19(2): 169–79.

Werner, Carol M., Altman Irwin and Oxley, David (1985) 'Temporal aspects of homes. a transactional perspective', in Irwin Altman and Carol M. Werner, (eds), *Home Environments*. NY: Plenum Press.

Williams, Rosalind H. (1982) *Dream Worlds. Mass Consumption in Late-Nineteenth Century France*. Berkeley: University of California Press.

Willis, Paul (1978) *Profane Culture*. London: Routledge and Kegan Paul.

Winnicott, D.W. (1971[1953]) *Playing and Reality*. London: Tavistock Publications.

Woodward, Ian (2001) 'Domestic objects and the taste epiphany. A resource for consumption methodology', *Journal of Material Culture*, 6(2): 115–36.

Woodward, Ian (2003) 'Divergent narratives in the imagining of the home amongst middle-class consumers: aesthetics, comfort and the symbolic boundaries of self and home', *Journal of Sociology*, 39(4): 391–412.

Woodward, Ian and Emmison, Michael (2001) 'From aesthetic principles to collective sentiments: the logics of everyday judgements of taste', *Poetics*, 29(6): 295–316.

Index